COMPREHENSIVE ASSURANCE
&
SYSTEMS TOOL

An Integrated Practice Set

THIRD EDITION

COMPREHENSIVE ASSURANCE
&
SYSTEMS TOOL

An Integrated Practice Set

THIRD EDITION

LAURA R. INGRAHAM
SAN JOSE STATE UNIVERSITY

J. GREGORY JENKINS
VIRGINIA POLYTECHNIC INSTITUTE AND STATE UNIVERSITY

PEARSON

Boston   Columbus   Indianapolis   New York   San Francisco   Upper Saddle River

Amsterdam   Cape Town   Dubai   London   Madrid   Milan   Munich   Paris   Montreal   Toronto

Delhi   Mexico City   Sao Paulo   Sydney   Hong Kong   Seoul   Singapore   Taipei   Tokyo

Editor in Chief: Donna Battista
Director, Product Development: Ashley Santora
Acquisitions Editor: Victoria Warneck
Editorial Project Manager: Christina Rumbaugh
Editorial Assistant: Jane Avery and Lauren Zanedis
Director of Marketing: Maggie Moylan Leen
Marketing Manager: Alison Haskins

Marketing Assistant: Kimberly Lovato
Production Manager: Meghan DeMaio
Creative Director: Jayne Conte
Cover Designer: Suzanne Behnke
Cover Images: Fotolia
Printer/Binder: Edwards Brothers Malloy
Cover Printer: Lehigh-Phoenix Color

Credits and acknowledgments borrowed from other sources and reproduced, with permission, in this textbook appear on appropriate page within text.

Many of the designations by manufacturers and seller to distinguish their products are claimed as trademarks. Where those designations appear in this book, and the publisher was aware of a trademark claim, the designations have been printed in initial caps or all caps.

Library of Congress Cataloging-in-Publication Data is available.

10 9 8 7 6 5 4 3 2 V0SV 16 15 14

PEARSON

ISBN 10: 0-13-325196-9
ISBN 13: 978-0-13-325196-8

Table of Contents

Manual Module

1.1   The Manual Accounting Information System .... Manual - 1
1.2   Transaction Set A .... Manual - 10
1.3   Chart of Accounts .... Manual - 14
1,4   Price List .... Manual - 16
1.5   Supporting Documents .... Manual - 17
1.6   General Journal .... Manual - 28
1.7   Sales Regsiter .... Manual – 31
1.8   Cash Receipts Register .... Manual – 32
1.9   Purchases Journal .... Manual – 33
1.10 Cash Disbursements Journal .... Manual – 34
1.11 Payroll Journal .... Manual – 35
1.12 Accounts Receivable Subsidiary Ledger .... Manual – 36
1.13 Perpetual Inventory Subsidiary Ledger .... Manual – 38
1.14 Accounts Payable Subsidiary Ledger .... Manual – 41
1.15 Employee Payroll Subsidiary Ledger .... Manual – 42
1.16 Fixed Asset Subsidiary Ledger .... Manual – 46
1.17 General Ledger .... Manual – 48
1.18 Transaction Set B .... Manual – 60
1.19 Transaction Set C .... Manual – 67

Computerized Module

2. Spreadsheet Applications Using Microsoft® Excel 2010 .... Computerized AIS - 1
   2.1   Protecting the Data .... Computerized AIS - 2
   2.2   Formula Auditing .... Computerized AIS - 4
   2.3   Data Integrity .... Computerized AIS - 7
   2.4   Simple Data Analysis .... Computerized AIS - 14
   2.5   What-If Analysis .... Computerized AIS - 15
   2.6   Information Needs .... Computerized AIS - 17
   2.7   Macros .... Computerized AIS – 20
   2.8   More Advanced Macros .... Computerized AIS – 24
   2.9   Database Functions .... Computerized AIS - 27
   2.10 Introduction to PivotTable Reports .... Computerized AIS - 30
   2.11 Detail in Reporting .... Computerized AIS - 36
   2.12 Flexible Budgeting Using PivotTables .... Computerized AIS – 42
   2.13 Creating Charts From PivotTables .... Computerized AIS – 44
   2.15 Wrap-Up .... Computerized AIS – 49

3. General Ledger Applications Using Peachtree Complete
   Accounting 2011® .... Computerized AIS - 50
   3.1   Setting Up a New Company .... Computerized AIS - 51
   3.2   Setting Up the General Ledger .... Computerized AIS - 56
   3.3   Setting Up Beginning Account Balances .... Computerized AIS - 61
   3.4   Setting Up User Security .... Computerized AIS - 63

3.5   Setting Up Accounts Receivable .... Computerized AIS - 65

3.6   Setting Up Accounts Payable .... Computerized AIS - 70

3.7   Setting Up Inventory .... Computerized AIS - 74

3.8   Setting Up Payroll .... Computerized AIS - 78

3.9   Setting Up Payroll Formulas .... Computerized AIS - 86

3.10 Entering Transactions .... Computerized AIS - 89

3.11 Transaction Set A ....Computerized AIS – 97

3.12 Month-End Procedures ....Computerized AIS – 98

3.13 Year-End Procedures ....Computerized AIS – 100

3.11 Transaction Set B ....Computerized AIS – 112

3.11 Transaction Set C ....Computerized AIS – 118

4. Database Applications Using Microsoft® Access 2010..... Computerized AIS - 128

    4.1   Creating a New Database and New Table .... Computerized AIS - 132

    4.2   Creating a Form .... Computerized AIS - 138

    4.3   Ensuring Sequential Integrity .... Computerized AIS - 143

    4.4   Creating Relations .... Computerized AIS - 148

    4.5   Integrating Forms within Forms .... Computerized AIS - 150

    4.6   Creating a Query .... Computerized AIS - 162

    4.7   Creating a Report .... Computerized AIS - 165

    4.8   Summary .... Computerized AIS - 169

Assurance Module

5.1 Client Acceptance .... Assurance - 1

5.2 Understanding the Business Environment .... Assurance - 15

5.3 Identification of Audit Tests for the Expenditure Cycle .... Assurance - 31

5.4 Selection of Audit Tests and Risk Assessment for the

5.5 Expenditure Cycle .... Assurance - 49

5.6 Performance of Audit Tests for the Revenue Cycle .... Assurance - 57

5.7 Completing the Audit .... Assurance - 107

Preface

The **C**omprehensive **A**ssurance and **S**ystems **T**ool (CAST) provides an integrated learning opportunity that encompasses financial statement assurance and accounting information systems. CAST uniquely exposes students to these issues at The Winery at Chateau Americana, a hypothetical company that is based on an actual domestic winery. Unlike traditional projects and assignments that may offer little or no context, students develop a rich knowledge and understanding of Chateau Americana and its industry as they provide assurance on the company's financial statements and address a variety of challenging accounting information systems issues.

CAST is comprised of three self-contained, but complementary modules:

- The *Manual AIS module* requires students to complete real-world business documents, journalize and post a variety of transactions, and prepare a year-end worksheet. The module now contains three alternative transaction sets to allow the instructor to rotate through them from semester to semester and to afford some variety among the transactions provided. This module may be completed before or during the completion of either the Computerized Accounting Information Systems module or the Assurance module. However, students are not required to complete this module before the other modules.
- The *Computerized Accounting Information Systems module* is comprised of three components: spreadsheets, general ledger software, and databases. Each of these components may be completed individually. However, the module itself is written so that each component strengthens the knowledge learned in the previous component. In addition, although self-contained, this module's value is greatest when combined with the Manual AIS module.
- The *Assurance module* provides students hands-on experience with fundamental elements of financial statement assurance. This module is comprised of components related to the client acceptance decision, understanding the business environment, understanding and testing internal controls, assessing risks and materiality, conducting substantive tests, evaluating attorney's letters, performing analytical review procedures, and determining the appropriate audit opinion. These components build upon one another and should be completed in the order in which they are presented.

CAST should be implemented in either an undergraduate or graduate setting and is ideally suited for simultaneous integration across assurance and information systems courses. In addition, each of the modules can be completed either as an in-class or an out-of-class assignment. CAST affords students the opportunity to develop and strengthen their analytical thinking, written and oral communication, problem solving, and team building skills.

The third edition has been updated in response to the changes that have occurred in the accounting environment, in technology, and in response to the many helpful comments and suggestions we have received from adopters and students alike. Specifically, we have incorporated new transactions in the Manual Module that are intended to reinforce more advanced accounting transaction processing. In the Computerized AIS Module, we have provided more advanced Macro instruction and additional PivotTable practice. And, in the Assurance Module we have updated materials for changes in professional standards and introduced new audit issues for students to address related to conflicting client inquiry and misstatements. We are excited about the changes we have made to this 3rd edition. We believe your students will benefit from using CAST and we once more encourage you to contact us with questions or suggestions about how we can improve the materials.

Finally, we would like to thank Monica Horenstein for her many hours spent checking and editing these Modules. Her contribution was invaluable.

Laura Ingraham
Greg Jenkins

We dedicate this book to our families:
Dan and Casey
Elaine, Anna, Claire and Will

THE MANUAL ACCOUNTING INFORMATION SYSTEM:
The Winery at Chateau Americana

LEARNING OBJECTIVES

After completing and discussing this module, you should be able to:

- Recognize and prepare common business documents
- Recognize and understand common control activities designed to capture, summarize, and report business activities
- Explain the objectives of maintaining an audit trail
- Recognize deficiencies in the design of common business documents
- Prepare journal entries, journals, and ledgers
- Understand the relationships among various documents, journals, and ledgers in the accounting cycle

BACKGROUND

In this module, you are required to prepare common source documents relating to the various accounting cycles, prepare journal entries, post entries to the general and subsidiary ledgers, prepare trial balances, and prepare a year-end worksheet and the financial statements. While working through this module, you will observe the data flows from their inception to their final reporting.

Due to constraints on students' and instructors' time and resources, the processes outlined in this module focus only on the wholesale segment of the business, picking up after the wine has been manufactured and bottled in the winery and is ready to be sold to distributors.

Company History
Since its founding by Edward Summerfield in 1980, Chateau Americana (CA) has been a small, family-owned winery located in northern California. While CA is comparatively new to the wine industry, it has already cultivated a reputation as one of America's finest wineries. The small, family-owned winery has an impressive vineyard whose 125 acres yields a variety of grapes including Cabernet Sauvignon, Cabernet Franc, Pinot Noir, Chardonnay and Riesling. They are now looking to purchase more acreage to begin growing additional varieties of their own, specifically Sauvignon Blanc, Merlot and Malbec. CA planted its first grapevines in 1983 and began selling wine in 1988. These vineyards yield approximately 25% of the grapes (or about 800 tons) it requires for wine production. The remaining grapes are purchased from CA's suppliers. In the last several years, CA's wines have received accolades at several highly regarded wine competitions that have

dramatically increased the demand for its wines. The company currently has annual sales of 3,850,000 cases.

OVERVIEW OF WINE PRODUCTION

Chateau Americana is a fully operational winery that produces red, white, and sparkling wines.

Red Wine Process

The process for making red wine begins by feeding the grapes into a destemmer/crusher machine. The crushed grapes, skin and seeds, called "must," is then piped into stainless steel fermentation tanks, each of which holds between 3,000 and 5,000 gallons. The must remains in the fermentation tanks at a temperature of 70-75° for a period of 8-21 days and is rotated 4 times a day to break up the skim containing the seeds which float to the surface. The fermentation tank is then emptied. Seventy percent of the juice comes out as "free run," much of which is later used for the more expensive wine labels. The solid remainder is then emptied into a presser that carefully extracts the remaining juice without breaking the seeds.

Red wine is typically aged in oak barrels. Aging of the wine depends upon the number of times the barrel has been used. If the barrel has never been used before, the aging process takes approximately six months. If it has been used once before, the aging process takes approximately 18 months. And if it has been used twice before, the aging process takes approximately 2 years.

White Wine Process

The process of making white wine begins by feeding the white grapes into a bladder press. Inside this machine, a bladder expands, pressing the white grapes between it and the outer shell. Only the juice is then piped into the fermentation tanks where it remains at a temperature of approximately 60° for approximately 30 days while the sugar in the grapes is converted to alcohol.

White wine is most often then aged in stainless steel tanks, although oak barrels may be used.

Bottling

The aged wine is bottled in an atmospherically controlled "clean" room where the air is filtered and exchanged every 60 seconds. Using an automated assembly line, bottles are sterilized, filled, corked, capped, and labeled at a rate of 50 per minute.

OPERATIONS

Organizational Structure and Personnel

CA presently employs 250 permanent employees. Its management team is widely respected in the industry. Because the winery is a family-owned business, the owners have invested considerable time and energies in hiring individuals whom they believe are competent and trustworthy.

Currently, members of the Summerfield family occupy most of the key management positions. Edward Summerfield is the family's patriarch and president of the company. He has received several entrepreneurship awards and is generally perceived as an astute business person. Edward's daughter, Taylor Summerfield, is vice president of marketing for the company. Prior to assuming this position, she had a successful career in sales and marketing. Taylor is well-educated and earned an MBA from an Ivy League school.

Edward's son-in-law, Jacques Dupuis, is vice-president of winery operations. He has an extensive background in viticulture (i.e., grape growing) and vinification (i.e., wine making). Rob Breeden, the company's CFO, is the sole individual to hold a key management position who is not a member of the Summerfield family. He has extensive financial experience and was previously employed in public accounting for nine years and served as controller and CFO for another California winery. Rob holds undergraduate and graduate degrees in accounting and is a CPA.

Chart of Accounts

Chateau Americana has developed a six-digit classification scheme for its Chart of Accounts. The Chart of Accounts is found behind the Year-End Procedures.

				CASH SALES INVOICE			Invoice Number	C2228

Chateau Americana, Inc.
3003 Vineyard Way
Huntington, CA 95394
(707) 368-8485
CA-NC-67

Invoice Date: 12/3/XX

Sold To:
Grapevine Selections
2864 Worth Street
Napa, CA 95748

Ship To:
Grapevine Selections
2864 Worth Street
Napa, CA 95748

Salesperson	Customer P.O. Number	Customer Number	ABC Number
RS	7563	0505	P45293X

Product	Description	Size	Quantity	Cost	Extended
W120019	Chenin Blanc	0.750	432	5.25	$ 2,268.00
R130056	Merlot	0.750	324	6.00	1,944.00
R130061	Cabernet Sauvignon	0.750	384	6.50	2,496.00
S140000	Sparkling Brut	0.750	228	11.00	2,508.00

Grand Total Bottles: 1,368

Total Cases: 114
Comments:

Grand Total Cost: $ 9,216.00

Date: 12/3/XX
Invoice Number: C2228
Customer Number: 0505

Distribution: Copy 1 — Accounting; Copy 2 – Shipping; Copy 3 – Customer; Copy 4 – Sales

Figure 1- Sample Invoice

Selling Prices and Costs

Chateau Americana maintains a list of wine costs and selling prices. Wine is sold by the case (12 bottles to a case). The list is found behind the Year-End Procedures.

Date	12/03/XX		Uniform Bill of Lading		

Ship From

Name:	Chateau Americana, Inc.
Address:	3003 Vineyard Way
City/State/Zip:	Huntington, CA 95394
SID No.:	122448

Bill of Lading Number: 136369

Carrier Name: *Pacific Freightliners*

Trailer number: *ABC 3899*

Serial number(s): *313734449*

Ship To

Name:	Grapevine Selections
Address:	2864 Worth Street
City/State/Zip:	Napa, CA 95748
CID No.:	542352

Special Instructions:

Freight Charge Terms: (Freight charges are prepaid unless marked otherwise)

Prepaid: ☐   Collect: ☒   3rd Party: ☐

☐ **(check box):** Master bill of lading with attached underlying bills of lading.

Customer Order Information

Description of Items	Quantity	Weight	Pallet/Slip (circle one)		Additional Shipper Information
Wine	*114*	*3,876*	(Y)	N	
			Y	N	
			Y	N	
			Y	N	
Grand Total					

Where the rate is dependent on value, shippers are required to state specifically in writing the agreed or declared value of the property as follows: "The agreed or declared value of the property is specifically stated by the shipper to be not exceeding _____ per _____."

COD Amount: $ 9,216.00

Free terms:

☐ Collect

☐ Prepaid

☒ Customer check acceptable

Note: Liability limitation for loss or damage in this shipment may be applicable. See 49 USC §14706(c)(1)(A) & (B)

Received, subject to individually determined rates or contracts that have been agreed upon in writing between the carrier and shipper, if applicable, otherwise to the rates, classifications and rules that have been established by the carrier and are available to the shipper, on request, and to all applicable state and federal regulations.

The carrier shall not make delivery of this shipment without payment of and all other lawful charges.

Shipper Signature   *Jerry Richards*

Shipper Signature/Date	**Trailer Loaded:**	**Carrier Signature/Pickup Date**
This is to certify that the above named materials are properly classified, packaged, marked and labeled, and are in proper condition for transportation according to the applicable regulations of the DOT.	☐ By shipper ☒ By driver	Carrier acknowledges receipt of packages and required placards. Carrier certifies emergency response information was made available and/or carrier has the DOT emergency response guidebook or equivalent documentation in the vehicle. **Property described above is received in good order, except as noted.**
Jerry Richards 12/03/XX		*Bruce Garrett* 12/03/XX

Distribution: Copy 1 — Accounting; Copy 2 – Shipping; Copy 3 – Customer

Figure 2 – Sample Bill of Lading

Processes

Sales. Chateau Americana sells its wine to most distributors on account and offers a few select distributors credit terms as detailed below. Sales to a small number of distributors are cash sales. When a purchase order is received from a distributor, a sales invoice (*Figure 1*) is generated and the requested items are pulled from finished goods inventory. Copies 1, 2 and 3 of the Invoice are sent to Shipping where the Bill of Lading (*Figure 2*) is prepared in triplicate. Copy 3 of the Bill of Lading and Copy 3 of the Invoice are sent to the Customer with the wine. Copy 2 of the Bill of Lading and Copy 2 of the Invoice are filed numerically by the Shipping department. Copy 1 of the Bill of Lading and Copy 1 of the Invoice are sent to Accounting where the Accounting Clerk updates the Sales Register. Copy 1 of the Bill of Lading and Copy 1 of the Invoice are then filed numerically.

The Sales Register is totaled monthly and then posted to the General Ledger.

		Credit Memo	
Chateau Americana, Inc. 3003 Vineyard Way Huntington, CA 95394 Phone: (707)368-8485		**Credit Memo :** **2753**	
		Date: 1/8/XX	**Salesperson:** CEZ
		Customer Number: 2201	**Customer PO No:** 10654
		Amount Net: $267.00	

Credit To: Veritas Distributors Inc

Comments:

Returned damaged cases of wine

Item # / Description	Quantity	Price Unit Price	Amount
R130061 / Cabernet Sauvignon	12	$6.50	$78.00
W120019 / Chenin Blanc	36	$5.25	$189.00

Customer Name: Veritas Distributors Inc

Credit: Amount:: $267.00

Chateau Americana, Inc.
3003 Vineyard Way
Huntington, CA 95394
Phone: (707)368-8485

Credit Date: 1/8/XX

Credit Memo #: **2753**

Customer Number: 2201

Distribution: Copy 1 – Accounting; Copy 2 -- Customer

Figure 3 – Sample Credit Memo

Sales Tax. Sales tax is not assessed on wholesale sales. Therefore, there is no sales tax applied to sales to distributors.

Credit Terms. Chateau Americana offers discounts for early payment to certain select distributors who have done business with CA for an extended period. The terms offered to these distributors are 3/15, net 30. Most other distributors are granted credit terms without early payment discounts.

Returns and Allowances. Credit memos (*Figure 3*) are issued for price corrections, overshipments, or when a shipment has been damaged in transit. Due to legal restrictions, wine cannot be returned to regular inventory. On the very rare occasions that wine is returned, it is put into special inventory for taxed wines.

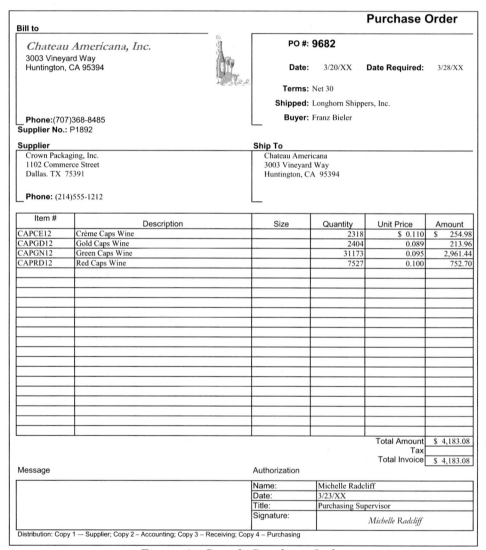

Figure 4 – Sample Purchase Order

Cash Receipts. The mail is received by the receptionist who opens it in the presence of another individual. At that time, all checks are restrictively endorsed by the receptionist. She also prepares and signs a cash receipts summary. The receptionist then prepares and takes a deposit slip, along with the checks, to the bank for deposit on a daily basis. The validated deposit slip received from the bank, remittance advices from the checks, and cash receipts summary are sent to accounting.

After receiving the validated deposit slip, remittance advices from the checks, and the cash receipts summary, the Accounting Clerk inputs the transactions, updates the cash receipts journal, and the accounts receivable subsidiary ledger if the cash received was from a credit customer. The validated deposit slip, cash receipts summary, and remittance advices are filed together chronologically. The cash receipts journal is totaled monthly and posted to the general ledger.

The Accounting Clerk prepares monthly customer statements in duplicate. Copy 2 is filed alphabetically in Accounting. Copy 1 is mailed to the customer.

Receiving Report

Date Received: *3/28/XX*

Receiving Report #: **14891**

Received from

Crown Packaging, Inc.

Purchase Order #

9682

Freight carrier

Longhorn Shippers, Inc.

Received by

BH

Quantity	Item #	Size	Description
2318	CAPCE12		Crème Cabs Wine
2404	CAPGD12		Gold Cabs Wine
31173	CAPGN12		Green Cabs Wine
7527	CAPRD12		Red Cabs Wine

Condition:

Excellent

Distribution: Copy 1 — Accounting; Copy 2 – Purchasing; Copy 3 – Receiving

Figure 5 – Sample Receiving Report

Purchases. As raw materials are needed for production and bottling, a prenumbered purchase order is completed (*Figure 4*) in quadruplicate. The purchase order must be approved and signed by a purchasing supervisor. Copy 1 of the purchase order is sent to the supplier. Copy 2 of the purchase order is sent to Accounting. Copy 3 of the purchase order is sent to Receiving. Copy 4 of the purchase order and the purchase requisition are held temporarily in Purchasing. As goods are received from suppliers, they are inspected, counted and compared to copy 3 of the purchase order. A prenumbered receiving report is prepared in triplicate (*Figure 5*). Copy 3 of the receiving report and copy 3 of the purchase order are filed numerically. Copy 2 of the receiving report is sent to Purchasing where it is matched with copy 4 of the purchase order and the purchase requisition and filed numerically. Copy 1 is sent to Accounting where it is matched with Copy 2 of the purchase order.

Cash Disbursements. When invoices are received for items or services not requiring a receiving report or a purchase order, they are first routed to the appropriate department for approval (by the receptionist when she opens the mail). The approved invoice is then sent to Accounting.

When invoices for inventory are received from suppliers, the receptionist sends them directly to Accounting. These invoices are matched with copy 1 of the receiving report and copy 2 of the purchase order. They are then entered into the purchases journal. The purchases journal is totaled monthly and then posted to the general ledger.

Supplier invoices, copy 1 of the receiving report, and copy 2 of the purchase order are then filed in a temporary file by due date to insure that they will be paid on a timely basis and that any discounts offered will be taken. Supplier invoices not requiring receiving reports and/or purchase orders are also included in this temporary file. As the invoices come due, the accounting clerk pulls them from the temporary file and writes the checks. The accounting supervisor reviews the supporting documentation such as the check, invoice, copy 1 of the receiving report, and copy 2 of the purchase order for completeness, initials the invoices, and sends the documentation (commonly referred to as a voucher package) to the chief financial officer (CFO) for signature.

The CFO reviews the package for reasonableness, signs the checks, stamps the documents "Paid," and returns the package to Accounting. The checks are then mailed. The remaining documents are filed numerically by check number.

The cash disbursements journal is totaled monthly and posted to the general ledger.

Inventory. Chateau Americana maintains a perpetual inventory system for both production inventory and for finished goods (bottled wines). The perpetual inventory records are updated based on the standard cost buildups for each bottled wine when inventory is moved from the bottling room to the warehouse. (Again, you are reminded that this module focuses only on the wholesale segment of the business and does not deal with production or selling of basic grape-stock).

A physical inventory is taken at the end of the year for production inventory and at the end of each quarter for finished goods inventory. Adjusting entries are made as necessary based on the physical inventory counts.

Payroll. Chateau Americana pays its employees on the 15th and the last day of each month. The department supervisors are responsible for approving and initialing the time cards for any hourly employees in their respective departments. The time cards are then sent to Accounting at the end of the payroll period. The accounting clerk calculates payroll for each employee using the current payroll information found in the employee payroll subsidiary ledgers. The accounting clerk enters the payroll into the payroll journal and posts to the employee payroll subsidiary ledgers. The time cards are then filed chronologically and alphabetically.

The accounting clerk prepares the payroll checks from the payroll checking account based upon the information from the payroll journal and enters the check number in the payroll journal. The accounting clerk also prepares a check drawn from the general checking account payable to the payroll checking account in the amount of the total payroll to cover the current period's payroll. The accounting supervisor reviews the payroll check and the check from the general checking account and initials the payroll journal before forwarding all the checks to the CFO for signature. The CFO reviews and signs the checks and returns them to Accounting. Accounting distributes the payroll checks to the employees and deposits the check for the payroll checking account in the bank.

For payroll purposes, you will be preparing the payroll for four employees: two members of middle management who are salaried employees (Anna Johnson and José Rodriguez) and two production workers who are hourly employees (Tom Bryan and Bob Hissom).

Anna Johnson is an Accounting Supervisor and has been with Chateau Americana for two years. José Rodriguez is a Shift Supervisor and has been with the company for 10 years. Both Bryan and Hissom are in the Operations Department. Bryan is a shift worker in the Wine Presses, and Hissom is a receiving clerk. Both have been with the company for several years.

Employees are paid for holidays. Hourly employees who work more than eight hours in one day receive overtime pay. Overtime hours are paid at a rate of 150% of the regular hourly pay per overtime hour worked.

The amount of federal income tax withheld for each employee is determined (a) by taking into account the employee's marital status and the number of withholding allowances claimed by the employee (both of which can be found in the employee payroll subsidiary ledgers) and (b) referring to the percentage method of withholding of IRS Publication 15. (**HINT:** You can find IRS Publication 15, also entitled "Circular E, Employer's Tax Guide, on the Internet.) You will also need to calculate FICA & Medicare withholdings.

NOTE: For simplification purposes, state withholdings are not calculated in this exercise. In addition, we will use 6.2% as the employee FICA withholding rate since the current reduced 4.2% rate that exists in 2012 is temporary and we cannot predict whether Congress will once more extend it. The Medicare rate remains at 1.45%

Fixed Assets. Depreciation expense is calculated monthly. All assets are depreciated on the straight-line basis using the half-year convention in the year of purchase and the year of sale. A portion of the Fixed Asset subsidiary ledgers has been reproduced for you. Date of acquisition, estimated useful life, acquisition value, and accumulated depreciation for each asset are listed in the ledgers.

TRANSACTION SET A

The books have been posted through December 15, 20XX. The following selected transactions have been extracted from the period December 16 through December 31, 20XX and are to be completed in accordance with the policies and procedures explained above. Documents to be completed can be found in the Document Packet. For all required signatures on these documents sign your name. Supporting documentation for the transactions is provided behind the Year-End Procedures followed by all necessary journals and ledgers.

Note that the current year transactions are denoted as 20XX; prior year transactions are denoted as 20XW; transactions for the subsequent year are denoted as 20XY. Your instructor will provide you with the appropriate current year and you can make the fill in the dates accordingly for all transactions.

December	Transaction
16	Receive a purchase order from California Premium Beverage (page 17). Fill and ship the order. Complete Invoice No. 15535, Bill of Lading No. 136480 and record the sale in the journals and ledgers. W. A. Bierkstahler is the sales account representative. Relevant data: shipment weight - 12,532 lbs., trailer # - 122302, serial # - 999356278. The carrier is CA Express. Leave the CID No. blank.
16	Order 29 tons of white grapes at $541.11 per ton from Mendocino Vineyards. The item number for the white grapes is WG1003. Complete Purchase Order No. 9682. Relevant data: date required - Dec. 22, shipper - Longhorn Shippers, Inc., buyer - Franz Bieler, supplier # - M0652.
16	Purchase a 20XW Ford truck for $26,750.00. The terms include a $4,750.00 down payment and a 3-year, 6% promissory note to Ford Credit for the remaining $22,000.00. Principal and interest on the note are due monthly beginning January 4, 20XY. The company expects the truck to have a useful life of 5 years and no salvage value. Prepare Check No. 19257 payable to Potter Valley Ford for the down payment and record the transaction in the journals and ledgers.
16	The Board of Directors of Chateau Americana authorized a $50,000 cash dividend payable on January 20th to the stockholders of record on January 15th.
17	Receive a phone complaint from Seaside Distributors about a case of Chenin Blanc that was damaged in shipment. The case was part of Invoice No. 15175, dated November 5, 20XX, in the amount of $20,438.40. Seaside paid the invoice on November 19, 20XX and took advantage of the discount (terms 3/15, net 30). Prepare Credit Memo No. 2753 to write-off the damaged inventory that was not returned, and prepare Check No. 19286 to reimburse Seaside for the damaged goods. Record the transactions in the journals and ledgers. W. A. Bierkstahler is the sales account representative. Relevant data: customer PO # - MZ5713. (Note: Be sure to review *Returns and Allowances* on Page 6.)

December	Transaction
19	Receive $850 refund from California Wine & Cheese Monthly for overpayment of advertising costs (page 18). Enter the receipt on Cash Receipts Summary No. 5712 and record the cash receipt in the journals and ledgers.
19	Receive payment in full from Pacific Distribution Co. on Invoice No. 15243 dated November 13, 20XX, in the amount of $19,576.80 (page 19). Enter the receipt on Cash Receipts Summary No. 5712 and record the cash receipt in the journals and ledgers.
19	Receive a purchase order (page 20) with payment (page 21) from Sonoma Distributors. Fill and ship the order. Complete Invoice No. C2489, enter the receipt on Cash Receipts Summary No. 5712, and record the sale in the journals and ledgers. W. A. Bierkstahler is the sales account representative. Relevant data: shipment weight - 7,650 lbs., trailer # - 279AJ1, serial # - 919515094. (Hint: Use the Other Account column to post Inventory and Cost of Goods Sold.) **DO NOT** create a Bill of Lading for this purchase order.
22	Receive 19 tons of red grapes at $703.40 per ton from Mendocino Vineyards. Also received Invoice No. M7634 from Mendocino Vineyards with the shipment (page 22). Terms on the invoice are 2/10, net 30. Complete Receiving Report No. 17251 and record the inventory in the journals and ledgers using the gross method.
26	Receive utility bill from Pacific Gas and Electric in the amount of $18,887.62 (page 23). Prepare Check No. 19402 and record the payment in the journals and ledgers.
30	Receive Brokerage Advice from Edwards Jones for purchase of 500 shares of Microsoft at $49.20 per share plus $400 broker's commission (page 24). Prepare Check No. 19468 and record the purchase in the journals and ledgers.
30	Prepare Check No. 19473 payable to Mendocino Vineyards for the shipment received on December 22 and record the payment in the journals and ledgers.
31	Receive payment in full for the December 16 purchase from California Premium Beverage (page 25). Enter the cash receipt on Cash Receipts Summary No. 5718 and record the cash receipt in the journals and ledgers.
31	Prepare Payroll Checks (Nos. 7111-7114) for Anna Johnson, José Rodriguez, Tom Bryan, and Bob Hissom. Time cards for Tom and Bob are on pages 26-27. Prepare Check No. 19474 to transfer cash from the general cash account to the payroll account. Record the payroll transactions and all appropriate *accruals* in the journals and ledgers.
31	Prepare Check No. 19475 to repay $50,000 of the principal on long-term debt to Bank of Huntington and record the payment in the journals and ledgers.

MONTH-END PROCEDURES

1. Calculate monthly accrued interest expense for the installment note to Ford Credit (based on 365 days per year and interest starting to accrue on December 17, 20XX). Make the appropriate adjusting entry. The payable is posted to Other Accrued Expenses Payable.

2. For your convenience, depreciation in the amount of $105,341.50 has been calculated on all assets for the month of December **except** for any current purchases of assets. Calculate the depreciation for the Ford Pickup purchased on December 16. Post the depreciation to the Fixed Asset Subsidiary Ledger and add the amount of depreciation expense to the rest of the December depreciation. Make the appropriate adjusting entry.

3. The accounting clerk receives the bank statement on a monthly basis and reconciles it to the cash receipts and cash disbursements journals, identifying the necessary adjusting journal entries such as bank services charges, etc. The bank statement for the General Checking Account (Account #111000) reports a balance of $_____ as of December 31, 20XX. (**NOTE:** You will need to obtain the bank statement balance for the current year from your instructor.) The accounting clerk notes that there are outstanding checks totaling $88,097.31 (checks 19469, 19470, and 19471) and deposits in transit of $41,261.47. In addition, the bank statement indicates bank charges of $30, a returned check from Alota Wine Distributors in the amount of $19,475.26, and a check printing fee of $60. Reconcile the cash balance for the General Checking Account.

4. Foot and cross foot the journals & registers. Post all monthly totals from the journals/registers to the General Ledger and post the individual entries in the General Journal to the General Ledger.

5. Reconcile the Accounts Receivable Subsidiary Ledger, Accounts Payable Subsidiary Ledger and the Perpetual Inventory Subsidiary Ledger to the General Ledger.

YEAR-END PROCEDURES

1. Prepare the unadjusted trial balance using the electronic year-end worksheet provided to you on the CAST web site (your instructor will provide you with the URL for this web site).

2. Foot and cross foot the Payroll Subsidiary Ledgers.

3. Prepare the year-end adjusting journal entries:

   a. Calculate the allowance for bad debts using the net sales method. Experience indicates that 0.05% of net sales should be set aside for bad debts. Make the appropriate adjusting entry.

   b. The calculation of federal income tax expense is a year-end adjusting entry but it cannot be made until all other entries have been made and net income before taxes has been determined. Therefore, you must first complete the year-end worksheet and calculate net income before taxes. Then calculate federal income tax expense and post the adjusting entry to the worksheet. (**HINT:** Use rates in effect as of January 20XX. You can find these rates in any tax textbook or by referring to the instructions for Schedule J, Form 1120.)

4. Complete the remainder of the electronic year-end worksheet.

5. Prepare the financial statements including the income statement, the statement of retained earnings, balance sheet, and the statement of cash flows (using the indirect method).

6. Prepare and record the closing journal entries in the journal and general ledger.

7. Prepare the electronic post-closing trial balance worksheet.

The Winery at Chateau Americana
Chart of Accounts

Assets (100000)		
Cash (110000)		
	General Checking Account	111000
	Payroll Checking Account	112000
	Money Market Account	113000
	Savings Account	114000
	Petty Cash	119000
Accounts Receivable (120000)		
	Accounts Receivable	121000
	Allowance for Bad Debts	129000
Inventory (140000)		
	Inventory – Production	141000
	Inventory – Finished Goods	145000
Prepaid Expenses		150000
Land and Buildings		160000
Equipment		170000
Accumulated Depreciation		180000
Investments		191000
Liabilities (200000)		
Accounts Payable		210000
Accrued Expenses (220000)		
	Federal Income Tax Withheld	222100
	FICA Withheld	222200
	Medicare Withheld	222300
Payroll Taxes Payable (223000)		
	FICA Payable – Employer	223100
	Medicare Payable – Employer	223200
	Unemployment Taxes Payable	223300
Other Accrued Expenses		230000
	Federal Income Taxes Payable	235000
	Property Taxes Payable	236000
	Dividends Payable	239000
Mortgages Payable		240000
Other Long-Term Payables (260000)		
	Notes Payable	261000
Owners' Equity (300000)		
Common Stock		310000
Paid-in Capital in Excess of Par – Common		311000
Dividends – Common		312000
Retained Earnings		390000
Income (400000)		
	Sales	410000
	Sales Discounts	420000
	Sales Returns and Allowances	430000

	Gain/Loss – Fixed Assets	451000
	Gain/Loss – Marketable Securities	452000
	Dividend Income	491000
	Interest Income	492000
Cost of Goods Sold		510000
Expenses (600000 – 700000)		
Payroll Expense (600000)		
	Wages and Salaries Expense	601000
	Sales Commission Expense	601500
	FICA Tax Expense	602100
	Medicare Tax Expense	602200
	FUTA Expense	602300
	SUTA Expense	602400
Occupancy Expense (610000)		
	Utilities Expense	611000
	Irrigation & Waste Disposal Expense	611300
	Landscaping Expense	612000
Marketing (620000)		
	Advertising Expense	621000
	Marketing Expense	623000
	Festivals & Competitions Expense	624000
Communications Expense (630000)		
	Telephone Expense	631000
	Internet & Computer Expense	632000
	Postage Expense	633000
Professional Services Expense (640000)		
	Legal & Accounting Fees	641000
	Other Consulting Fees	643000
Supplies Expense (650000)		
	Office Supplies Expense	651000
Data Processing Expense		660000
Depreciation Expense		670000
Travel and Entertainment Expense		680000
Insurance Expense (690000)		
	Other Insurance	691000
	Medical Insurance	692000
	Workmen's Compensation Insurance	693000
	Other Employee Benefits Expense	699000
Dues and Subscriptions Expense		700000
Tax Expense (710000)		
	Federal Income Tax Expense	711000
	Property Tax Expense	712000
Maintenance Expense (720000)		
	Repairs and Maintenance Expense	721000
Automobile Expense		731000
Lease Expense		740000
Other Operating Expense (790000)		
	Bad Debt Expense	791000

Miscellaneous Expense		792000
Interest Expense		793000

The Winery at Chateau Americana
Price List

Inventory Code	Description	Standard Cost (per bottle)	Selling Price (per bottle)
R130064	Cabernet Franc	$ 7.50	$ 10.00
R130061	Cabernet Sauvignon	7.20	9.50
R130056	Merlot	7.62	9.00
R130072	Shiraz	7.58	9.25
W120080	Chardonnay	7.54	10.00
W120019	Chenin Blanc	6.34	8.25
W120015	Riesling	5.86	7.85
W120016	Sauvignon Blanc	5.86	7.85
S140000	Sparkling Brut	10.28	14.00

California Premium Beverage

PURCHASE ORDER

39848 South Street
Santa Rosa, CA 95402
Phone (707) 555-7451 Fax (707) 555-7452

To:
Chateau Americana
3003 Vineyard Way
Huntington, CA 95394

Ship To:
California Premium Beverage
39848 South Street
Santa Rosa, CA 95402

ABC Permit #: A59782

P.O. DATE	P.O. NUMBER	SHIPPED VIA	F.O.B. POINT	TERMS
12/13/XX	8746	CA Express	Destination	3/15, net 30

ITEM NO	QTY	SIZE	DESCRIPTION	UNIT PRICE	TOTAL
W120015	1512	0.750	Riesling	7.85	11,869.20
W120016	504	0.750	Sauvignon Blanc	7.85	3,956.40
W120019	336	0.750	Chenin Blanc	8.25	2,772.00
R130061	1176	0.750	Cabernet Sauvignon	9.50	11,172.00
R130056	672	0.750	Merlot	9.00	6,048.00
S140000	240	0.750	Sparkling Brut	14.00	3,360.00
W120080	336	0.750	Chardonnay	10.00	3,360.00
				TOTAL	42,537.60

Jorge Gonzalez   12/13/XX
Authorized by   Date

California Wine and Cheese Monthly
573 Parkins Ave.
Ukiah, CA 95482

Lone Star Bank
Dallas, TX 27540

23545

Date ____12/15/XX____

PAY____Eight Hundred Fifty and 00/100 Dollars -- $ ____850.00____

To the
order of   Chateau Americana
              3003 Vineyard Way
              Huntington, CA 95394

- SAMPLE, DO NOT CASH -

|:000000|: :000000000: 23545

California Wine and Cheese Monthly   **23545**

Reference	Amount
Overpayment of monthly advertising	$850.00

Pacific Distribution Company   Bank of America   **69712**
10034 Westborough Boulevard   San Francisco, CA 94104
San Francisco, CA 94080

Date ____ 12/16/XX ____

PAY___ Nineteen Thousand Five Hundred Seventy Six and 80/100 Dollars ----------------- $ ___ 19,576.80

To The   ⌐ Chateau Americana   ¬
Order Of   3003 Vineyard Way
             Huntington, CA 95394
                                                                - SAMPLE, DO NOT CASH -

|:000000|: :000000000: 69712

Pacific Distribution Company   **69712**

Reference	Net Amount
Invoice #15243, customer # 0505	$19,576.80

PURCHASE ORDER

PO Number: 4376
Date: 12/19/XX

To:
Chateau Americana
3003 Vineyard Way
Huntington, CA 95394

Ship To:

SONOMA Distributors

3224 Greenlawn Street
Ukiah, CA 95482
Phone (707) 555-1705 Fax (707) 555-1706

SHIPPED VIA	ABC #	F.O.B. POINT	TERMS
United Express	A557912	Huntington	Cash

ITEM NO	QTY	SIZE	DESCRIPTION	UNIT PRICE	TOTAL
W120015	480	0.750	Riesling	7.85	3,768.00
W120080	468	0.750	Chardonnay	10.00	4,680.00
W120019	300	0.750	Chenin Blanc	8.25	2,475.00
R130072	780	0.750	Shiraz	9.25	7,215.00
R130056	672	0.750	Merlot	9.00	6,048.00
				TOTAL	24,186.00

Chrystal Harrington   *12/19/XX*

Authorized by   Date

Sonoma Distributors	Humboldt Bank	**17003**
3224 Greenlawn Street	Ukiah, CA 95482	
Ukiah, CA 95482		

Date ___ 12/19/XX ___

PAY ___ Twenty-four Thousand One Hundred Eighty Six and 00/100 Dollars ---------------- $ ___ 24,186.00 ___

To the
order of Chateau Americana
3003 Vineyard Way
Huntington, CA 95394

- SAMPLE, DO NOT CASH -

⑆000000⑆⑆ ⑆000000000⑆ 17003

Sonoma Distributors		**17003**
Reference	Discount	Net Amount
Payment for PO 4376		$24,186.00

| CUSTOMER INVOICE | | Invoice Number | M7634 |

Mendocino Vineyards
8654 Witherspoon Way
Hopland, CA 95449
Phone: (707) 555-1890

Invoice Date   12/20/20XX

Sold To:

Chateau Americana, Inc.
3003 Vineyard Way
Huntington, CA 95394

Credit Terms: 2/10, Net 30

Ship To:

Chateau Americana, Inc.
3003 Vineyard Way
Huntington, CA 95394

Customer I.D	Customer P.O. Number
CHATAM	9660

Description	Product Number	Quantity	Cost	Extended
Cabernet Sauvignon Grapes	CS1250	19 tons	$703.40	$13,364.60

Total Cost: $13,364.60

Comments:

Payment Coupon

Bill Date: 12/23/20XX

| Please Pay by 01/17/20XX |
| $18,887.62 |

Amount Enclosed

Account No. 21790-1879

Chateau Americana, Inc.
3003 Vineyard Way
Huntington, CA 95394

Send Payment to:

Pacific Gas and Electric
P.O. Box 2575
San Francisco, CA 94103

- -

Retain bottom portion for your records, detach and return stub with payment.

Service	Chateau Americana, Inc.	Your Account Number	Rate Class	Billing Date
For:	3003 Vineyard Way Huntington, CA 95394	**21790-1879**	**Commercial**	**12/23/20XX**

Meter Number	Service Period	Days	Type of Reading	Multiplier	Units	Meter Readings Current	Past	Usage
68869800	**11/23/XX – 12/23/XX**	**31**	**Actual**	**1**	**KWH**	**1098412**	**1001301**	**97111**
Previous Balance								16,895.53
Payment								16,895.53
Balance Forward								0.00
Current Charges								18,887.62
							Due Date	**Total Due**
							01/17/20XX	18,887.62

Pacific Gas and Electric
1000 Energy Drive, San Francisco, CA 94103, (415) 973-8943

Edward Jones Financial Services

100 Market Street
San Francisco, CA 94109
(415)504-9000

Customer
Chateau Americana, Inc.
3003 Vineyard Way
Huntington, CA 95394

	Account Number	**Tax Identification #**
	02334-85763	23-7788954

SAVE THIS STATEMENT FOR TAX PURPOSES

Date	Description	Symbol	Fees and/or Commissions($)	Net Dollar Amount ($)	Share Price ($)	Transaction Shares
12/30/03	Microsoft Corporation Common Shares	MSFT	400.00	24,600.00	49.20	500.0000

California Premium Beverage   Bay View Bank   **21803**
39848 South Street   Santa Rosa, CA 95407
Santa Rosa, CA 95402

Date ___ 12/29/XX ___

PAY ___ Forty-One Thousand Two Hundred Sixty-One and 47/100 Dollars ------------------ $ ___ 41,261.47 ___

To The ⌐ Chateau Americana ¬
Order Of   3003 Vineyard Way
           Huntington, CA 95394

- SAMPLE, DO NOT CASH -

⑆000000⑆ ⑈000000000⑈ 21803

California Premium Beverage   **21803**

Reference	Discount	Net Amount
# 0504 Invoice 15535	$1,276.13	$41,261.47

Time Card — Period Ending December 31, 20XX

Employee Name: Thomas P. Bryan
Signature: Tom Bryan
Approved: PJB

Day	In	Out	In	Out	Approved (AM / PM)
1st Day					
2nd Day	07:29 AM	11:30 AM	12:01 PM	05:00 PM	4 / 5
3rd Day	07:31 AM	11:30 AM	11:59 AM	04:33 PM	4 / 4.5
4th Day	06:45 AM	11:30 AM	11:58 AM	04:02 PM	4.75 / 4
5th Day					
6th Day					
7th Day					

Time Card — Period Ending December 26, 20XX

Employee Name: Thomas P. Bryan
Signature: Tom Bryan
Approved: PJB

Day	In	Out	In	Out	Approved (AM / PM)
1st Day					
2nd Day	07:28 AM	11:31 AM	12:02 PM	04:04 PM	4 / 4
3rd Day	07:30 AM	11:33 AM	12:01 PM	04:00 PM	4 / 4
4th Day	07:29 AM	11:30 AM	12:02 PM	04:00 PM	4 / 4
5th Day	Holiday				4
6th Day	Holiday				4
7th Day					

Time Card — Period Ending December 19, 20XX

Employee Name: Thomas P. Bryan
Signature: Tom Bryan
Approved: PJB

Day	In	Out	In	Out	Approved (AM / PM)
1st Day					
2nd Day					
3rd Day	07:31 AM	11:30 AM	11:59 AM	04:03 PM	4 / 4
4th Day	07:30 AM	11:30 AM	11:58 AM	04:02 PM	4 / 4
5th Day	07:31 AM	11:30 AM	12:00 PM	04:01 PM	4 / 4
6th Day	07:29 AM	11:30 AM	12:01 PM	04:00 PM	4 / 4
7th Day					

Time Card — December 31, 20XX

Employee Name: Robert T. Hissom
Signature: *Bob Hissom*
Approved: PJB

Day	In	Out	In	Out	Approved
1st Day					
2nd Day	07:26 AM	11:30 AM	11:55 AM	03:57PM	4
3rd Day	07:30 AM	11:30 AM	11:59 AM	04:01 PM	4
4th Day	07:32 AM	11:32 AM	11:58 AM	04:00 PM	4
5th Day					4
6th Day					4
7th Day					4

Time Card — December 26, 20XX

Employee Name: Robert T. Hissom
Signature: *Bob Hissom*
Approved: PJB

Day	In	Out	In	Out	Approved
1st Day					
2nd Day	07:31 AM	11:31 AM	12:01 PM	04:03 PM	4
3rd Day	07:30 AM	11:33 AM	12:00 PM	04:00 PM	4
4th Day	07:29 AM	11:30 AM	12:04 PM	04:03 PM	4
5th Day	Holiday				4
6th Day	Holiday				4
7th Day					4

Time Card — December 19, 20XX

Employee Name: Robert T. Hissom
Signature: *Bob Hissom*
Approved: PJB

Day	In	Out	In	Out	Approved
1st Day					
2nd Day					
3rd Day					4
4th Day	07:30 AM	11:34 AM	12:02PM	04:03 PM	4
5th Day	07:31 AM	11:30 AM	11:59 AM	04:00 PM	4
6th Day	07:27 AM	11:30 AM	12:02 PM	03:59 PM	4
7th Day	07:29 AM	11:30 AM	12:01 PM	04:02 PM	4

Ingraham & Jenkins

GENERAL JOURNAL

Date	GL Acct #	Explanation	Post Ref*	Debit			Credit		

*Note: Posting reference is "GL and Page Number." For example, GL52.

Initials _____
Date _____

GENERAL JOURNAL

Date	GL Acct #	Explanation	Post Ref*	Debit				Credit			

*Note: Posting reference is "GL and Page Number." For example, GL52.

Initials _____
Date _____

Ingraham & Jenkins

GENERAL JOURNAL

Date	GL Acct #	Explanation	Post Ref*	Debit					Credit				

*Note: Posting reference is "GL and Page Number." For example, GL52.

Initials _____
Date _____

SALES REGISTER

Date	Customer	Invoice/ Document Number	A/R Acct #	Accounts Receivable 121000	Sales 410000	Inventory 145000	Cost of Goods Sold 510000

Initials _____
Date _____

Hint: A/R is debited; Sales is credited. Inventory is credited; COGS is debited.

Ingraham & Jenkins

CASH RECEIPTS JOURNAL

Date	Description	Cash 111000	Sales Discount 420000	Accounts Receivable 121000		Sales 410000	Other Account		
				A/R Acct #	Transaction Amount		GL Acct #	Transaction Amount	Post Ref*

Initials _____
Date _____

*Note: Posting reference is "GL and Page Number." For example, GL52.

Hint: Cash and Sales Discount are debited; A/R and Sales are credited. Other Account is typically credited, although there may also be entries that are debited.

PURCHASES JOURNAL

Date	Vendor	Vendor Invoice #	Inventory 141000	Other Account			Accounts Payable 210000	
				G/L Acct #	Transaction Amount	Post Ref*	A/P Acct #	Transaction Amount

Initials _____
Date _____

*Note: Posting reference is "GL and Page Number." For example, GL52.

Hint: Inventory is debited; Other Account and Accounts Payable are credited.

Ingraham & Jenkins

CASH DISBURSEMENTS JOURNAL

Date	Check Number	Description	Cash 111000			Inventory 141000	Accounts Payable 210000			Other Account			
							A/P Acct #	Transaction Amount		GL Acct #	Transaction Amount	Post Ref

Initials _____
Date _____

*Note: Posting reference is "GL and Page Number." For example, GL52.

Hint: Cash and Inventory are credited; Accounts Payable are credited; Accounts Payable is debited. Other Account is typically debited, although there may be entries that are credited.

PAYROLL JOURNAL [1]

Date	Employee/ SSN	Hours: Regular/ Overtime	Pay: Regular/ Overtime	Gross Pay 601000	FICA Withheld 222200	Medicare Withheld 222300	Federal Income Tax 222100	Net Pay 112000	Check No.

Initials _____
Date _____

[1] Use two lines for each employee. For example, for an hourly employee, the employee's name, regular hours and regular pay are written on the first line, while the social security number, overtime hours, overtime pay, and all other information are written on the second line.

Hint: Gross Pay is debited; FICA Withheld, Medicare Withheld, Federal Income Tax and Net Pay are credited.

ACCOUNTS RECEIVABLE SUBSIDIARY LEDGER

0509	**Alota Wine Distributors** Pier 32, The Embarcadero San Francisco, CA 94111 Phone: (415) 975-8566						**Terms:** **3/15, net 30** **Credit Limit:**		
Date		**Description**		**Debit**		**Credit**		**Balance**	
12	15	Balance Forward						3	340	283	15

0501	**Bock Wines and Vines** Pier 19, The Embarcadero San Francisco, CA 94111 Phone: (415) 834-9675						**Terms:** **3/15, net 30** **Credit Limit:**		
Date		**Description**		**Debit**		**Credit**		**Balance**	
12	15	Balance Forward						39	824	24

0555	**California Pacific Wine** Pier 81, The Embarcadero San Francisco, CA 94111 Phone: (415) 827-8455						**Terms:** **3/15, net 30** **Credit Limit:**		
Date		**Description**		**Debit**		**Credit**		**Balance**	
12	15	Balance Forward						47	147	71

0504	**California Premium Beverage** 39848 South Street Santa Rosa, CA 95402 Phone: (707) 555-7451 Fax: (707) 555-7452						**Terms:** **3/15, net 30** **Credit Limit:**		
Date		**Description**		**Debit**		**Credit**		**Balance**	
12	15	Balance Forward								

Initials _____
Date _____

0511	**Diversita Wine and Beer Distributors** 1328 L Street Sacramento, CA 95814 Phone: (916) 441-5517				**Terms:** **3/15, net 30** **Credit Limit:**			

Date		Description	Debit			Credit			Balance			
12	15	Balance Forward							1	885	031	06

0505	**Pacific Distribution Co.** 10034 Westborough Boulevard San Francisco, CA 94080 Phone: (415) 555-1532				**Terms:** **3/15, net 30** **Credit Limit:**			

Date		Description	Debit			Credit			Balance			
12	15	Balance Forward								39	153	60

0506	**Seaside Distributors, Inc.** 9835 West Hills Road Ukiah, CA 95481 Phone: (707) 555-3102				**Terms:** **3/15, net 30** **Credit Limit:**			

Date		Description	Debit			Credit			Balance			
12	15	Balance Forward										

0527	**Ukiah Beer, Wines and Vines** 782 Talmadge Street Ukiah, CA 95482 Phone: (707) 555-8247				**Terms:** **3/15, net 30** **Credit Limit:**			

Date		Description	Debit			Credit			Balance			
12	15	Balance Forward								15	231	10

Initials _____
Date _____

Ingraham & Jenkins

PERPETUAL INVENTORY SUBSIDIARY LEDGER

145000 - R130056 Merlot

Date		Description	Trans. Quantity	Cost		Extended Cost		Quantity on Hand	Total Balance		
Dec	15	Balance Forward						83484	385	696	08

145000 - R130061 Cabernet Sauvignon

Date		Description	Trans. Quantity	Cost		Extended Cost		Quantity on Hand	Total Balance		
Dec	15	Balance Forward						65784	276	292	80

145000 - R130064 Cabernet Franc

Date		Description	Trans. Quantity	Cost		Extended Cost		Quantity on Hand	Total Balance		
Dec	15	Balance Forward						5964	26	838	00

Initials _____
Date _____

145000 - R130072 Shiraz

Date		Description	Trans. Quantity	Cost		Extended Cost			Quantity on Hand	Total Balance		
Dec	15	Balance Forward							75888	347	567	04

145000 - W120015 Riesling

Date		Description	Trans. Quantity	Cost		Extended Cost			Quantity on Hand	Total Balance		
Dec	15	Balance Forward							118596	339	184	56

145000 - W120016 Sauvignon Blanc

Date		Description	Trans. Quantity	Cost		Extended Cost			Quantity on Hand	Total Balance		
Dec	15	Balance Forward							93636	267	798	96

Initials _____
Date _____

Ingraham & Jenkins

145000 - W120019 Chenin Blanc

Date		Description	Trans. Quantity		Cost		Extended Cost			Quantity on Hand		Total Balance		
Dec	15	Balance Forward								44532		148	736	88

145000 - W120080 Chardonnay

Date		Description	Trans. Quantity		Cost		Extended Cost			Quantity on Hand		Total Balance			
Dec	15	Balance Forward								420552	1	909	306	08

145000 - S140000 Sparkling Brut

Date		Description	Trans. Quantity		Cost		Extended Cost			Quantity on Hand		Total Balance		
Dec	15	Balance Forward								47064		342	625	91

Initials _____
Date _____

ACCOUNTS PAYABLE SUBSIDIARY LEDGER

D2538	Delicio Vineyards 12701 South Fernwood Livermore, CA 94550 Phone: (925) 555-1890							Terms: 2/10, net 30		
Date	**Description**	**Debit**			**Credit**			**Balance**		
11	4	Invoice No. 45354				14	563	56	14	563	56

D0999	Diversi Vineyards 8713 Montauk Drive Napa, CA 94558 (707)515-8575							Terms: 2/10, net 30		
Date	**Description**	**Debit**			**Credit**			**Balance**		
12	15	Balance Forward							2	675	814	93

M0652	Mendocino Vineyards 8654 Witherspoon Way Hopland, CA 95449 Phone: (707) 555-1890							Terms: 2/10, net 30		
Date	**Description**	**Debit**			**Credit**			**Balance**		
12	15	Balance Forward							28	942	78

M5170	Molti Vineyards 12773 Calma Court Geyersville, CA 95441 (707)956-8626							Terms: 2/10, net 30		
Date	**Description**	**Debit**			**Credit**			**Balance**		
12	15	Balance Forward							2	268	654	52

Initials _____
Date _____

EMPLOYEE PAYROLL SUBSIDIARY LEDGER

Employee Name (Last name, First Name, MI): Bryan, Thomas P.

Social Security No: 014-39-4215

Address: 35 Winchester Street

Phone: (707) 555-1495

Huntington, CA 95394

Date of Birth: 6/14/65

Date of Employment: 4/25/95

Date of Termination:

PAY RATE HISTORY

Effective Date	Pay Rate	Pay Type	Position	Filing Status	Withholding Allowances		
4/25/XW	14.00	Hourly	Presses	Single	1		
4/25/XX	15.00	Hourly	Presses	Single	1		

Date		Hours		Gross Pay 601000		FICA Withheld 222200		Medicare Withheld 222300		Federal Income Tax 222100		Net Pay		
Period Ending	Payroll Date	Regular	Overtime											
11-30-XX Balance Forward				32	040	58	1	986	52	464	59	3	588	42	26	001	05
12	15	12	15	88	00	4	25	1	415	63	87	77	20	53	157	00	1	150	33

Initials _____
Date _____

Employee Name (Last name, First Name, MI): Hissom, Robert T.	Social Security No: 349-43-6417
Address: 3187 Heckert Way	Phone: (707) 555-1219
Apt. 4A	
Huntington, CA 95394	Date of Birth: 11-9-77
	Date of Employment: 1-4-98
	Date of Termination:

PAY RATE HISTORY

Effective Date	Pay Rate	Pay Type	Position	Filing Status	Withholding Allowances
1-4-XX	14.25	Hourly	Receiving	Single	0

Date		Hours		Gross Pay 601000		FICA Withheld 222200		Medicare Withheld 222300		Federal Income Tax 222100		Net Pay	
Period Ending	Payroll Date	Regular	Overtime										
11-30-XX Balance Forward				30 438	32	1 887	18	441	36	3 870	46	24 219	32
12 15	12 15	88 00	2 75	1 312	78	81	39	19	04	165	32	1 047	03

Initials _____
Date _____

Employee Name (Last name, First Name, MI): Johnson, Anna C.

Address: 175 Bunker Hill Lane

Huntington, CA 95394

Social Security No: 296-49-3438

Phone: (707) 555-3856

Date of Birth: 9-7-68

Date of Employment: 2-14-01

Date of Termination:

PAY RATE HISTORY

Effective Date	Pay Rate	Pay Type	Position	Filing Status	Withholding Allowances
2-14-XW	1,600	Salary	Payroll	Married	3
2-16-XX	1,750	Salary	Acct Sup	Married	3

| Date | | Hours | | Gross Pay 601000 | FICA Withheld 222200 | Medicare Withheld 222300 | Federal Income Tax 222100 | Net Pay |
Period Ending	Payroll Date	Regular	Overtime					
11-30-XX Balance Forward				36 300 00	2 250 60	526 35	2 294 60	31 228 45
12 15	12 15			1 750 00	108 50	25 38	104 30	1 511 82

Initials _____
Date _____

Employee Name (Last name, First Name, MI): Rodriguez, José G.

Social Security No: 124-11-7755

Address: 2953 Whistler Hill Lane
Huntington, CA 95394

Phone: (707) 555-2024

Date of Birth: 7-7-71

Date of Employment: 11-3-93

Date of Termination:

PAY RATE HISTORY

Effective Date	Pay Rate	Pay Type	Position	Filing Status	Withholding Allowances
1-1-XX	2,550	Salary	Supervisor	Married	4

Date		Hours		Gross Pay 601000	FICA Withheld 222200	Medicare Withheld 222300	Federal Income Tax 222100	Net Pay
Period Ending	Payroll Date	Regular	Overtime					
11-30-XX Balance Forward				56 100 00	3 478 20	813 45	4 412 10	47 396 25
12 15	12 15			2 550 00	158 10	36 98	200 55	2 154 37

Initials _____
Date _____

FIXED ASSET SUBSIDIARY LEDGER

Asset: Fork Lift

Purchased from: Northern California Equipment

Depreciation Method: SL

Estimated Life: 10 years

Estimated Salvage Value: $ 0

Date			Asset Debit	Asset Credit	Asset Balance	Depreciation Debit	Depreciation Credit	Depreciation Balance	Net Book Value
12	23	XW	18 881 00		18 881 00				18 881 00
12	31	XW					944 05	944 05	17 936 95
1	31	XX					157 34	1 101 39	17 779 61
2	28	XX					157 34	1 258 73	17 622 27
3	31	XX					157 34	1 416 07	17 464 93
4	30	XX					157 34	1 573 41	17 307 59
5	31	XX					157 34	1 730 75	17 150 25
6	30	XX					157 34	1 888 09	16 992 91
7	31	XX					157 34	2 045 43	16 835 57
8	31	XX					157 34	2 202 77	16 678 23
9	30	XX					157 34	2 360 11	16 520 89
10	31	XX					157 34	2 517 45	16 363 55
11	30	XX					157 34	2 674 79	16 206 21
12	31	XX					157 36	2 832 15	16 048 85

Initials _____

Date _____

Ingraham & Jenkins

Asset:				Depreciation Method:				
Purchased from:				Estimated Life:				
				Estimated Salvage Value:				

Date	Asset								Depreciation						Net Book Value
	Debit		Credit		Balance				Debit		Credit		Balance		

Initials _____
Date _____

GENERAL LEDGER

111000 - General Checking Account			Ref	Debit				Credit				Debit Balance			
Dec	15	Balance Forward										2	222	927	47

112000 - Payroll Checking Account			Ref	Debit				Credit				Debit Balance			
Dec	15	Balance Forward											1	000	00

113000 - Money Market Account			Ref	Debit				Credit				Debit Balance			
Dec	15	Balance Forward											782	546	49

114000 - Savings Account			Ref	Debit				Credit				Debit Balance			
Dec	15	Balance Forward											51	745	56

119000 - Petty Cash			Ref	Debit				Credit				Debit Balance			
Dec	15	Balance Forward												500	00

121000 - Accounts Receivable			Ref	Debit				Credit				Debit Balance			
Dec	15	Balance Forward										5	366	670	86

*Note: Use the Reference column to refer to the applicable journal. For example, use SR and the page number (e.g., SR29) to refer to the appropriate page of the sales register. Similarly, use CD and the page number to refer to the appropriate page of the cash disbursements journal.

Initials _____
Date _____

129000 – Allowance for Bad Debts			Ref	Debit			Credit			Credit Balance		
Dec	15	Balance Forward								95	401	58

141000 – Inventory -- Production			Ref	Debit			Credit			Debit Balance		
Dec	15	Balance Forward								11	564	851	56

145000 - Inventory – Finished Goods			Ref	Debit			Credit			Debit Balance		
Dec	15	Balance Forward								4	044	046	31

150000 - Prepaid Expenses			Ref	Debit			Credit			Debit Balance		
Dec	15	Balance Forward								142	465	96

160000 - Land and Buildings			Ref	Debit			Credit			Debit Balance		
Dec	15	Balance Forward								16	358	487	34

170000 - Equipment			Ref	Debit			Credit			Debit Balance		
Dec	15	Balance Forward								13	844	881	10

Initials _____
Date _____

Ingraham & Jenkins

180000 - Accumulated Depreciation			Ref	Debit					Credit					Credit Balance			
Dec	15	Balance Forward											15	233	662	97

191000 - Investments			Ref	Debit					Credit					Debit Balance			
Dec	15	Balance Forward											3	070	227	56

210000 - Accounts Payable			Ref	Debit					Credit					Credit Balance			
Dec	15	Balance Forward											4	987	975	79

222100 - Federal Income Tax Withheld			Ref	Debit					Credit					Credit Balance			
Dec	15	Balance Forward												66	739	08

222200 - FICA Withheld			Ref	Debit					Credit					Credit Balance			
Dec	15	Balance Forward												12	237	64

222300 - Medicare Withheld			Ref	Debit					Credit					Credit Balance			
Dec	15	Balance Forward												2	862	01

Initials _____
Date _____

223100 - FICA Payable – Employer			Ref	Debit			Credit			Credit Balance		
Dec	15	Balance Forward								12	237	64

223200 - Medicare Payable – Employer			Ref	Debit			Credit			Credit Balance		
Dec	15	Balance Forward								2	862	01

223300 - Unemployment Taxes Payable			Ref	Debit			Credit			Credit Balance		
Dec	15	Balance Forward									943	57

230000 – Other Accrued Expenses			Ref	Debit			Credit			Credit Balance		
Dec	15	Balance Forward								599	348	98

235000 - Federal Income Taxes Payable			Ref	Debit			Credit			Credit Balance		
Dec	15	Balance Forward									0	00

239000 - Dividends Payable			Ref	Debit			Credit			Credit Balance		
Dec	15	Balance Forward									0	00

Initials _____
Date _____

240000 - Mortgages Payable			Ref	Debit				Credit				Credit Balance			
Dec	15	Balance Forward										7	639	067	73

261000 - Notes Payable			Ref	Debit				Credit				Credit Balance			
Dec	15	Balance Forward											841	000	00

310000 - Common Stock			Ref	Debit				Credit				Credit Balance			
Dec	15	Balance Forward											90	000	00

311000 - PIC in Excess of Par - Common			Ref	Debit				Credit				Credit Balance			
Dec	15	Balance Forward										3	567	265	00

312000 - Dividends - Common			Ref	Debit				Credit				Debit Balance			
Dec	15	Balance Forward												0	00

390000 - Retained Earnings			Ref	Debit				Credit				Credit Balance			
Dec	15	Balance Forward										22	064	134	78

Initials _____
Date _____

410000 - Sales			Ref	Debit			Credit			Credit Balance			
Dec	15	Balance Forward								22	264	431	15

420000 - Sales Discounts			Ref	Debit			Credit			Debit Balance			
Dec	15	Balance Forward									346	741	36

430000 - Sales Returns and Allowances			Ref	Debit			Credit			Debit Balance			
Dec	15	Balance Forward									15	588	47

451000 - Gain/Loss – Fixed Assets			Ref	Debit			Credit			Credit Balance			
Dec	15	Balance Forward										0	00

452000 - Gain/Loss – Marketable Securities			Ref	Debit			Credit			Credit Balance			
Dec	15	Balance Forward										0	00

491000 - Dividend Income			Ref	Debit			Credit			Credit Balance			
Dec	15	Balance Forward									4	000	00

Initials _____
Date _____

Ingraham & Jenkins

492000 - Interest Income	Ref	Debit	Credit	Credit Balance
Dec	15	Balance Forward														23	482	56

510000 - Cost of Goods Sold	Ref	Debit	Credit	Debit Balance
Dec	15	Balance Forward														11	514	092	11

601000 - Wages and Salaries Expense	Ref	Debit	Credit	Debit Balance
Dec	15	Balance Forward													1	965	164	11

601500 - Sales Commission Expense	Ref	Debit	Credit	Debit Balance
Dec	15	Balance Forward														771	665	60

602100 - FICA Tax Expense	Ref	Debit	Credit	Debit Balance
Dec	15	Balance Forward														244	124	52

602200 - Medicare Tax Expense	Ref	Debit	Credit	Debit Balance
Dec	15	Balance Forward														57	093	62

Initials _____
Date _____

602300 - FUTA Expense			Ref	Debit			Credit			Debit Balance		
Dec	15	Balance Forward								7	392	00

602400 - SUTA Expense			Ref	Debit			Credit			Debit Balance		
Dec	15	Balance Forward								22	176	00

611000 - Utilities Expense			Ref	Debit			Credit			Debit Balance		
Dec	15	Balance Forward								307	067	05

611300 - Irrigation & Waste Disp. Expense			Ref	Debit			Credit			Debit Balance		
Dec	15	Balance Forward								230	910	91

612000 - Landscaping Expense			Ref	Debit			Credit			Debit Balance		
Dec	15	Balance Forward								142	475	69

621000 - Advertising Expense			Ref	Debit			Credit			Debit Balance		
Dec	15	Balance Forward								296	794	33

Initials _____
Date _____

Ingraham & Jenkins

623000 - Marketing Expense	Ref	Debit	Credit	Debit Balance
Dec	15	Balance Forward										192	865	67

624000 - Festivals & Competitions Expense	Ref	Debit	Credit	Debit Balance
Dec	15	Balance Forward										238	654	75

631000 - Telephone Expense	Ref	Debit	Credit	Debit Balance
Dec	15	Balance Forward										37	584	73

632000 - Internet & Computer Expense	Ref	Debit	Credit	Debit Balance
Dec	15	Balance Forward										14	475	00

633000 - Postage Expense	Ref	Debit	Credit	Debit Balance
Dec	15	Balance Forward										35	117	66

641000 - Legal & Accounting Fees	Ref	Debit	Credit	Debit Balance
Dec	15	Balance Forward										88	425	50

Initials _____
Date _____

643000 - Other Consulting Fees			Ref	Debit			Credit			Debit Balance		
Dec	15	Balance Forward								12	500	00

651000 - Office Supplies Expense			Ref	Debit			Credit			Debit Balance		
Dec	15	Balance Forward								58	689	68

660000 - Data Processing Expense			Ref	Debit			Credit			Debit Balance		
Dec	15	Balance Forward								9	743	89

670000 - Depreciation Expense			Ref	Debit			Credit			Debit Balance		
Dec	15	Balance Forward								1 092	832	66

680000 - Travel and Entertainment Expense			Ref	Debit			Credit			Debit Balance		
Dec	15	Balance Forward								169	405	86

691000 – Other Insurance Expense			Ref	Debit			Credit			Debit Balance		
Dec	15	Balance Forward								115	058	55

Initials _____
Date _____

Ingraham & Jenkins

692000 – Medical Insurance			Ref	Debit				Credit				Debit Balance		
Dec	15	Balance Forward										192	154	80

693000 - Workmen's Compensation Insurance			Ref	Debit				Credit				Debit Balance		
Dec	15	Balance Forward										139	750	00

699000 - Other Employee Benefits Expense			Ref	Debit				Credit				Debit Balance		
Dec	15	Balance Forward										175	643	90

700000 - Dues and Subscriptions Expense			Ref	Debit				Credit				Debit Balance		
Dec	15	Balance Forward										32	076	00

711000 - Federal Income Tax Expense			Ref	Debit				Credit				Debit Balance		
Dec	15	Balance Forward										857	595	76

712000 - Property Tax Expense			Ref	Debit				Credit				Debit Balance		
Dec	15	Balance Forward										19	875	00

Initials _____
Date _____

721000 - Repairs and Maintenance Expense			Ref	Debit			Credit			Debit Balance		
Dec	15	Balance Forward								71	974	93

731000 - Automobile Expense			Ref	Debit			Credit			Debit Balance		
Dec	15	Balance Forward								81	493	45

740000 - Lease Expense			Ref	Debit			Credit			Debit Balance		
Dec	15	Balance Forward								113	607	56

791000 - Bad Debt Expense			Ref	Debit			Credit			Debit Balance		
Dec	15	Balance Forward									0	00

792000 - Miscellaneous Expense			Ref	Debit			Credit			Debit Balance		
Dec	15	Balance Forward								26	575	63

793000 - Interest Expense			Ref	Debit			Credit			Debit Balance		
Dec	15	Balance Forward								359	915	53

Initials _____
Date _____

TRANSACTION SET B

The books have been posted through December 15, 20XX. The following selected transactions have been extracted from the period December 16 through December 31, 20XX and are to be completed in accordance with the policies and procedures explained above. Documents to be completed can be found in the Document Packet. For all required signatures on these documents sign your name. Supporting documentation for many of the transactions is provided behind the Year-End Procedures on page 12, followed by all necessary journals and ledgers. Additional documentation is found behind the Transaction Set B.

Note that the current year transactions are denoted as 20XX; prior year transactions are denoted as 20XW; transactions for the subsequent year are denoted as 20XY. Your instructor will provide you with the appropriate current year and you can make the fill in the dates accordingly for all transactions.

December	Transaction
16	Receive a purchase order from California Premium Beverage (page 63). Fill and ship the order. Complete Invoice No. 15535, Bill of Lading No. 136480 and record the sale in the journals and ledgers. W. A. Bierkstahler is the sales account representative. Relevant data: shipment weight - 12,532 lbs., trailer # - 122302, serial # - 999356278. The carrier is CA Express. Leave the CID No. blank.
16	Order 29 tons white grapes at $541.11 per ton from Mendocino Vineyards. The item number for the white grapes is WG1003. Complete Purchase Order No. 9682. Relevant data: date required - Dec. 22, shipper - Longhorn Shippers, Inc., buyer - Franz Bieler, supplier # - M0652.
16	Purchase a 2004 Ford truck for $30,250.00. The terms include a $4,750.00 down payment and a 3-year, 6% promissory note to Ford Credit for the remaining $25,500.00. Principal and interest on the note are due monthly beginning January 4, 20XY. The company expects the truck to have a useful life of 5 years and no salvage value. Prepare Check No. 19257 payable to Potter Valley Ford for the down payment and record the transaction in the journals and ledgers.
16	The Board of Directors of Chateau Americana authorized a $50,000 cash dividend payable on December 31st to the stockholders of record on December 26th. Use Check No. 19476 when paid.
17	Receive a phone complaint from Seaside Distributors about a case of Chenin Blanc that was damaged in shipment. The case was part of Invoice No. 15175, dated November 5, 20XX, in the amount of $20,438.40. Seaside paid the invoice on November 19, 20XX and took advantage of the discount (terms 3/15, net 30). Prepare Credit Memo No. 2753 to write-off the damaged inventory that was not returned, and prepare Check No. 19286 to reimburse Seaside for the damaged goods. Record the transactions in the journals and ledgers. W. A. Bierkstahler is the sales account representative. Relevant data: customer PO # - MZ5713. (Note: Be sure to review **Returns and Allowances** on Page 6.)

December	Transaction
19	Receive notification of $850 interest income that was deposited directly into the checking account from a certificate of deposit from State Employees' Credit Union. Record the cash receipt in the journals and ledgers.
19	Receive payment in full from Pacific Distribution Co. on Invoice No. 15243 dated November 13, 20XX, in the amount of $19,576.80 (page 19). Enter the receipt on Cash Receipts Summary No. 5712 and record the cash receipt in the journals and ledgers.
19	Receive a purchase order (page 64) with payment (page 65) from Sonoma Distributors. Fill and ship the order. Complete Invoice No. C2489, enter the receipt on Cash Receipts Summary No. 5712, and record the sale in the journals and ledgers. W. A. Bierkstahler is the sales account representative. Relevant data: shipment weight - 7,650 lbs., trailer # - 279AJ1, serial # - 919515094. (Hint: Use the Other Account column to post Inventory and Cost of Goods Sold.) **DO NOT** create a Bill of Lading for this purchase order.
22	Receive 19 tons red grapes at $703.40 per ton from Mendocino Vineyards. Also received Invoice No. M7634 from Mendocino Vineyards with the shipment (page 22). Terms on the invoice are 2/10, net 30. Complete Receiving Report No. 17251 and record the inventory in the journals and ledgers using the gross method.
26	Receive utility bill from Pacific Gas and Electric in the amount of $18,887.62 (page 23). Prepare Check No. 19402 and record the payment in the journals and ledgers.
30	Receive Brokerage Advice from Edwards Jones for purchase of 500 shares of Microsoft at $49.20 per share plus $400 broker's commission (page 24). Prepare Check No. 19468 and record the purchase in the journals and ledgers.
31	Receive payment in full for the December 16 purchase from California Premium Beverage (page 66). Enter the cash receipt on Cash Receipts Summary No. 5718 and record the cash receipt in the journals and ledgers.
31	Prepare Check No. 19473 payable to Mendocino Vineyards for the shipment received on December 22 and record the payment in the journals and ledgers.
31	Prepare Payroll Checks (Nos. 7111-7114) for Anna Johnson, José Rodriguez, Tom Bryan, and Bob Hissom. Time cards for Tom and Bob are on pages 26-27. Prepare Check No. 19474 to transfer cash from the general cash account to the payroll account. Record the payroll transactions in the journals and ledgers.
31	Prepare Check No. 19475 to repay $50,000 of the principal on long-term debt to Bank of Huntington and record the payment in the journals and ledgers.

Refer to Pages 12-13 for **Month-End** and **Year-End Procedures**.

The Winery at Chateau Americana
Price List

Inventory Code	Description	Standard Cost (per bottle)	Selling Price (per bottle)
R130064	Cabernet Franc	$ 7.80	$ 12.80
R130061	Cabernet Sauvignon	7.90	12.40
R130056	Merlot	8.02	12.00
R130072	Shiraz	8.14	12.15
W120080	Chardonnay	7.95	13.10
W120019	Chenin Blanc	6.71	11.15
W120015	Riesling	6.49	10.75
W120016	Sauvignon Blanc	6.34	10.90
S140000	Sparkling Brut	10.48	16.70

California Premium Beverage

PURCHASE ORDER

39848 South Street
Santa Rosa, CA 95402
Phone (707) 555-7451 Fax (707) 555-7452

To:
Chateau Americana
3003 Vineyard Way
Huntington, CA 95394

Ship To:
California Premium Beverage
39848 South Street
Santa Rosa, CA 95402

ABC Permit #: A59782

P.O. DATE	P.O. NUMBER	SHIPPED VIA	F.O.B. POINT	TERMS
12/13/XX	8746	CA Express	Destination	3/15, net 30

ITEM NO	QTY	SIZE	DESCRIPTION	UNIT PRICE	TOTAL
W120015	1512	0.750	Riesling	10.75	16,254.00
W120016	504	0.750	Sauvignon Blanc	10.90	5,493.60
W120019	336	0.750	Chenin Blanc	11.15	3,746.40
R130061	1176	0.750	Cabernet Sauvignon	12.40	14,582.40
R130056	672	0.750	Merlot	12.00	8,064.00
S140000	240	0.750	Sparkling Brut	16.70	4,008.00
W120080	336	0.750	Chardonnay	13.10	4,401.60
				TOTAL	56,550.00

Jorge Gonzalez   *12/13/XX*

Authorized by   Date

PURCHASE ORDER

PO Number: 4376
Date: 12/19/XX

To:
Chateau Americana
3003 Vineyard Way
Huntington, CA 95394

Ship To:
SONOMA Distributors
3224 Greenlawn Street
Ukiah, CA 95482
Phone (707) 555-1705 Fax (707) 555-1706

SHIPPED VIA	ABC #	F.O.B. POINT	TERMS
United Express	A557912	Huntington	Cash

ITEM NO	QTY	SIZE	DESCRIPTION	UNIT PRICE	TOTAL
W120015	480	0.750	Riesling	10.75	5,160.00
W120080	468	0.750	Chardonnay	13.10	6,130.80
W120019	300	0.750	Chenin Blanc	11.15	3,345.00
R130072	780	0.750	Shiraz	12.15	9,477.00
R130056	672	0.750	Merlot	12.00	8,064.00
				TOTAL	32,176.80

Chrystal Harrington   *12/19/XX*
Authorized by   Date

Sonoma Distributors	Humboldt Bank	**17003**
3224 Greenlawn Street	Ukiah, CA 95482	
Ukiah, CA 95482		

Date   12/19/XX

PAY   Thirty-two Thousand One Hundred Seventy-Six and 80/100 Dollars ----------------- $ 32,176.80

To the   Chateau Americana
order of   3003 Vineyard Way
               Huntington, CA 95394

- SAMPLE, DO NOT CASH -

⑊:000000⑊: :000000000: 17003

Sonoma Distributors		**17003**
Reference	Discount	Net Amount
Payment for PO 4376		$32,176.80

California Premium Beverage
39848 South Street
Santa Rosa, CA 95402

Bay View Bank
Santa Rosa, CA 95407

21803

Date ___12/29/XX___

PAY___Fifty-Four Thousand Eight Hundred Fifty-Three and 50/100 Dollars ------------------ $ ___54,853.50___

To The
Order Of ⌐ Chateau Americana ¬
3003 Vineyard Way
Huntington, CA 95394

- SAMPLE, DO NOT CASH -

⑆000000⑆ ⑈000000000⑈ 21803

California Premium Beverage

21803

Reference	Discount	Net Amount
# 0504 Invoice 15535	1,696.50	$54,853.50

TRANSACTION SET C

The books have been posted through December 15, 20XX. The following selected transactions have been extracted from the period December 16 through December 31, 20XX and are to be completed in accordance with the policies and procedures explained above. Documents to be completed can be found in the Document Packet. For all required signatures on these documents sign your name. Supporting documentation for many of the transactions is provided behind the Year-End Procedures on page 12, followed by all necessary journals and ledgers. Additional documentation is found behind the Transaction Set C.

Note that the current year transactions are denoted as 20XX; prior year transactions are denoted as 20XW; transactions for the subsequent year are denoted as 20XY. Your instructor will provide you with the appropriate current year and you can make the fill in the dates accordingly for all transactions.

December	Transaction
16	Receive a purchase order from California Premium Beverage (page 70). Fill and ship the order. Complete Invoice No. 15535, Bill of Lading No. 136480 and record the sale in the journals and ledgers. W. A. Bierkstahler is the sales account representative. Relevant data: shipment weight - 12,532 lbs., trailer # - 122302, serial # - 999356278. The carrier is CA Express. Leave the CID No. blank.
16	Order 31 tons white grapes at $591.11 per ton from Mendocino Vineyards. The item number for the white grapes is WG1003. Complete Purchase Order No. 9682. Relevant data: date required - Dec. 22, shipper - Longhorn Shippers, Inc., buyer - Franz Bieler, supplier # - M0652.
16	Purchase a 2004 Ford truck for $32,750.00. The terms include a $4,750.00 down payment and a 3-year, 6% promissory note to Ford Credit for the remaining $28,000.00. Principal and interest on the note are due monthly beginning January 4, 20XY. The company expects the truck to have a useful life of 5 years and no salvage value. Prepare Check No. 19257 payable to Potter Valley Ford for the down payment and record the transaction in the journals and ledgers.
16	Sell Fork Lift that was purchased on December 23, 20XW for $19,250.00 to Castle Vineyards. Record the transactions in the journals and ledgers (the Fork Lift depreciation for December was calculated before the sale took place and depreciation for the year needs to be adjusted). Enter receipt on Cash Receipts Summary No. 5712.
17	Receive a phone complaint from Seaside Distributors about a case of Chenin Blanc that was damaged in shipment. The case was part of Invoice No. 15175, dated November 5, 20XX, in the amount of $20,438.40. Seaside paid the invoice on November 19, 20XX and took advantage of the discount (terms 3/15, net 30). Prepare Credit Memo No. 2753 to write-off the damaged inventory that was not returned, and prepare Check No. 19286 to reimburse Seaside for the damaged goods. Record the transactions in the journals and ledgers. W.A. Bierkstahler is the sales account representative. Relevant data: customer PO # - MZ5713. (Note: Be sure to review *Returns and Allowances* on Page 6.)

December	Transaction
19	Receive notification of $850 interest income that was deposited directly into the checking account from a certificate of deposit from State Employees' Credit Union. Record the cash receipt in the journals and ledgers.
19	Receive payment in full from Pacific Distribution Co. on Invoice No. 15243 dated November 13, 20XX, in the amount of $20,164.30 (page 19). Enter the receipt on Cash Receipts Summary No. 5712 and record the cash receipt in the journals and ledgers.
19	Receive a purchase order (page 71) with payment (page 72) from Sonoma Distributors. Fill and ship the order. Complete Invoice No. C2489, enter the receipt on Cash Receipts Summary No. 5712, and record the sale in the journals and ledgers. W. A. Bierkstahler is the sales account representative. Relevant data: shipment weight - 7,650 lbs., trailer # - 279AJ1, serial # - 919515094. (Hint: Use the Other Account column to post Inventory and Cost of Goods Sold.) **DO NOT** create a Bill of Lading for this purchase order.
22	Receive 21 tons red grapes at $718.63 per ton from Mendocino Vineyards. Also received Invoice No. M7634 from Mendocino Vineyards with the shipment (page 74). Terms on the invoice are 2/10, net 30. Complete Receiving Report No. 17251 and record the inventory in the journals and ledgers using the gross method.
26	Receive utility bill from Pacific Gas and Electric in the amount of $19,271.12 (page 73). Prepare Check No. 19402 and record the payment in the journals and ledgers.
30	Receive Brokerage Advice from Edwards Jones for purchase of 500 shares of Microsoft at $49.20 per share plus $400 broker's commission (page 24). Prepare Check No. 19468 and record the purchase in the journals and ledgers.
31	Receive payment in full for the December 16 purchase from California Premium Beverage (page 75). Enter the cash receipt on Cash Receipts Summary No. 5718 and record the cash receipt in the journals and ledgers.
31	Prepare Check No. 19473 payable to Mendocino Vineyards for the shipment received on December 22 and record the payment in the journals and ledgers.
31	Prepare Payroll Checks (Nos. 7111-7114) for Anna Johnson, José Rodriguez, Tom Bryan, and Bob Hissom. Time cards for Tom and Bob are on pages 26-27. Prepare Check No. 19474 to transfer cash from the general cash account to the payroll account. Record the payroll transactions in the journals and ledgers.
31	Prepare Check No. 19475 to repay $80,000 of the principal on long-term debt to Bank of Huntington and record the payment in the journals and ledgers.

Refer to Pages 12-13 for **Month-End** and **Year-End Procedures**.

The Winery at Chateau Americana
Price List

Inventory Code	Description	Standard Cost (per bottle)	Selling Price (per bottle)
R130064	Cabernet Franc	$ 9.30	$ 13.40
R130061	Cabernet Sauvignon	9.40	14.00
R130056	Merlot	9.52	13.60
R130072	Shiraz	9.64	13.75
W120080	Chardonnay	9.45	14.70
W120019	Chenin Blanc	8.31	12.75
W120015	Riesling	8.09	12.35
W120016	Sauvignon Blanc	7.94	12.50
S140000	Sparkling Brut	11.98	18.30

California Premium Beverage

PURCHASE ORDER

39848 South Street
Santa Rosa, CA 95402
Phone (707) 555-7451 Fax (707) 555-7452

To:
Chateau Americana
3003 Vineyard Way
Huntington, CA 95394

Ship To:
California Premium Beverage
39848 South Street
Santa Rosa, CA 95402

ABC Permit #: A59782

P.O. DATE	P.O. NUMBER	SHIPPED VIA	F.O.B. POINT	TERMS
12/13/XX	8746	CA Express	Destination	3/15, net 30

ITEM NO	QTY	SIZE	DESCRIPTION	UNIT PRICE	TOTAL
W120015	1512	0.750	Riesling	12.35	18,673.20
W120016	504	0.750	Sauvignon Blanc	12.50	6,300.00
W120019	336	0.750	Chenin Blanc	12.75	4,284.00
R130061	1176	0.750	Cabernet Sauvignon	14.00	16,464.00
R130056	672	0.750	Merlot	13.60	9,139.20
S140000	240	0.750	Sparkling Brut	18.30	4,392.00
W120080	336	0.750	Chardonnay	14.70	4,939.20
				TOTAL	64,191.60

Jorge Gonzalez
Authorized by

12/13/XX
Date

PURCHASE ORDER

PO Number: 4376
Date: 12/19/XX

To:
Chateau Americana
3003 Vineyard Way
Huntington, CA 95394

Ship To:
SONOMA Distributors
3224 Greenlawn Street
Ukiah, CA 95482
Phone (707) 555-1705 Fax (707) 555-1706

SHIPPED VIA	ABC #	F.O.B. POINT	TERMS
United Express	A557912	Huntington	Cash

ITEM NO	QTY	SIZE	DESCRIPTION	UNIT PRICE	TOTAL
W120015	480	0.750	Riesling	12.35	5,928.00
W120080	468	0.750	Chardonnay	14.70	6,879.60
W120019	300	0.750	Chenin Blanc	12.75	3,825.00
R130072	780	0.750	Shiraz	13.75	10,725.00
R130056	672	0.750	Merlot	13.60	9,139.20
				TOTAL	36,496.80

Chrystal Harrington   *12/19/XX*
Authorized by   Date

Sonoma Distributors	Humboldt Bank	**17003**
3224 Greenlawn Street Ukiah, CA 95482	Ukiah, CA 95482	

Date ___12/19/XX___

PAY___ Thirty-six Thousand Four Hundred Ninety-six and 80/100 Dollars ----------------- $ ___36,496.80___

To the order of
Chateau Americana
3003 Vineyard Way
Huntington, CA 95394

- SAMPLE, DO NOT CASH -

|:000000|: :000000000: 17003

Sonoma Distributors		**17003**
Reference	Discount	Net Amount
Payment for PO 4376		$36,496.80

CUSTOMER INVOICE

Mendocino Vineyards
8654 Witherspoon Way
Hopland, CA 95449
Phone: (707) 555-1890

Invoice Number **M7634**

Invoice Date   12/20/20XX

Sold To:

Chateau Americana, Inc.
3003 Vineyard Way
Huntington, CA 95394

Credit Terms: 2/10, Net 30

Ship To:

Chateau Americana, Inc.
3003 Vineyard Way
Huntington, CA 95394

Customer I.D	Customer P.O. Number
CHATAM	9660

Description	Product Number	Quantity	Cost	Extended
Cabernet Sauvignon Grapes	CS1250	21 tons	$718.63	$15,091.23

Total Cost: $15,091.23

Comments:

Distribution: Copy 1 — Accounting; Copy 2 – Shipping; Copy 3 – Customer

Payment Coupon

Bill Date: 12/23/20XX

Please Pay by 01/17/20XX
$19,271.12

Amount Enclosed

Account No. 21790-1879

Chateau Americana, Inc.
3003 Vineyard Way
Huntington, CA 95394

Send Payment to:

Pacific Gas and Electric
P.O. Box 2575
San Francisco, CA 94103

- -

Retain bottom portion for your records, detach and return stub with payment.

Service	Chateau Americana, Inc.	Your Account Number	Rate Class	Billing Date
For:	3003 Vineyard Way Huntington, CA 95394	**21790-1879**	**Commercial**	**12/23/20XX**

Meter Number	Service Period	Days	Type of Reading	Multiplier	Units	Meter Readings Current	Past	Usage
68869800	**11/23/XX – 12/23/XX**	**31**	**Actual**	**1**	**KWH**	**1098412**	**1001301**	**97111**
Previous Balance								16,895.53
Payment								16,895.53
Balance Forward								0.00
Current Charges								19,271.12
							Due Date	**Total Due**
							01/17/20XX	19,271.12

Pacific Gas and Electric
1000 Energy Drive, San Francisco, CA 94103, (415) 973-8943

California Premium Beverage		Bay View Bank	**21803**
39848 South Street		Santa Rosa, CA 95407	
Santa Rosa, CA 95402			

Date _____ 12/29/XX _____

PAY_____ Sixty-two Thousand Two Hundred Sixty-five and 85/100 Dollars ------------------ $ _____ 62,265.85 _____

To The
Order Of   Chateau Americana
                3003 Vineyard Way
                Huntington, CA 95394

- SAMPLE, DO NOT CASH -

|:000000|: :000000000: 21803

California Premium Beverage		**21803**
Reference	Discount	Net Amount
# 0504 Invoice 15535	1,925.75	$62,265.85

SPREADSHEET APPLICATIONS
USING MICROSOFT® EXCEL 2010:
The Winery at Chateau Americana

LEARNING OBJECTIVES

After completing and discussing this module, you should be able to:

- Recognize the managerial and technological issues and risks associated with designing and utilizing a spreadsheet application as the primary accounting information system
- Understand and evaluate data integrity issues associated with spreadsheet utilization
- Understand and perform data analysis techniques using spreadsheet applications
- Understand the advantages and disadvantages of various presentation formats
- Understand the advantages and disadvantages of database functions in spreadsheet applications

BACKGROUND

When Chateau Americana began operations in 1980, accounting records were maintained manually. As the winery grew, the former CFO decided it was time to computerize various aspects of the system. As an initial step, he decided to use a spreadsheet program to assist in preparing journal entries, the year-end worksheet, and the financial statements. He also wanted to be able to create a single set of financial statements that could be used to present differing amounts of information to the various users. His goal was to simplify the bookkeeping functions, while improving the accuracy and usefulness of the financial statements. He knew reducing the amount of redundancy inherent in manual recordkeeping could do this. If the data was entered once and was verified at that time, this data could then be transmitted to other spreadsheets without the risk of incurring clerical errors that might appear upon re-entering the same data. He, therefore, had created various spreadsheets for Chateau Americana that would assist in these goals.

Assume that you had been asked to create these spreadsheets for Chateau Americana, given the current year-end data. The following exercises were written assuming that you will be working in *Microsoft® Excel 2010*. Tutorials follow many of the sections, providing hints and additional explanations for some of the more advanced Excel skill requirements. As you read through the text, you will periodically come across the symbol ⌘. This symbol denotes areas for which additional tutorial explanation is provided.

NOTE: This book has consistently left the year as a variable. Your instructor will inform you as to the appropriate years to be used.

DOWNLOAD THE FILE

Download the Excel file entitled "CA Computerized Excel Workbook.xlsx" from the CAST web site (your instructor will provide you with the URL for this web site) and save it as *"yourlastname_your firstname.xls"*⌘. This workbook contains several worksheets that will be necessary for the completion of the various exercises contained in the Spreadsheet assignment. We will continue to refer to this file as the **CA Computerized Excel Workbook** file throughout the text, although you have now renamed it using your own name.

Save As
The **Save As** function in *Excel 2010* can be found by clicking on the **File** on the Excel spreadsheet.

As you have undoubtedly learned by now, one internal control for computerized accounting information systems is to maintain backups. Therefore, as with any other computer file, it is important to **save your work often**. In addition, it is strongly suggested that you **back up your file** to another storage medium frequently to avoid problems in the event that you experience a crash, virus, etc.

PROTECTING THE DATA

Open the **CA Computerized Excel Workbook** file you have downloaded. This file contains several worksheets including a blank year-end worksheet similar to the one you may have completed in the Manual AIS Module of CAST entitled **Y-E Worksheet**. Examine the set-up of the year-end worksheet, familiarizing yourself with the ways in which the creation of formulas in Excel can be used to minimize the amount of data input.

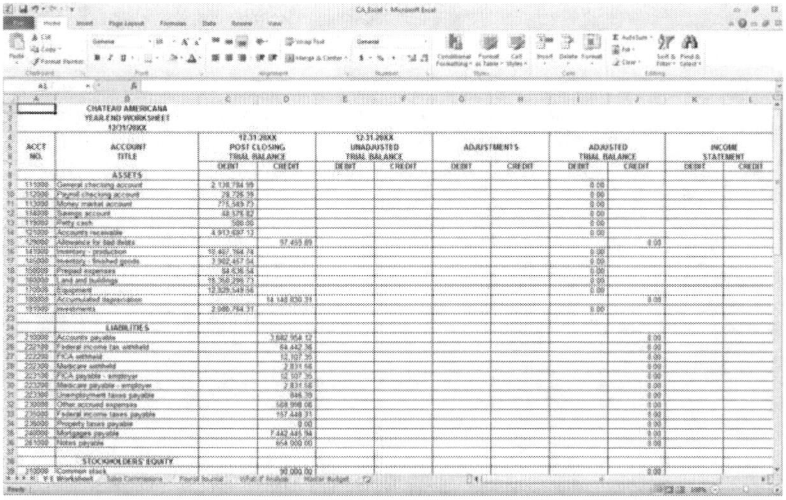

Figure 1

Requirements

1. With the file open to the **Y-E Worksheet**, enter the data for the 12-31-XX Unadjusted Trial Balance and the 12-31-XX Adjustments columns, allowing the formulas contained in the spreadsheet to calculate the totals and carry the figures from one column of the spreadsheet to the next (i.e., from those columns to the Adjusted Trial Balance, Balance Sheet, and Income Statement columns). Make sure that you change the years so that they reflect the appropriate date (ask your instructor if you are uncertain as to the years you should be using). The data for completion of this worksheet are available on the CAST web site.

2. Review the worksheet to be sure that your column totals are accurate and that you have entered the correct data for each account.

3. Once you have made certain that the embedded formulas are being calculated correctly, you should lock (or protect) the cells that contain them so that no one can change the formulas at a later date. To do this, highlight cells **I9** through **N91** and then protect them ⌘.

Protecting the Data Tutorial

Highlight the cells to be protected. Click on **File** tab. Under the Info tab [Info],

click on **Protect Workbook** [Protect Workbook]. Now select "Protect Current Sheet" from the pull-down menu. Make sure that the boxes entitled "Protect Worksheet and Contents of Locked Cells," "Select locked cells," and "Select unlocked cells" are checked. You will need to enter a password to protect the cells. For purposes of this assignment, use "protect" as the password. You will then be prompted to confirm the password by reentering it. Note: The password is **case sensitive**!

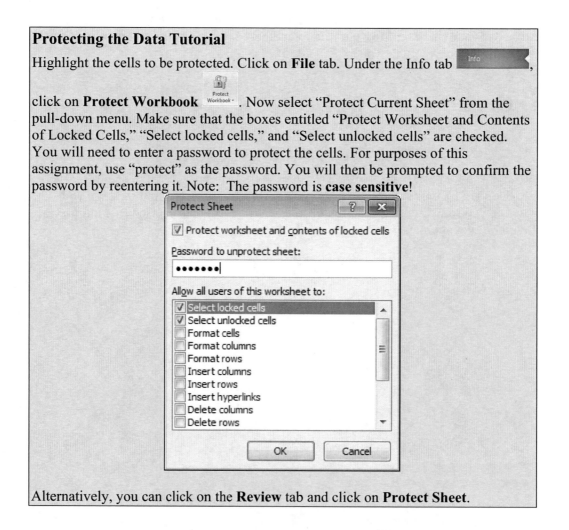

Alternatively, you can click on the **Review** tab and click on **Protect Sheet**.

---

4. Verify that the cells have been locked properly by attempting to alter any of the formulas contained in columns I through N. If the worksheet has been properly protected, you should get the following warning:

Figure 2

FORMULA AUDITING

The spreadsheet is now ready to be used for the creation of the financial statements and manipulation of the data for various managerial tasks. Before you begin, however, it is important to recognize that, despite the fact that you will be using a computer to deal with many of the clerical tasks previously done manually, the computer can do so accurately only insofar as the formulas are entered correctly. Statistics show that the number of errors on computer worksheets exceeds 25%.

Some of the more common errors are:

# NAME?	Occurs when Excel cannot evaluate a defined name used in the formula because the name may never have existed, may be misspelled, or may have been inadvertently deleted.
# N/A	Dependent upon the formula. For example, it may mean that no value was available in a vlookup function.
#REF!	Indicates a problem with a cell reference due, perhaps, to deleting cells, rows or columns used in a formula.
# VALUE!	Typically due to trying to use a cell containing text in a calculation or entering incorrect arguments.

The **Formula Auditing** tool in Excel enables the user to audit the worksheet to find and correct many of the errors that inevitably occur.

Requirements

As you work through the following steps, you will occasionally be asked questions. Please respond to these questions in the space provided in the **Sales Commissions** worksheet.

1. Open the **CA Computerized Excel Workbook** file and click on the **Sales Commissions** worksheet. Click on the **Formulas** tab to display the **Formula Auditing** toolbar.

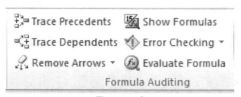

Figure 2

The following table describes some of the buttons on the toolbar:

Option	Description
Trace Precedents	Displays an arrow from all cells that supply data to the selected cell.
Trace Dependents	Displays an arrow to the cell that is dependent upon the selected cell for data.
Remove Arrows	Removes all tracer arrows throughout the worksheet.
Remove Precedent Arrows	Removes all precedent arrows for each level displayed. The button must be pushed for each level from which the data are supplied. Found under the Remove Arrows pull-down menu.
Remove Dependent Arrows	Removes all dependent arrows for each level displayed. The button must be pushed for each level to which the data are supplied. Found under the Remove Arrows pull-down menu.
Show Formulas	Displays the formulas in each cell rather than the resulting values.
Error Checking	Describes the error that has occurred and allows the user to obtain help on the error, to walk through the calculation steps, to ignore the error, or to edit the error in the formula bar.
Trace Errors	Allows the user to find the source of an error by displaying a blue arrow from the source of the error to the selected cell. Found under the Error Checking pull-down menu.
Circular References	Occurs when a formula refers back to its own cell, either directly or indirectly. Found under the Error Checking pull-down menu.
Evaluate Formula	Allows the user to display the result of any underlined or italicized portion of a formula.

2. Go to cell **G30**. Click on **Trace Precedents** on the **Formula Auditing** toolbar. From what cell is cell **G30** obtaining its data? (Enter your response in cell **B48**.)

3. Now click on **Remove Precedent Arrows** on the **Formula Auditing** toolbar.

4. While cell **G30** is highlighted, click on **Error Checking** on the **Formula Auditing** toolbar.

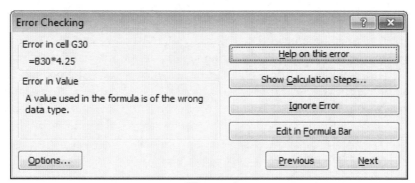

Figure 4

5. Note that an explanation for the error is provided for you in the window. More detailed explanations can be obtained by clicking on **Help on this error**. Obtain two other possible causes for the error by clicking on **Help on this error** and enter them in cell **B49**. Close the **Error Checking** window.

6. While cell **G30** is highlighted, click on **Evaluate Formula** on the **Formula Auditing** toolbar. Next, click on **Evaluate**. Based upon what you find when Excel evaluates this formula, explain why has this error occurred. Enter your response in cell **B50**. Close the **Evaluate Formula** window.

7. Examine the cells surrounding **G30** and then fix the error in cell **G30**.

8. Go to cell **F35**. Click on **Trace Precedents** on the **Formula Auditing** toolbar. What happens? (Enter your response in cell **B51**.)

9. While cell **F35** is highlighted, click on **Trace Dependents** on the **Formula Auditing** toolbar. What happens? (Enter your response in cell **B52**.)

10. While cell **F35** is highlighted, click on **Evaluate Formula** on the **Formula Auditing** toolbar. Next, click on **Evaluate** and determine why the error has occurred and then fix it. (Enter your response as to why the error occurred in cell **B53**.)

11. Check to be sure that all errors on this worksheet have been fixed.

DATA INTEGRITY

Using the **Y-E Worksheet** you can create the Statement of Income and Retained Earnings and the Balance Sheet with very little additional data entry. This is beneficial because you have already verified the accuracy of the data on the **Y-E Worksheet**. If you access this data directly, you will only need to verify the logic on the other spreadsheets you are preparing to be sure that they are operating as intended and achieving the correct results. One method by which this can be accomplished is to utilize the "=" sign to tell Excel that a particular cell is equal to the amount in another cell on another spreadsheet. Another method is to create a Name for a particular amount to be used later in a formula. You will utilize both of these methods.

The Statement of Income and Retained Earnings is to be prepared as a **single-year, multi-step income statement**. This statement is to be formatted so that it can provide differing amounts of detail to the users when viewed or printed at a later date. To do this, you will need to pay careful attention to the formatting instructions provided below. Do not attempt to enter any formulas or data until you are finished formatting. Then carefully read the directions in step 8 to continue with the data entry. You may find it helpful to refer to the sample shown in *Figure 5* as you work through the income statement instructions.

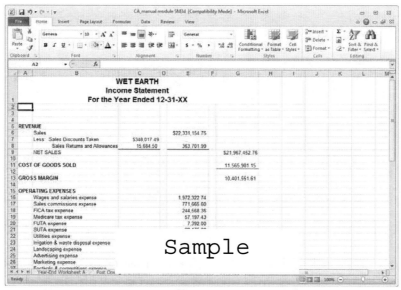

Figure 5

Requirements

1. Open the **CA Computerized Excel Workbook** file and insert a new worksheet by clicking on **Insert > Insert Sheet** (under the **Cells** section of the **Home** tab).

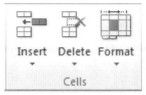

Figure 6

2. Format the columns for the following widths ⌘e:

A	B	C	D	E	F	G
31	38	14	3	14	3	17

Column A will contain the category headings. Column B will contain the account titles. Columns C, E and G will contain amounts.

Set the row height for row 1 at 71 ⌘. It is not necessary to adjust the heights of the remaining rows.

Rename the newly inserted worksheet "**Income Statement.**" ⌘

3. Column B will be used for individual revenue and expense account titles such as Sales, Wages and Salaries Expense, etc. Starting in **row 6 of column B**, enter the revenue and expense account titles listed on the **Y-E Worksheet**. (**HINT**: Be sure that you have copied and pasted on the new worksheet all account titles needed to create the Statement of Income and Retained Earnings. The ordering and presentation of the account titles should be consistent with that commonly used on income statements, not that found on the **Y-E Worksheet**. When you past the cells into the **Income Statement Worksheet**, be sure to use the **Values** function so that you don't include the formatting from the prior worksheet.)

4. Column A will be used for category headings. Beginning on **row 5** of **column A**, enter the category heading "REVENUE." Enter the following headings in subsequent rows in column A: COST OF GOODS SOLD, GROSS MARGIN, OPERATING EXPENSES, INCOME FROM OPERATIONS, OTHER INCOME AND EXPENSES, INCOME (LOSS) BEFORE TAXES, FEDERAL INCOME TAX, NET INCOME (LOSS), RETAINED EARNINGS - 12/31/20XW, RETAINED EARNINGS - 12/31/20XX, and EARNINGS PER SHARE.

5. Capitalize the main headings in column A using bold Arial 10. Use non-bold Arial 10 for the account titles in column B. Be sure to underline when appropriate using borders ⌘.

6. Columns C and E should be used for amounts that must be added to arrive at subtotals. For example, the amounts for Sales Returns and Allowances and

Sales Discounts should be placed in column C. These are combined to arrive at the amount that is subtracted from Sales (both of these amounts should be in Column E) to compute Net Sales, which is then presented in column G along with the other main category totals (see *Figure 5*).

7. Copy the appropriate amounts to the **Income Statement** worksheet by typing an "=," locating the appropriate cell on the **Y-E Worksheet** (**HINT**: Most of these amounts should be taken from columns K through L), and hitting **Enter**. For example, when you have finished entering the value for Sales, the formula should read: "='Y-E Worksheet'!L45." This has the effect of returning the value located on the **Y-E Worksheet** to the **Income Statement** sheet. The benefit of doing this is that you know the numbers in the Income Statement are correct since you have already proofed the **Y-E Worksheet**. There is no redundancy or inconsistency in your workbook since you are pulling the data from its original source of data entry.

   Note, however, that Retained Earnings on the **Y-E Worksheet** has not yet been updated for the current year Net Income. Therefore, the amount in cell **N42** on the **Y-E Worksheet** represents Retained Earnings as of 12-31-XW. You will have to use a formula on the **Income Statement** worksheet to calculate Retained Earnings as of 12-31-XX.

8. Skip steps 11 through 13 if your instructor does not want you to calculate federal income taxes on the **Income Statement** worksheet using a nested "IF" statement ⌘. A nested "IF" statement is a powerful tool that allows Excel to evaluate several logical conditions in a single function. For example, it can be used for searching an Excel database or in complex calculations such as that of federal or state income tax where the calculation varies depending upon the level of net income before taxes, or payroll taxes where the calculation is dependent upon the amount of gross pay an individual earns.

9. You will need to calculate the amount to be entered into Federal Income Tax Expense using a nested "IF" statement. To minimize future changes to the nested "IF" statement, insert a new worksheet and name it "**Reference Data.**" Create a heading in this worksheet for Corporate Tax Brackets and Rates. You should provide any text necessary for the bracket descriptions in column A (e.g., "Greater than or equal to," etc.), the amounts for the brackets in column B (e.g., $50,000, etc.) and the rates in column C (e.g., 15%, etc.). Column D should contain any adjustments needed for your formula. Creating the brackets and associated rates will take some thought on your part as they are to be used in your nested IF statement for the corporate tax calculation to eliminate the need to recreate the formula if the brackets or rates are changed by Congress at a later date. (**Note:** Current tax rates may be found in any tax textbook or by referring to the instructions for Schedule J, Form 1120.)

10. It is much easier for both the creator and for later users of a worksheet to understand and maintain the worksheet if it is created using meaningful names for the data values contained in the cells rather than by using the cell references for those data values. For example, it would probably make more

sense to you if you saw a formula written as =NetSales-CostOfGoodsSold instead of =G9-G11. For this reason, it is a good practice to use cell names whenever possible, but particularly when creating complex formulas.

Create cell names ⌘ for the brackets, rates and adjustments (e.g., Bracket0, Rate0, Bracket1, Rate1, etc.)

11. Create the nested IF ⌘ statement using the cell names on the Reference Data sheet.

12. Create the following cell names ⌘ for the Statement of Income and Retained Earnings:
    - Cost Of Goods Sold
    - Net Sales
    - Interest Expense
    - NIBT (i.e., net income before tax)
    - Federal Income Tax
    - Net Income

13. Properly format your amounts for currency (i.e., with dollar signs, commas, decimal points, etc.) ⌘ where appropriate. REMEMBER: Decimal points are supposed to line up!

14. Create a multiple-line heading ⌘ in cell **A1**. The information for this heading is as follows:

    Chateau Americana, Inc. (using bold Arial 14)
    Statement of Income and Retained Earnings (using bold Arial 12)
    For the Year ended 12/31/XX (using bold Arial 12)

    Center the heading across columns A through E.

15. Use formulas to calculate subtotals and totals on the income statement.

16. Be sure to include Earnings Per Share on your income statement. *There are 45,000 shares issued and outstanding.*

    NOTE: At this point, the only amount that you should have typed into your worksheet is the number of shares issued and outstanding needed to calculated earnings per share. All other amounts should be formula-driven.

17. Insert a new worksheet entitled "**Balance Sheet**" and create a **comparative, classified Balance Sheet** employing the same general formatting techniques and utilizing formulas as before (see *Figure 7)*. Determine your column widths as you deem appropriate. Use a single column to present the various account balances for 20XW and a single column to present the account balances for 20XX.

	A	B	C	D	E	F	G	H	I	J	K
					WET EARTH						
					Balance Sheet						
1					**For the Year Ending 12-31-XX**						
2											
3							20XW		20XX		
4						**ASSETS**					
5											
6	**CURRENT ASSETS**										
7		Cash & Cash Equivalents					$2,992,137.93		$2,984,718.65		
8		Accounts Receivable					4,913,697.13		5,366,569.32		
9		Less: Allowance for bad debts					(97,459.89)		(106,374.32)		
10		Inventory					14,309,621.78		15,593,099.63		
11		Prepaid Expenses					84,636.54		142,465.96		
12		Investments - Available for Sale					2,080,764.31		3,095,227.56		
13		**Total Current Assets**					$24,283,397.80		$27,075,706.80		
14											
15	**PROPERTY, PLANT & EQUIPMENT**						$28,179,845.29		$30,230,118.44		
16		Less: Accumulated Depreciation					(14,1				
17							$14,0				
18											
19		**TOTAL ASSETS**					$38,3				
20											
21		**LIABILITIES AND STOCKHOLDER'S EQUITY**									
22											
23	**CURRENT LIABILITIES**										
24		Accounts Payable					$3,682,954.12		$4,987,975.79		
25		Accrued Expenses					568,998.06		599,403.23		
26		Payroll Taxes Withheld and Payable					95,166.57		99,558.04		

Sample (appears in cells G17–I19 area)

Figure 7

18. Create the following cell or range names for the Balance Sheet:
    - Beginning Inventory
    - Ending Inventory
    - Current Assets (for 20XX only)
    - Beginning Total Assets
    - Ending Total Assets
    - Current Liabilities (for 20XX only)
    - Ending Total Liabilities
    - Beginning Stockholders Equity
    - Ending Stockholders Equity

19. (*Optional*) Insert a new worksheet entitled "**Statement of Cash Flows**" and create a Statement of Cash Flows (indirect method) using the same general formatting techniques and utilizing formulas as before.

Data Integrity Tutorial

Adjust the column width. There are three ways in which you can adjust the column width. First, columns may be formatted by clicking on the applicable column letter. Then click on **Format > Column Width** (in the **Cells** section of the **Home** tab) and type in the desired column width.

Insert Delete Format

Cells

Alternatively, you can right-click on the appropriate column letter, select **Column Width** from the pull-down menu and enter the desired column width. Finally, you can adjust the column width by placing the cursor on the line separating the heading for columns A and B on the gray bar above the cells. You will notice that the cursor turns to a cross and the column width is displayed in the box above the column separator. Drag the cursor to the desired width. Repeat for every column whose width should be changed.

Adjust the row height. Rows may be formatted by clicking on the applicable row number and then clicking on **Format > Row Height** (in the **Cells** section of the **Home** tab) and typing in the desired row height. Alternatively, you can right-click on the appropriate row number, select **Row Height** from the pull-down menu and enter the desired row height. Finally, you can adjust the row height by placing the cursor on the line separating rows 1 and 2. You will notice that the cursor turns to a cross and the row height is displayed in the box above the row separator. Drag the cursor to the desired height. Repeat for every row whose height should be changed.

Rename the worksheet. To rename a worksheet, left double-click on the worksheet's name tab and enter the new name. To illustrate, insert the first new worksheet into your workbook, left double-click on the tab at the bottom of the worksheet entitled 'Sheet 1' and enter the new worksheet title.

Underlining. To underline totals and subtotals use the border Icon found in the **Font** section of the **Home** tab. For subtotals, after placing the cursor in the appropriate cell, pull down the border menu by placing the cursor on the arrow next to the Icon and select the **Bottom Border**. For totals, select **Bottom Double Border**.

Another way to place a border in a cell is to select the cell by clicking on it with the right mouse button to bring up the ShortCut Menu, select **Format Cells > Border**. Select the appropriate style and select the placement in the picture.

Formatting numbers and currency. Click **Format > Format Cells** found in the **Cells** section of the **Home** tab. Select **Number** and make sure the **Decimal places** box has "2" and the **Use 1000 Separator (,)** box has a check to format for commas with two decimal points. Be sure that you also select one of the choices that uses parentheses for negative numbers. If you desire a dollar sign, select **Currency** and make sure the **Decimal places** box has "2" and the **Symbol** box has "$" to ensure that your amounts will be formatted for currency with two decimal points.

Multiple line heading. To enter a multiple line heading in one cell, type the first line. Hold down the **Alt** key and hit the **Enter** key to go on to the second line, and repeat this process for the third line. To center the heading across columns, highlight the cells in which you would like to center the heading and click on the **Merge and Center** button. Increase the font on each line to the desired size. Resize the height of the row.

Data Integrity Tutorial (continued)

Entering and using formulas. A formula always begins with an "=" sign. Formulas use an operator (+ - / * > < % etc.) combined with values that can be cell references or range names. Note that the following are only examples of formulas you might need:

    =Gross_Revenue-SUM(Sales_Adjustments)
    =C15+C16
    =$E9-$E19
    =SUM(C24:C32)

Note the "**$**" in the third example above. This has the effect of holding the column **E** as an absolute reference; in other words, if this formula is moved to another place in the worksheet, it will still reference column **E** but the row number will change. If a dollar sign is placed on either side of the **E (\$E\$9)**, both the column and row reference will be absolute. Without the dollar signs, EXCEL treats cell references as relative; that is, when they are moved, the references will change relative to the new cell position.

To enter a formula in a cell:
  a) Select the cell into which you want to enter the formula.
  b) Type an "=" to activate the formula bar.
  c) Type the formula. If you make a mistake, edit to correct it.
  d) Press Enter or click on the enter box (the green checkmark) next to the
     formula bar.

Nested "IF" statement. An "IF" statement returns one of two values based on a specified logical condition. They are what we call 'If, then, else' statements. For example, if X is less than Y, then return the value of 5, else return the value of 10. "IF" statements begin with the "=" sign and use comparison operators (=, >, <, >=, <=, <>) to specify the logical condition. The format for an "IF" statement is:

  "=IF(**A1***comparison operator***B1,C1,D1**)."

  For example, =IF(**A1<=B1,C1,D1**)

This "IF" statement specifies that if cell **A1** is less than or equal to cell **B1** (logical condition) then return the value in cell **C1** else return the value in cell **D1**. Note that numerical values, cell references or range names can be used in "IF" statements.

A nested "IF" statement returns one of three or more values based on the specified logical conditions. For example, if X is greater than Y then return the value of 10 else if X is greater than Z then return the value of 5 else return the value of 1. The general format for a nested "IF" statement is:

  "=IF(**A1>=B1,A2**, IF(**A1>=C1,B2,C2**))."

Data Integrity Tutorial (continued)

Nested "IF" statement (cont).
This "IF" statement specifies that if cell **A1** is greater than or equal to cell **B1** (first logical condition) then return the value in cell **A2** else if cell **A1** is greater than or equal to cell **C1** (second logical condition) then return the value in cell **B2** else return the value in cell **C2**. The else condition represented by **C2** can be replaced by additional "IF" statements as necessary until all logical conditions have been met.

Naming cells. You can create a name for a single cell or an array (a range) of cells. Names cannot include spaces; instead you can capitalize the first letter of each word or use the underscore ("_") between words (e.g., either of the following are acceptable cell names: CostOfGoodsSold or Cost_of_goods_sold). Names can be up to 255 characters.

To create a cell name, first select the cell or cells that you wish to name. Use only those cells that contain the amounts you want to name. It is **not** necessary to include the cells with the text describing those numbers. Click on the **Name** box at the left side of the **Formula bar** . Type the name for the cell(s) into the **Name** box to refer to your selection.

Alternatively, you can select the cell or cells that you wish to name. Click on **Define**

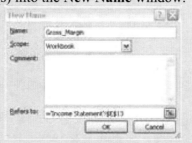

Name in the **Defined Names** section of the **Formulas** tab. Type the name for the cell(s) into the **New Name** window.

You can see a list of all named cells and edit them if you need to by clicking on **Name Manager** in the **Defined Names** section.

SIMPLE DATA ANALYSIS

With the data you now have in the financial statements and with the cell names that you have created in those financial statements, you can now easily explore the power of data analysis that a spreadsheet offers. For example, it is very easy to calculate some common ratios.

Requirements

1. Open the **CA Computerized Excel Workbook** file and insert a new worksheet entitled "**Ratio Analysis**."

2. On this new worksheet, calculate the ratios listed below by using formulas that refer to cell or range names that you have created. Do not use direct cell references (e.g., N42, G18, etc.) in these calculations.

   - Current ratio
   - Inventory turnover
   - Return on assets
   - Return on equity
   - Debt to equity ratio
   - Times interest earned

   In addition to increasing the understandability of your formulas, using cell names rather than cell references also increases the flexibility and auditability of your Excel workbook. At the same time, it decreases the maintenance necessary for your Excel workbook. For example, rows and columns can more easily be inserted and deleted without altering cell and range names, or formulas that refer to them. **You may have to create new cell names to complete these formulas.**

3. Format your Ratio Analysis worksheet so that one column contains the ratio name and one column contains the ratio itself. In addition, the spreadsheet should include an appropriate heading.

WHAT-IF ANALYSIS

There are also a variety of business modeling tools and analytic techniques that can be brought to bear on data. The what-if analysis is one of the most fundamental methods that can be used for analyzing worksheet data. In a what-if analysis, you calculate a formula and then change the variables to see what happens. For example, assume the formula is (A*B) + C = D. What would happen to D if you increase A? Or decrease C?

Assume that Chateau Americana is going to begin funding a pension plan. The president of the company, Edward Summerfield, has asked you to determine how much the fund would have in it if he were to deposit $250,000 initially and then make ten annual deposits of $100,000 each (at the end of each year), assuming an annual interest rate of 5%. You recognize this as a future value problem and turn to Excel knowing that it can calculate this for you very quickly.

Requirements

1. Open the **CA Computerized Excel Workbook** file and click on the **What-If Analysis** worksheet.

2. Enter the interest rate in cell **C4**. The interest rate entered here will represent the interest rate per period in the future value formula.

3. Enter the time period in cell **C5**. The number entered here represents the total number of payment periods for the entire investment period.

4. Enter the annual deposit in cell **C6**. This amount is the payment made each period. It should be entered as a negative amount since this represents a cash disbursement (i.e., money paid out).

5. Enter the initial deposit in cell **C7**. The initial deposit is the present value of the investment, i.e., what it is worth now. Again this should be entered as a negative amount because we are disbursing this amount.

6. Enter the deposit type in cell **C8**. The type indicates the timing of the payment. If the payment is going to be made at the end of the period, enter a 0; if it will be made at the beginning of the period, enter a 1.

7. Go to cell **B10**. Click on **Financial > FV** in the **Function Library** section of the **Formulas** tab (*Figure 8*).

Figure 8

Enter the cells (from requirements 1-6) into the appropriate arguments and click **OK** (*Figure 9*).

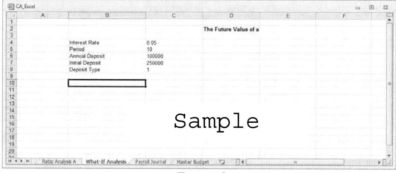

Figure 9

This gives you the amount that the pension plan will grow to if $250,000 is invested now and ten annual deposits are made, assuming 5% interest.

Now assume that Mr. Summerfield wants to know 'what-if' the interest rate is not 5% (rates ranging from 4.5% to 7%, in 0.5% increments) and 'what-if' the company decides to make a different annual deposit (anything from $70,000 to $130,000, in $10,000 increments). You can answer these questions quickly by creating a Data Table for the what-if analysis.

8. To set up the Data Table for the What-If Analysis, enter the interest rates in cells **C10** through **H10**. Enter the payment amounts in cells **B11** through **B17** (*Figure 10*).

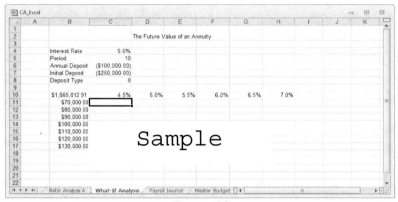

Figure 10

9. Highlight cells **B10** through **H17**. Click **What-If Analysis > Data Table** in the **Data Tools** section of the **Data** tab (*Figure 11*).

Figure 11

10. Enter the interest rate (**C4**) into the row input cell.

11. Enter the annual deposit (**C6**) into the column input cell. Click **OK**. The table is then populated with the future values of all the 'what-if' possibilities.

One final note: You can make changes to any of the variables in the formula and Excel will automatically recalculate the entire table IF the spreadsheet has been set to automatic recalculation. To do this, click on **Calculation Options** in the **Calculation** section of the **Formulas** tab (*Figure 12)* and make sure that it is set to **Automatic**.

Figure 12

INFORMATION NEEDS

Information needs vary among the users of the accounting information system and information overload is a very real problem in businesses. Spreadsheets are very flexible and have very powerful reporting capabilities. Using the spreadsheets and the financial statements you have prepared, you can easily report information to each user according to his or her needs by grouping and ungrouping data from a single spreadsheet without changing the format of the spreadsheet. For example, a company's president may only want to see the overall picture, rather than the detail of the accounts, while the vice president of sales might want to see details related to a specific product or line of products and the production manager would need to see the manufacturing costs broken down, line item by line item.

Spreadsheets can also be used to sort and query large bodies of data to extract only the desired information. For example, the controller may want to see a listing of only those expense accounts that exceed a certain dollar amount.

The following requirements will help you create an outline for the income statement that will let you show or hide varying levels of detail without changing the income statement format itself.

Requirements

1. Open the **CA Computerized Excel Workbook** file and click on the **Income Statement** worksheet. Highlight columns B through F.

2. Click on **Group** in the **Outline** section of the **Data** tab (see *Figure 13*). Then click on **Group** in the pull-down menu.

Figure 13

Notice that a bar with a minus sign appears above the column G.

3. Click on the minus sign to see what happens.

4. Highlight rows 6 through 9 and repeat the **Group** command.

5. Repeat the **Group** command for "OPERATING EXPENSES" and "OTHER INCOME AND GAINS" (see *Figure 14*).

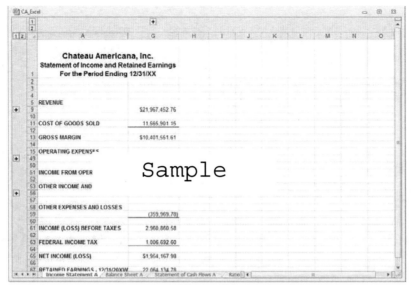

Figure 14

Now assume that the CFO has heard about your Excel skills and has asked you to help him determine which of the expense accounts for Chateau Americana, Inc. exceeded $200,000 for 20XX. Filter the expense accounts to provide this information as follows:

6. Insert a new worksheet entitled "**Operating Expenses**" into the **CA Computerized Excel Workbook** file. For all operating expenses copy the account title and amount from the **Y-E Worksheet** to the new worksheet.

7. Insert a row at the top of the data and enter the column headings "**Operating Expenses**" in cell **A1** and "**Amount**" in cell **B1**.

8. Extract, or filter, all operating expenses in excess of $200,000 ⌘. Insert a row at the top of the spreadsheet and create an appropriate heading for the worksheet (see *Figure 15*).

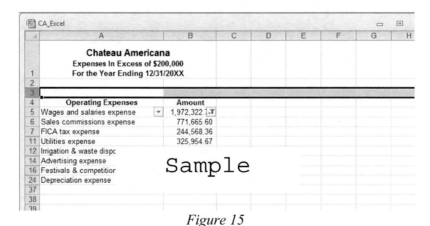

Figure 15

Information Needs Tutorial

Filtering data. Highlight the cells to be filtered including cells containing descriptions for other cells. Click on **Filter** in the **Sort & Filter** section of the **Data** tab.

Notice that arrows for the pull-down menus appear in the top cells. Click on the arrow in the column to be filtered to obtain the appropriate pull-down menu (i.e., the column containing the amounts). Click on **Number Filters** and select **Custom Filter** from the pull-down menu. In the **Custom Filter** window, click on the pull-down menu next to the box containing "equal" to select the applicable logical condition and input the desired amount in the box to the right.

NOTE: You can restore the worksheet to its original format by selecting **Filter** and clicking on **Clear**. Therefore, it is not necessary to copy the data you are filtering to a new worksheet although it is advisable such that you are sure that you do not permanently alter the original format in any way.

MACROS

When preparing spreadsheets or workpapers, it is typical to add the name of the preparer and the date prepared to the work product. However, this is a repetitious task that can be automated through the use of macros. Excel macros are written in a programming language called Visual Basic for Applications (or VBA), which is a shorter version of the popular Visual Basic programming language.

There are two ways to create macros in Excel. The first is to learn VBA and write them in code. However, learning VBA takes a great deal of time and is outside the scope of this book. Fortunately, there is a much simpler way to create macros using an Excel tool called the **macro recorder**. This tool functions in much the same way as a tape recorder, recording each keystroke that you make once you turn the recorder on and continues recording until you turn the recorder off. You can then 'play back' the macro and it will repeat those keystrokes.

Requirements

1. Open the **CA Computerized Excel Workbook** file and click on the **Ratio Analysis** worksheet. Move to cell **A2**.

2. Select **Macros > Record Macro** under the **Macros** section of the **View** tab (*Figure 16*).

Figure 16

3. Type "**PreparerInfo**" in the **Macro name** section (*Figure 17*). Click **OK**.

Figure 17

4. Keep in mind that entering preparer information is often an afterthought. Therefore, you will often have to make room for this data. Make sure that row 3 is blank; if it is not, insert a row(s) so that it is. Now begin the macro by highlighting the **3 through 5 simultaneously** in the row number column (using the left mouse button) and then right-click to reach the pull-down menu. Select **Insert** to insert two rows.

5. Move your cursor to **A3**. Type "**Preparer:**".

6. Move your cursor to **B3** and type your name (first and last name).

7. Go to cell **A4** and type "**Date:**".

8. The date that is entered should be entered automatically. This can be accomplished using the **TODAY** function in Excel. Go to cell **B4** and type "**=TODAY()**".

9. Highlight cells **A3** and **A4** and click on the Italics *I* icon in the **Font** section of the **Home** tab.

10. Click on **Macros** > **Stop Recording** in the **Macros** section of the **View** tab. Note that you might have to widen column B to view the date properly.

11. Save your file at this time. Note that you will get a warning that your file cannot be saved at this time (see *Figure 18*). Click on **No** and select **Excel Macro-Enabled Workbook** under the **Save as type** pull-down menu.

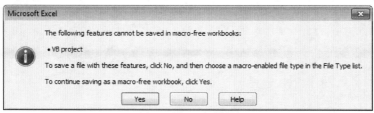

Figure 18

Macros can be a problem for your computer. They are potentially dangerous since they can be programmed to harm your computer. Many viruses and worms are based upon macros. As a result, you should not trust any file that contains macros unless it has been digitally signed or you created it yourself and you know what is in it. Excel files with an .xlsx extension can always be trusted since they are incapable of storing macros. The default setting in *Excel 2010* is to disable all macros with notification. Therefore, despite the fact that you saved the file as an **Excel Macro-Enabled Workbook**, the macros will be disabled before the file is opened again.

12. Open the file at this time. Note the Security Warning message under the Toolbar.

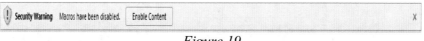

Figure 19

However, since this is a macro that you created and that you might want to use in several worksheets, you will want to click on **Enable Content**. You will also need to click **Yes** on the Security Warning window that pops up.

Figure 20

One way to get around this warning is to create a 'Trusted Files' folder on your computer. Then, in Excel, click on **File**, the click on **Options**, and finally click on **Trust Center**. Once in the **Trust Center** option, you can click on **Trust Center Settings > Trusted Locations > Add new location > Browse** and search your computer for the folder you set up. Once found, click the **OK** button three times to accept the location and close the dialog windows. Now any files saved in the 'Trusted Files' folder will be saved with their macros enabled and you won't have to deal with warnings.

13. As we said, the macro you created in the previous steps is one that you might want to use in several worksheets in this workbook. We can make it readily available by adding it to the *Quick Access toolbar* located at the top of the Excel window so that you get to it whenever you need it. To add the macro, click on the **File** section. Now click on the **Options** 🗋 Options icon at the bottom of the list on the left.

Figure 21

14. On the left-hand side of the Options window, click on the **Quick Access Toolbar** | Quick Access Toolbar icon. The **Quick Access Toolbar** [icon] is the toolbar in the upper left corner of the Excel window.

15. Select **Macros** from the **Choose commands from:** pull-down menu (*Figure 22*).

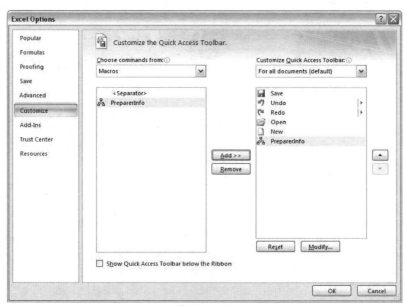

Figure 22

16. Select **PreparerInfo** from the list in the lower left window and click the Add button. Click **OK**. You will see now that there is a new icon in the **Quick Access Toolbar** at the top of your workbook.

Now you can try out your newly created macro on another worksheet.

17. Select the **Operating Expenses** worksheet.

18. Move to cell **A3**. Click on the newly created macro icon . The preparer information is now inserted (*Figure 23*).

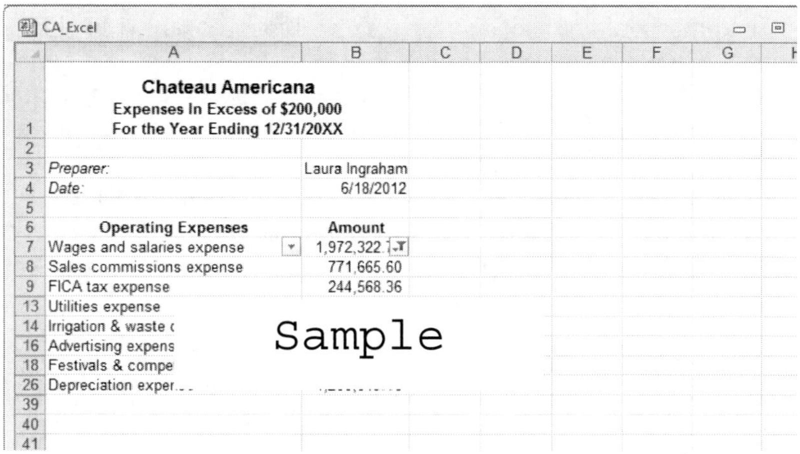

Figure 23

MORE ADVANCED MACROS

The macro you created in the previous section was a very simple one. Macros have a great deal of power and can simplify tasks that would otherwise take a great deal of time to perform. Let's assume that you asked the Payroll clerk for payroll information so that you could create a Master Payroll file. Unfortunately, the clerk did not understand the purpose of the request and the information was provided to you in a columnar format. You could, of course, ask that the spreadsheet be redone in the format would be conducive to your ultimate goal but you can also create a macro that will do the job in a matter of minutes (including the time it takes to create the macro).

Requirements

1. Open the **CA Computerized Excel Workbook** file and insert a new worksheet entitled "**Payroll Information**."

2. Beginning in cell **A1** and continuing on down in column **A**, enter the Social Security Number, Employee Name, Pay Type, Regular Pay Rate, and FIT Withheld. In cell **A5** (and for each subsequent employee), you will need to calculate Federal Income Tax Withheld based upon each employee's filing status and number of allowances. Leave two rows before beginning the next

employee. All of the necessary information has been provided for you in the table below.

Social Security Number	Employee Name	Pay Type	Regular Pay Rate	Filing Status	FIT W/H Allowance
124-11-7755	Rodriguez, José G.	Salaried	2550.00	Married	4
296-49-3438	Johnson, Anna C.	Salaried	1750.00	Married	3
349-43-6417	Hissom, Robert T.	Hourly	14.25	Single	0
014-39-4215	Bryan, Thomas P.	Hourly	15.00	Single	1

NOTE: The employee ID is the employee's social security number. The pay type is "S" for salaried employees or "H" for hourly employees. The FIT withholding should be the amount of federal income tax withheld for the pay period ending December 31, 20XX. If you have already completed the *Manual AIS Module*, you can refer to the Payroll Subsidiary Ledger in the *Manual AIS Module* for the withholding information. If you have not, you will need to determine the proper amount of federal income tax withheld for each employee by using the Percentage Method. You can simply look at the withholdings in the (**HINT**: You can find this information in Publication 15 from the IRS publications website. This form is also entitled "Circular E, Employer's Tax Guide.)

3. Insert a new row 1 into the worksheet. Click on cell **A1** and type "**ID**". Move cell to the right and type "**EMPLOYEE NAME**". Move one cell to the right and type "**PAY TYPE**". Move one cell to the right and type "**REGULAR PAY RATE**". Move one more cell to the right and type "**FIT W/H**".

4. Format the column widths so that column A is 11.86; column B is 18.43; column C is 7.29; column D is 9.43; and column E is 8.43.

5. Right click on row 1 and click on **Format Cells** in the pull-down menu. Click on the **Alignment** tab and select **Wrap text** under the **Text Control** section. Click **OK**. While the row is still highlighted, click on **Bold** in the **Home** section to bold the column headings you just created. Finally, click on **Center** to center these headings.

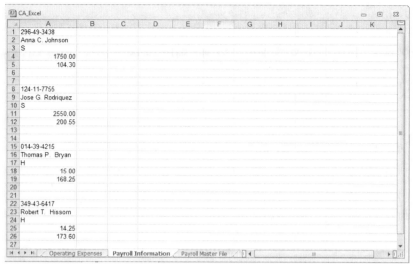

Figure 24

6. When recording macros, Excel defaults to 'absolute referencing' of the cells. In other words, it records the cell you start in and will always default to that cell. Because of the format of this sheet, we will need to use relative referencing in our macro so that our payroll information for subsequent employees is not pasted again and again into the first cell of the first row. We can do this by telling the macro that we are using relative referencing when we set it up. Click on the **View** section and click on the **Macros** icon. Then select **Use Relative References**.

7. In our prior exercise we want cell **A3** to be the active cell and you were instructed to make sure that row 3 was blank and you were given instructions to insert a row if it was not. If you had to insert a row, those steps were recorded by the Macro Recorder in the **PreparerInfo** macro.

   In this exercise, we want to begin with cell **A2** as the active cell.

8. Click on the **Macros** icon once more and select **Record Macro**. Name the macro '**MasterPayroll**'.

9. We will also set up a shortcut that will allow us to call up this macro with a click of the keyboard, rather than having to utilize the menu. Enter **p** in the **Shortcut key** box.

10. You can also provide a description for the macro to help subsequent users understand what the macro does. In this case, the description should read: 'This macro will take the columnar payroll information and create a Master Payroll table.' Click **OK**.

11. Right-click on cell **A3** and select **Cut**. Right-click on cell **B2** and select **Paste**. Continue this for the remaining information for the first employee (i.e., right-click on **A4** and cut, right-click on **C2** and paste, etc.)

12. Highlight rows 3 through 8. Right-click on the selected rows and select **Delete** from the pull-down menu.

13. Click in cell **A3**. This is now the active cell. Since this macro needs to be run for all employees, making cell **A3** active puts the cursor in the correct position to convert the remaining employee information.

14. Click on the **View** section once more. Now click on **Macros** and select **Stop Recording**. We now have the macro set up for multiple usage.

15. While still in cell **A3**, hold down the **Control (Ctrl) key** and press **p**. You should now see the second employee's payroll information and the cursor should now be in cell **A4** (the new active cell).

16. Repeat step 13 for the two remaining employees.

17. Highlight columns D and F and select **Format Cells**. Click on **Number**, make sure that the **Decimal places** is set to 2 and click **OK**.

18. Rename the worksheet **Payroll Master File**.

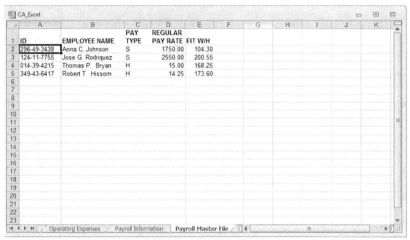

Figure 25

DATABASE FUNCTIONS

One of the benefits of a database is the reduction or elimination of data redundancy, which in turn, reduces or eliminates data inconsistency. As we stated earlier, this is one of the reasons you have been instructed to use formulas whenever possible. Excel contains a variety of functions that allow you to query or search for data in the worksheets. **VLOOKUP** is one of these Excel functions. **VLOOKUP** searches for a value that is located in the first column of a table array and, based upon the criteria requested, returns a value in the same row from another column in that table array. As a result, there is no need to reenter the data in a new worksheet. For example, you can enter employee data into a master payroll file and then pull that data into a payroll journal.

Requirements

1. Open the **CA Computerized Excel Workbook** file and insert a new worksheet. Name the new worksheet "**Payroll Master File**".

2. The **Payroll Master File** worksheet will be used as a database for the **Payroll Journal** worksheet provided for you in the **CA Computerized Excel Workbook** file. To accomplish this, you must designate an array for the database (i.e., create a range name). To do this, highlight cells **A2:E5** and designate the range name (i.e., the table array) as **Payroll_Master**.

3. Click on the **Payroll Journal** worksheet provided for you in your file. For each employee listed above, enter the payroll pay date (December 31, 20XX) and employee ID in cells **A3** through **B6** on the **Payroll Journal** worksheet.

   NOTE: While the **Payroll Journal** worksheet has already been created and formatted, it does not contain any data, formulas, or functions. *However, the worksheet does contain various cell names that you must use in creating the required formulas and functions.* These cell names were saved in the worksheet before you received it. Take some time now to acquaint yourself with all the cell names that are in your worksheet so that you will be familiar with what is available for use in this portion of the assignment.

4. Click on **Formulas** tab and pull down the **Lookup & Reference** ⬚ Lookup & Reference ▾ menu. Use the **VLOOKUP** function ⌘ in cells **C3** and **D3** in the **Payroll Journal** worksheet to return the employee's name and pay type to these cells.

   NOTE: The **Payroll Journal** worksheet requires no entry for salaried employees in columns **E** or **H**. However, both Thomas Bryan and Robert Hissom worked 96 hours of regular time and Thomas worked 2.25 hours of overtime.

5. Use the **VLOOKUP** function to return the pay rate in cell **F3** in the **Payroll Journal** worksheet.

6. In the **Payroll Journal** worksheet, create formulas to calculate the regular pay and overtime pay for cells **G3** and **I3**, respectively. **HINT:** Keep in mind that you are trying to create a Payroll Journal that will calculate the payroll for both salaried and hourly individuals based upon formulas. Therefore, we must create a formula (i.e., an **IF** statement) that will calculate pay for an employee regardless of their pay type. This formula should accommodate salaried employees whether or not they have entries for the number of hours worked. Otherwise, it would be easy for someone to commit fraud by, for example, paying a salaried individual overtime.

7. In the **Payroll Journal** worksheet, create formulas in cells **J3** and **K3** to calculate gross pay and FICA, respectively. Recall that Medicare is 1.45% of gross pay and Social Security is 6.2% of gross pay. Together, the deduction for FICA is 7.65%.

8. Use the **VLOOKUP** function in cell **L3** in the **Payroll Journal** worksheet to return the amount of federal income tax to be withheld.

9. In the **Payroll Journal** worksheet, create a formula in cell **M3** to calculate net pay and enter the appropriate check number in cell **N3** beginning with check number **7111**.

10. For internal control purposes, a formula should also be created in cell **N4** in the **Payroll Journal** worksheet as a sequential number check for the check number (i.e., "=**N3** +1").

11. To facilitate the entry of payroll data for any other employees, you will need to copy the formulas and functions you created. For this assignment, you only need to copy them into the next 3 rows.

12. Note that the final column is reserved for the Subsidiary Journal Posting Reference. You do not need to enter anything in this column for this exercise. However, if you were completing the posting of this data to the payroll subsidiary ledgers, you would fill in this column.

Database Functions Tutorial

VLOOKUP function. **The VLOOKUP function in EXCEL searches a previously defined database (i.e., array designated by an appropriate range name) for a specified value and returns a desired field (i.e., a data value) from that database. The syntax for the VLOOKUP function is**

=VLOOKUP(lookup_value,table_array,col_index_num,range_lookup)

where

lookup_value names the value to that you want to search for that is located in the first column of the table array. The **lookup_value** is typically a value that is unique to each row of data. For example, in a customer database, the **lookup_value** might be the Customer ID number. Therefore, in an employee database, the **lookup_value** would be the Employee ID number.

table_array contains two or more columns of data. It provides the name of the database that stores the data you want to bring into the current worksheet.

col_index_num specifies the number of the column in the database in which the desired data value is located. For example, if the data value is located in column C, column C is the third column and, therefore, the col_index_num would be 3. (NOTE: you must count the columns beginning with A=1, etc., and enter the appropriate column number).

range_lookup is a logical value specifying whether or not you want an exact match; FALSE indicates an exact match must be returned; TRUE indicates that an approximate match may be returned.

INTRODUCTION TO PIVOTTABLE REPORTS

Budgeting is a critical managerial accounting tool and Excel has a variety of tools that make it very easy to work with large bodies of data for budgeting purposes.

You have been asked to prepare Chateau Americana's budget for next year. Obviously, Excel can be used to assist in the preparation of the budget. You can set up a worksheet providing columns for the accounts, year, month, and amount. You can further break down the accounts by providing columns for type, code, and titles. You can also provide columns for departments and cost centers. And, lastly, you can provide a column that provides explanations for any months in which there are amounts that are out of the ordinary. Such a worksheet, entitled "**Master Budget**" has been prepared for you in the **CA Computerized Excel Workbook** workbook.

If all the data for the budget for an entire company is entered into one worksheet, you could easily end up with hundreds, if not thousands of rows of data; in other words, a worksheet that has become so large that working with the data has become slow, unwieldy and impractical. It becomes difficult to find the data you are looking for quickly and analyses on the data are slow and cumbersome. Fortunately, as we have discussed, Excel has powerful data analysis capabilities and we can employ these tools on large worksheets through the use of a PivotTable Report.

A PivotTable Report is an interactive table that enables you to quickly sift through and summarize large amounts of data. You can rotate rows and columns to see different summaries of the source data, filter the data by displaying different pages, or display details for certain areas of interest. You can do all this without writing a single formula or copying a single cell. In addition, these PivotTables are dynamic. In other words, once you have created them, you can rearrange the table so that it summarizes the data based on another grouping. For example, if you create a PivotTable for sales broken down by each quarter, you can then rearrange the data so that it focuses on sales by product, by salesperson, or by territory.

Before creating a PivotTable, you must prepare the data source. An excerpt from the Chateau Americana budget has been provided for you. You will find it on the "**Master Budget**" worksheet contained in the **CA Computerized Excel Workbook** file. Certain assumptions have been made and constraints have been imposed to facilitate your handling of the budget and the PivotTable, as detailed below.

The budget is for the entire year but contains only selected accounts. For purposes of this assignment, only three departments have been selected and the number of employees per department has been limited, as follows:

> Administration (Edward and Rob)
> Marketing (Taylor, Daniel and Cameron)
> Operations (Jacques and Sam)

Review the **Master Budget** worksheet. Notice that the worksheet has the following headings: **ACCT_TYPE**, **ACCT_CODE**, **ACCT_TITLE**, **DEPT**,

COST_CENTER, YR, MON, BUDGET, EXPLANATIONS. These represent the fields that you will use to create the PivotTable.

Requirements

1. Open the **CA Computerized Excel Workbook** file and click on the **Master Budget** worksheet. Be sure that the cursor is placed somewhere in the data on the worksheet. From the **Tables** section of the **Insert** tab, click on **PivotTable > PivotTable**.

Figure 26

2. The Create PivotTable window (*Figure 27*) appears.

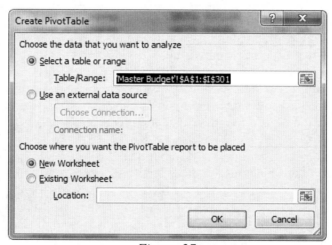

Figure 27

Be sure that the entire master budget has been selected (the range should be **A1** to **I301**). Also be sure that the radio button for "New worksheet" is selected. Click on **OK**.

3. Notice that Excel has generated (and moved you to) a new worksheet to create the PivotTable. You should see a **PivotTable1** table and a **PivotTable Field List** window that contains the column headings from your **Master Budget** spreadsheet (see *Figure 28*).

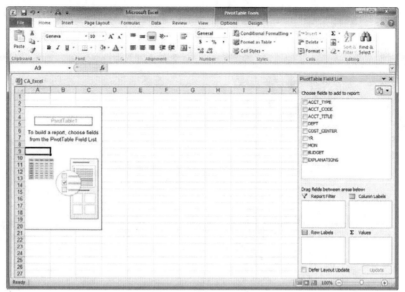

Figure 28

Drag the **ACCT_CODE** into the **Row Labels** area located in the lower left hand side of the **PivotTable Field List** window. Notice that the Account Codes are now listed in **Column A**.

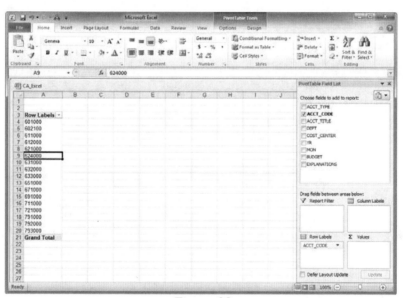

Figure 29

4. Now drag the **BUDGET** into the **Σ Values** area. Notice that the sums of the various account codes are now totaled in **Column B** and that the label for **BUDGET** has now changed "**Sum of BUDGET**." The **Grand Total** at the bottom of the sheet should be $4,321,018. Excel has now generated a PivotTable that summarizes the master budget by GL code.

5. Notice that the **Master Budget** worksheet is still intact. Now rename the new worksheet "**Pivot**".

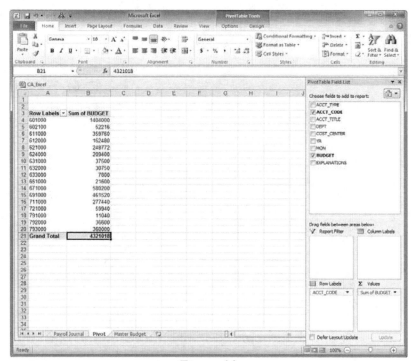

Figure 30

6. General ledger codes do not provide much information without the account titles. To add the general ledger account titles, click on the box next to the **ACCT_TITLE** field in the PivotTable Field List on the right side of the screen. **ACCT_TITLE** will be added to the Row Labels window at the bottom on the right side of the screen and the account titles will be added to your PivotTable.

Figure 31

7. The general ledger codes, descriptions and their totals are now in the PivotTable. This contains much more detail than we need in the budget. For example, the total lines are repetitious and should be removed.

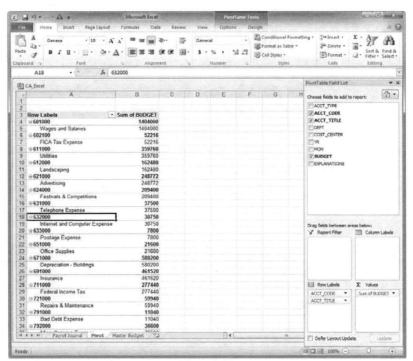

Figure 32

To do this, right-click on the **ACCT_CODE** cell (this should be Cell **A4**). From the pull-down menu, select **Field Settings**. In the **Subtotals & Filters** tab, click on the radio button for **None.** This should deselect the **Automatic** button. Click on **OK** and the subtotals disappear.

Figure 33

8. To provide managers with more detailed budget information, the time periods should be added to the PivotTable. Click anywhere within the

PivotTable. Select **MON**. Again, notice that it automatically drops into the **Row Labels**. This is not particularly useful for analyzing the data. It would be preferable to have the months appear as Column labels. Drag **MON** into the **Column Labels** area. The PivotTable should now break down the GL account totals by month.

9. Now add **ACCT_TYPE** to the list of **Row Labels**. In terms of hierarchy, **ACCT_TYPE** should come before **ACCT_CODE**. However, when it is added, it appears below **ACCT_TITLE**. Click on the pull-down menu for **ACCT_TYPE** and click on **Move to Beginning**. The **Row Labels** window now contains **ACCT_TYPE**, **ACCT_CODE** and **ACCT_TITLE**. The PivotTable should now be divided into "**601 – Salaries**", "**602 – Payroll Taxes**," "**610 – Occupancy**," etc, each with a total.

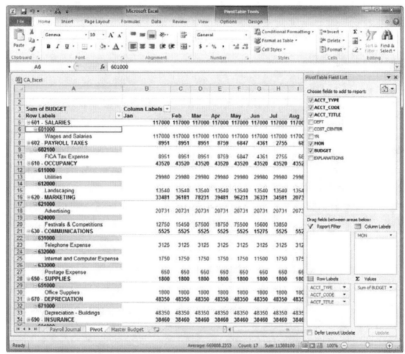

Figure 34

DETAIL IN REPORTING

The PivotTable allows the user to query or "drilldown" into a particular value in the PivotTable report to examine that item more closely. This provides a great deal of power and flexibility to the PivotTable report, whether the report is for budgeting applications, reporting monthly costs to department managers, or for reporting the results of sales to territory managers. The user can query a balance to view any of the underlying detail by simply double clicking on the entry in question.

The CFO has asked you to identify any unusual items in the budgeted amounts and report them to him. A quick review of the budget reveals *two months* under **Festivals** and **Competitions** and *one month* under **Internet and Computer** that appear to have higher than usual amounts of expenditures, when compared to other months.

Requirements

1. Open the **CA Computerized Excel Workbook** file and click on the **Pivot** worksheet. To determine what has caused this spike in costs, query one of the amounts in question by double clicking on an amount in question. A new worksheet appears that provides all the detail for the amount queried (*Figure 35*).

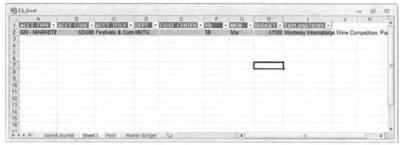

Figure 35

2. Return to the **Pivot** worksheet. Drill down on each of the other amounts to investigate the nature of their variance in cost.

   Return to the **Pivot** worksheet again. There may be occasions when you would want to limit other users' abilities to drill down into the data, particularly if the costs deal with payroll. This is done by right-clicking anywhere in the PivotTable report, selecting **PivotTable Options** from the shortcut menu, clicking on the **Data** tab, and deselecting the **Enable show details** box.

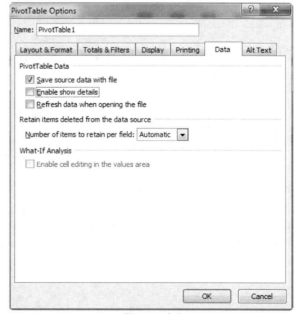

Figure 36

3. As you have seen, the PivotTable can be used to display only the data of interest. You might, for example, want to view the data for a particular department rather than for all departments or view data by cost centers. Either of these views can be obtained by dropping a particular field of interest in the **Column** area of the PivotTable or by filtering the entire PivotTable report to display data for a single item or all the items, using the **Page** field.

Access the **Pivot Table Field List** box again (under the **PivotTable Tools** Toolbar). Remove **MON** from **Column** by clicking on **Remove Field** in the pull-down menu beside it. Drag and drop **DEPT** into the **Column** area. Notice that the departmental totals for the Administrative, Marketing, and Operations departments now appear.

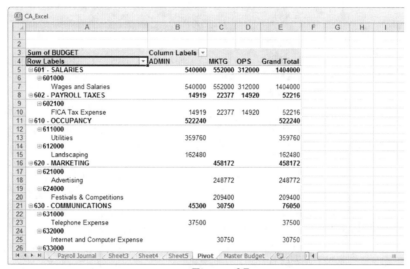

Figure 37

4. You can also view the data by department and month by using the **Report Filter** area in the lower right area of the screen. Drag **DEPT** to the **Report Filter** area and drop it. Drag and drop **MON** back into the **Column** area. Notice that the data is now broken down by period again. Notice also that cell **A1** now contains a box entitled "**DEPT**" and cell **B1** says, "**(All)**" and has a pull-down menu. **DEPT** is now a **Report Filter** field. It allows the user to see the information for the entire organization or by department (see *Figure 38*).

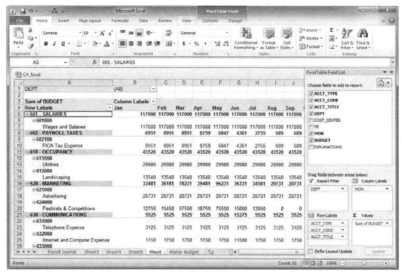

Figure 38

5. Click on the down arrow in the right of cell **B1** and notice that, in addition to **(All)**, the choices **ADMIN**, **MKTG**, and **OPS** appear. Click on **ADMIN** and click **OK**. The PivotTable now shows the costs for the Administrative department. You can click on the pull-down arrow again to look at the budgets for the Marketing department and for Operations. Note that the **(All)** option allows you to view the company totals.

6. View the **ADMIN** data again. This data can be broken down further into individual cost centers. Drag and drop **COST_CENTER** below **ACCT_TITLE** and remove the subtotals. The PivotTable is now broken down further to show the costs attributed to the individual cost centers in the Administrative department (i.e., Rob and Edward). Some of the cells in the **COST_CENTER** column contain "**(blank)**." This indicates that the costs for these accounts were not allocated to individual cost centers within the Administrative department, but were allocated instead to the entire Administrative department.

7. As more data is included in a worksheet, the threat of *information overload* or *analysis paralysis* increases. In addition, as more data is included, the PivotTable will likely require more levels to facilitate analysis of the data. However, increasing levels also increases complexity making data analysis more difficult. To address the issue of complexity, the PivotTable can be expanded or collapsed between different levels of detail using the **Expand Entire Field** and **Collapse Entire Field** commands found in the **Active Field** section of the **PivotTable Options** toolbar.

Figure 39

8. Click on cell **B1** and select **(All)** and click **OK**. The entire budget is now displayed.

9. Click on the **Options** tab and make sure that **ACCT_TYPE** is the **Active Field** in the **Active Field** section.

10. Select **Collapse Entire Field** in the **Active Field** section of the **PivotTable Tools** toolbar. Only the top level data (i.e., the account types) should now be visible (*Figure 40*).

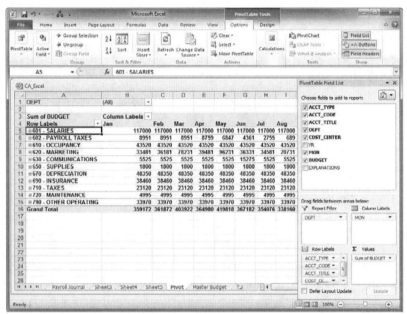

Figure 40

11. The detail can then be expanded for one or more account types. However, if you deselected the drilldown option in step 2 above, you will need to re-enable it before you go on. Show the detail for the costs associated with Communications by clicking on the "+" next to "**630 – Communications**" in column **A**. The Communications detail is now shown down to the **COST_CENTER** level (see *Figure 41*).

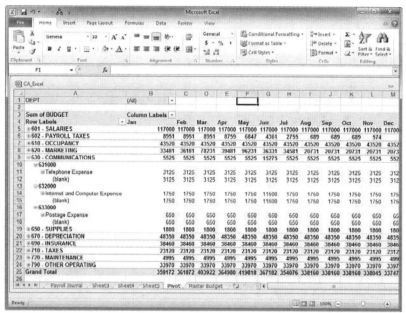

Figure 41

12. To return to the more concise view, click the "-" next to the "**630 – Communications**" title.

13. Return the entire PivotTable to its full detail again by clicking on **Expand Entire Field** in the **Active Field** section.

14. It is also sometimes desirable to focus on certain periods in a budget. The PivotTable enables you to hide the detail for some periods while leaving the detail for others showing and simultaneously recalculate the cumulative totals to show totals for just the periods of interest. Look at the data for the second quarter only by pulling down the **Column Labels** menu. Uncheck the **Select All** box and check the boxes for April, May and June and click **OK**. The PivotTable now contains the data only for April, May and June and the cumulative totals for each **ACCT_CODE** have been recalculated to include only the amounts from the second quarter months (see *Figure 42*). Notice also that a filter icon has appeared next to **Column Labels** to indicate that the columns have been filtered.

Figure 42

15. Unhide the rest of the year by clicking on the pull-down menu for **Column Labels** and checking the **Select All** box again and click on **OK**.

FLEXIBLE BUDGETING USING PIVOTTABLES

Flexible budgets are an important tool in accounting. PivotTables facilitate flexible budgeting. It is very easy to make changes, the results appear immediately, and any formulas that are affected are automatically updated. To see how revisions work, perform the following *independent* steps.

1. Open the **CA Computerized Excel Workbook** file and click on the **Master Budget** worksheet.

    After the budget was established, it was decided that some changes would be made. To allow for these changes, insert a new column before the **EXPLANATIONS** column by right-clicking on column **I** and selecting **Insert** from the pull-down menu. Copy the **BUDGET** values into the new column **I** by selecting the entire **BUDGET** column and copying and pasting it to the new column. Change the column heading **BUDGET** in Column **I** to **REV_BUDGET**. You should now have the original and revised budgets side by side. Daniel will be transferring from Marketing to Administration as of March 1. At that time, his salary will increase by $1,000. To adjust the budget for this change, click onto the **Master Budget** worksheet. Be sure the entire budget is highlighted (from A1 to J301). Click on **Filter** in the **Sort & Filter** section of the **Data** tab.

Figure 43

2. Now click on the **Cost Center** pull-down menu and click on **Select All** (to deselect all) and then click on **Daniel** to select him. Twelve records for Daniel should appear. Change Daniel's department for the appropriate periods and increase his salary for only those periods (*Figure 44*).

	ACCT_TYPE	ACCT_CODE	ACCT_TITLE	DEPT	COST_CENTER	F	MO	BUDG	REV_BUDG	EXPLANATIONS
14	601 - SALARIES	601000	Wages and Salaries	MKTG	DANIEL	'08	Jan	14000	14000	
15	601 - SALARIES	601000	Wages and Salaries	MKTG	DANIEL	'08	Feb	14000	14000	
16	601 - SALARIES	601000	Wages and Salaries	ADMIN	DANIEL	'08	Mar	14000	15000	
17	601 - SALARIES	601000	Wages and Salaries	ADMIN	DANIEL	'08	Apr	14000	15000	
18	601 - SALARIES	601000	Wages and Salaries	ADMIN	DANIEL	'08	May	14000	15000	
19	601 - SALARIES	601000	Wages and Salaries	ADMIN	DANIEL	'08	Jun	14000	15000	
20	601 - SALARIES	601000	Wages and Salaries	ADMIN	DANIEL	'08	Jul	14000	15000	
21	601 - SALARIES	601000	Wages and Salaries	ADMIN	DANIEL	'08	Aug	14000	15000	
22	601 - SALARIES	601000	Wages and Salaries	ADMIN	DANIEL	'08	Sep	14000	15000	
23	601 - SALARIES	601000	Wages and Salaries	ADMIN	DANIEL	'08	Oct	14000	15000	
24	601 - SALARIES	601000	Wages and Salaries	ADMIN	DANIEL	'08	Nov	14000	15000	
25	601 - SALARIES	601000	Wages and Salaries	ADMIN	DANIEL	'08	Dec	14000	15000	

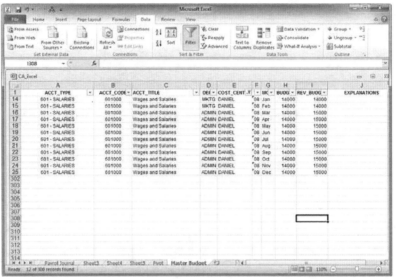

Figure 44

3. Go to the **Pivot** worksheet. Notice that Daniel's salary has not changed. Make sure that **the PivotTable Options** toolbar is active and click on **Refresh** in the **Data** section of the **PivotTable Tools** toolbar.

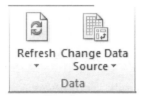

Figure 45

4. Drag **Sum of Budget** from the **Σ Values** section of the **Pivot Table Field List** and drag **Rev_Budget** to that section (*Figure 46*)**.** Daniel's salary should now be updated.

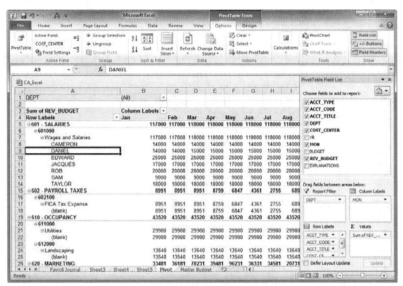

Figure 46

5. Go back to the **Master Budget** worksheet. Turn off the filter by clicking on the **Filter** ![filter icon] icon next to **COST_CENTER** and clicking on **(Select All)**.

6. Turn on the **Filter** again. Select Cameron and update her salary to reflect a $1,000 raise in the **REV_BUDGET** column beginning in June and extending into the subsequent months. Click onto the **Pivot** worksheet. Click **Refresh** in the **Data** section of the **PivotTable Options** toolbar.

7. Once the first budget has been created using PivotTables, it can be used to produce others very quickly. In the **Pivot** worksheet, show all departments. Pull down the **Options** menu in the **PivotTable** section of the **PivotTable Options** toolbar and select **Show Report Filter Pages**.

Figure 47

The three departmental budget PivotTables (one for **ADMIN**, one for **MKTG** and one for **OPS**) are created as three new worksheets in your workbook.

CREATING CHARTS FROM PIVOTTABLES

You are probably already aware that Excel contains powerful charting tools. You can also create charts from PivotTables. When you do this, it is important to remember that the charts you create are directly linked to the data in the PivotTable. If you change the data in the PivotTable, you will also modify the chart. Assume that management asks you to provide comparative data on Salaries paid by Department.

1. You already know that you can view the data in the three departmental worksheets. You could pull the information requested from each of these three sheets and provide that to management. However, you also know that charts are an excellent way to view comparative data.

2. Go to the **Pivot** worksheet. Click on the **Row Label** pull-down menu and deselect **Select All**. Click on **Salaries** and click **OK**. You should now see only the data for **Salaries**.

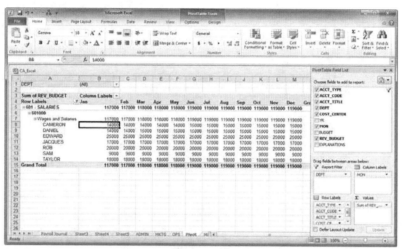

Figure 48

3. Drag **Cost_Center** from the **Row Labels** window and drop it in the **PivotTable Field List** window.

4. Drag **Dept** from the **Report Filter** window and drop it in the **Row Labels** window.

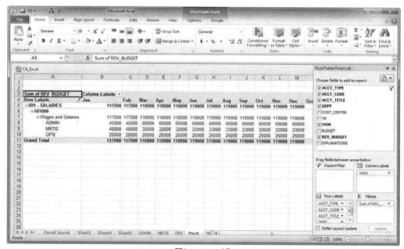

Figure 49

5. You do not need the **ACCT_CODE** so you can drag the field from the **Row Labels** window to the **PivotTable Field List** window. In addition, you have not been asked for a breakdown by month so drag **MON** from the Column Labels window to the **PivotTable Field List** window.

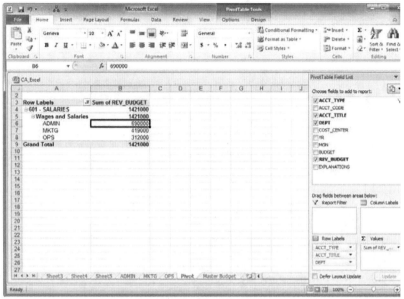

Figure 50

6. Click inside the PivotTable and click on the **Options** tab of the **PivotTable Tools** menu. Click on the **PivotChart** icon in the **Tools** section.

Figure 51

7. The **Insert Chart** window appears. Select **Pie** from the choices and click **OK**.

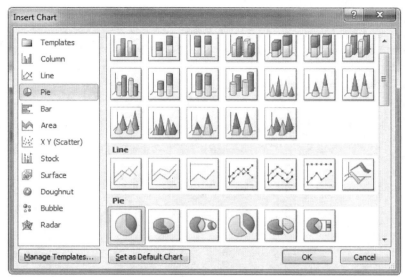

Figure 52

8. A pie chart appears, embedded in the **Pivot** worksheet. Notice that the Legend for the chart appears to the right of the pie chart. However, there is no other information (e.g., amounts or percentages) that has been provided. Right click on the center of the pie chart and select **Add Data Labels**. The totals by department are now added to the chart.

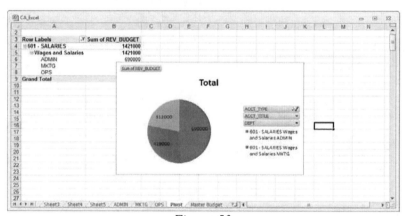

Figure 53

9. You can add more information by right clicking on the pie chart again and clicking on **Format Data Labels**. Click on Category Name and Percentage in the **Format Data Labels** window.

Figure 54

10. The placement of the chart in the middle of the **Pivot** worksheet is not optimal. Click on the **PivotChart Tools** toolbar and click on **Move Chart** in the **Location** section of the toolbar.

Figure 55

11. In the **Move Chart** window, click on **New Sheet** and name the sheet **Salary by Department**.

12. Notice that the newly created pie chart is entitled "**Total**". This is not very descriptive if you were to print the pie chart. Select the chart title by double clicking on it and change the title to "**Salary Expense by Department**".

13. Finally, note that if you were to return to the **Pivot** worksheet and restore the **DEPT, MON, ACCT_CODE,** and **COST_CENTER** fields to their appropriate places (in their proper order) and then click on the worksheet containing your pie chart, the formatting of the chart will change. As mentioned at the beginning of this exercise, the chart is linked to and matches the data shown in the PivotTable. If you change that data, the chart changes with it. If you experiment with the PivotTable from this point on, be sure to restore the settings for the chart discussed above.

WRAP-UP

You have now completed the Excel assignment. Be sure to save your work. Your instructor may provide you with an appropriate file naming convention, in which case you will have to rename your file.

o

GENERAL LEDGER APPLICATIONS USING *PEACHTREE COMPLETE ACCOUNTING 2012* ®:
The Winery At Chateau Americana

LEARNING OBJECTIVES

After completing and discussing this assignment, you should be able to:

- Recognize the managerial and technological issues associated with the implementation of a general ledger package
- Complete sample transactions
- Understand the implications of the design of the user interface
- Recognize and evaluate the strengths and weaknesses of controls embedded in a general ledger package
- Compare and contrast a general ledger package with a manual accounting information system

BACKGROUND

As the winery has grown, Rob Breeden, the chief financial officer, has realized that management does not have timely information about the financial condition of the company. This has resulted in several instances in which the decisions made were not optimal. Therefore, he has determined that it is time to convert the current system to a general ledger package. After investigating the possibilities, he has decided to utilize *Peachtree Complete Accounting 2012®*. Chateau Americana has hired you to convert the system.

REQUIREMENTS

Using the *Peachtree Complete Accounting 2012®* software program contained in your *CAST* package or in your school computer lab, you are to convert Chateau Americana from a manual system to a general ledger software package. If you are working on this assignment on your home computer, load the software following the instructions contained on the CD envelope.

As with any other computer file, it is important to **back up frequently** to another storage medium.

SETTING UP A NEW COMPANY

Requirements

1. Start *Peachtree Complete Accounting 2012®* and click on **Create a new company**.

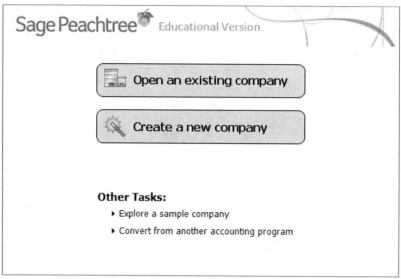

Figure 1

2. The Introduction screen that appears next alerts the user to information that will be required throughout the set-up procedure. Click on **Next**.

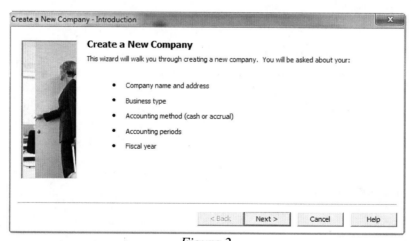

Figure 2

3. Enter the following company information and then click on **Next:**

> The Winery at Chateau Americana, Inc.
> 3003 Vineyard Way
> Huntington, CA 95394
> Phone: (707) 368-8485
> Fax: (707) 368-8486

Do not enter any information in the remaining input boxes.

Figure 3

4. You are now asked to select a method for setting up the Chart of Accounts. Peachtree provides you with sample charts of accounts in the event that you are setting up a start-up company. However, because Chateau Americana already has a Chart of Accounts, select **Build your own chart of accounts** and click on **Next**.

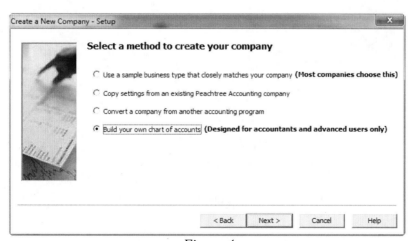

Figure 4

5. The next screen provides options for the company's accounting method. If you examine the Chart of Accounts you will notice various accounts that provide evidence that Chateau Americana utilizes the accrual method of accounting. Identify what these accounts are. Then click on **Next**.

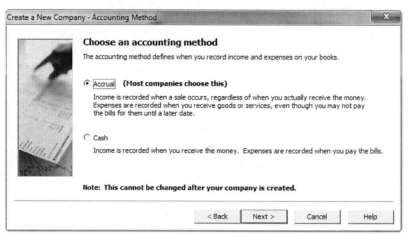

Figure 5

6. Peachtree offers two posting methods. In Real Time mode, each transaction is posted as it is written and the General Ledger is always up to date. In Batch mode, transactions are posted in batches or groups, resulting in processing efficiencies but delaying the updating of the General Ledger. Since one of Rob Breeden's concerns is that of timely information, select the **Real Time** posting method and click on **Next**.

Figure 6

7. The next two screens address the company's accounting period. The first asks you to select the number of accounting periods within a year. The company's fiscal year is a calendar year with 12-monthly accounting periods. Make sure the correct accounting period is selected and click on **Next**.

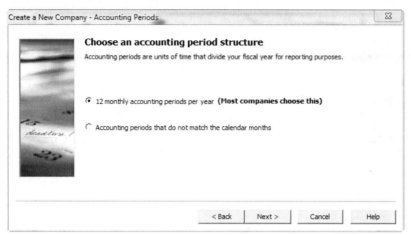

Figure 7

8. Now you are prompted to provide the month and year that the fiscal year begins (i.e., January 20XX). We will refer to the current year as 20XX but your instructor will provide you with the year you are to use. You have been given the general ledger balances as of December 15, 20XX. Note that this implies that the fiscal year begins as of January 20XX. Make sure the correct information is input and click on **Next**.

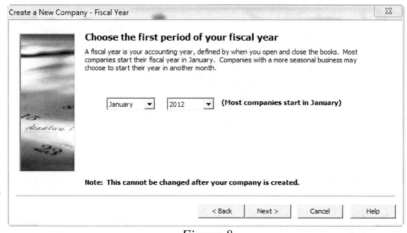

Figure 8

9. You have now completed the set-up procedures for converting Chateau Americana to Peachtree. Click on **Finish**.

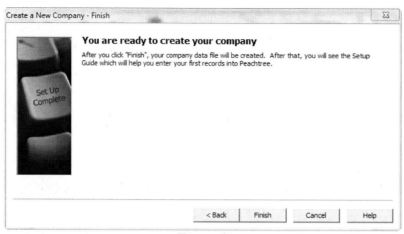

Figure 9

10. Close the **What's New in Peachtree 2012** window. (Before closing the window, you might also want to check the "Do not show this screen again" box.)

11. The **Setup Guide** window appears with the **Chart of Accounts** highlighted.

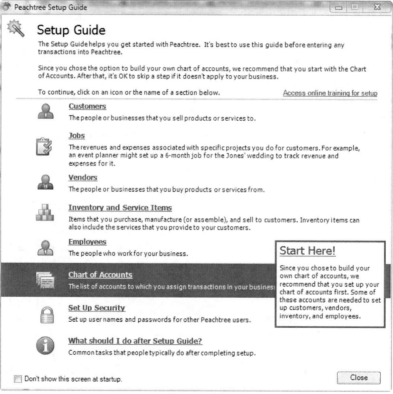

Figure 10

If you wish, you may close the file at this time and Peachtree will automatically save the contents. If you do so, the **Setup Guide** should reappear the next time you start up Peachtree. If the **Setup Guide** doesn't reappear, you may retrieve it at this or any other time by clicking on **File** in the Menu bar and the clicking on **Setup Guide**.

SETTING UP THE GENERAL LEDGER

Requirements

1. If you have closed the file, reopen the Chateau Americana file. Click on the **Chart of Accounts** now. After familiarizing yourself with the information on this window, you can click the **Next** button in the lower right-hand corner of the window.

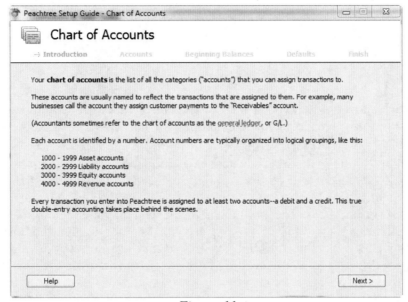

Figure 11

2. The next window describes the process for adding new accounts. Once you have read this information, you may click **Add New Accounts**.

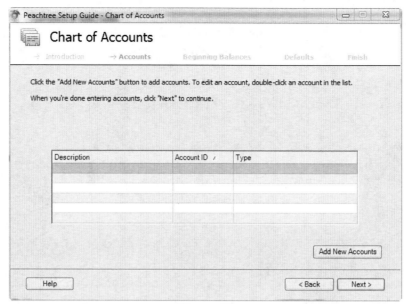

Figure 12

3. You can now set up your **Chart of Accounts**. It is extremely important that you set up the chart of accounts properly. Click on the **Add New Accounts** [Add New Accounts] icon. Use the account numbers and related descriptions that follow. (Note: All of the accounts have normal balances.) Begin by entering the Cash account. Type the account number (111000) in the field entitled **Account ID** field. Then enter "General Checking Account" in the **Description** field. The pull-down menu next to the **Account Type** field requires you to select the type of account for each account number. Scroll through the various Account Types to acquaint yourself with the listings there but leave the Account Type as Cash. **Do not enter balance information** for the accounts at this time.

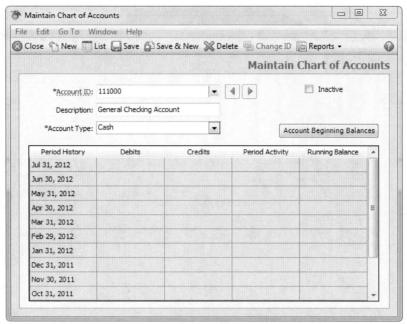

Figure 13

Click the **Save & New** ⌷Save & New button after you enter each account's information. As you enter the account titles, notice that the full title does not always fit in the space provided and you will, therefore, need to abbreviate the descriptions slightly. In addition, the **Account Type** for many of these accounts is obvious. For those that are not obvious, you will need to refer to the information provided below.

- Common Stock and Paid-In Capital in Excess of Par are "Equity-doesn't close" accounts
- Dividends is an "Equity-gets closed" account type
- "Income" accounts include Sales, Sales Returns and Allowances, Sales Discounts Taken, Gain/Loss on Sale of Assets, Gain/Loss on Sale of Securities, Interest/Dividend Income, and Miscellaneous Revenue

Account Title	Account #	12/15/XX Balance
Assets (100000)		
General Checking Account	111000	$ 2,222,927.47
Payroll Checking Account	112000	1,000.00
Money Market Account	113000	782,546.49
Savings Account	114000	51,745.56
Petty Cash	119000	500.00
Accounts Receivable	121000	5,366,670.86
Allowance for Bad Debts	129000	95,401.58
Inventory – Production	141000	$ 11,564,851.56
Inventory – Finished Goods	145000	4,044,046.31
Prepaid Expenses	150000	142,465.96

Land and Buildings	160000	16,358,487.34
Equipment	170000	13,844,881.10
Accumulated Depreciation	180000	15,233,662.97
Investments	191000	3,070,227.56
Liabilities (200000)		
Accounts Payable	210000	4,987,975.79
Federal Income Tax Withheld	222100	66,739.08
FICA Withheld	222200	12,237.64
Medicare Withheld	222300	2,862.01
FICA Payable – Employer	223100	12,237.64
Medicare Payable – Employer	223200	2,862.01
Unemployment Taxes Payable	223300	943.57
Other Accrued Expenses	230000	599,348.98
Federal Income Taxes Payable	235000	0.00
Property Taxes Payable	236000	0.00
Dividends Payable	239000	0.00
Mortgages Payable	240000	7,639,067.73
Notes Payable	261000	841,000.00
Owners' Equity (300000)		
Common Stock	310000	90,000.00
Paid-in Capital in Excess of Par – Common	311000	3,567,265.00
Dividends – Common	312000	0.00
Retained Earnings	390000	22,064,134.78
Income (400000)		
Sales	410000	22,264,431.15
Sales Discounts	420000	346,741.36
Sales Returns and Allowances	430000	15,588.47
Gain/Loss – Fixed Assets	451000	0.00
Gain/Loss – Marketable Securities	452000	0.00
Dividend Income	491000	4,000.00
Interest Income	492000	23,482.56
Cost of Goods Sold	510000	11,514,092.11
Expenses (600000 – 700000)		
Wages and Salaries Expense	601000	1,965,164.11
Sales Commission Expense	601500	771,665.60
FICA Tax Expense	602100	244,124.52
Medicare Tax Expense	602200	57,093.62
FUTA Expense	602300	7,392.00
SUTA Expense	602400	22,176.00
Utilities Expense	611000	307,067.05
Irrigation & Waste Disposal Expense	611300	230,910.91
Landscaping Expense	612000	142,475.69
Advertising Expense	621000	296,794.33
Marketing Expense	623000	192,865.67
Festivals & Competitions Expense	624000	238,654.75
Telephone Expense	631000	37,584.73
Internet & Computer Expense	632000	14,475.00
Postage Expense	633000	35,117.66
Legal & Accounting Fees	641000	88,425.50
Other Consulting Fees	643000	12,500.00
Office Supplies Expense	651000	58,689.68

Data Processing Expense	660000	9,743.89
Depreciation Expense	670000	1,092,832.66
Travel and Entertainment Expense	680000	169,405.86
Other Insurance	691000	115,058.55
Medical Insurance	692000	192,154.80
Workmen's Compensation Insurance	693000	139,750.00
Other Employee Benefits Expense	699000	175,643.90
Dues and Subscriptions Expense	700000	32,076.00
Federal Income Tax Expense	711000	857,595.76
Property Tax Expense	712000	19,875.00
Repairs and Maintenance Expense	721000	71,974.93
Automobile Expense	731000	81,493.45
Lease Expense	740000	113,607.56
Bad Debt Expense	791000	0.00
Miscellaneous Expense	792000	26,575.63
Interest Expense	793000	359,915.53

You can go back and forward to view or edit your work at any time by clicking on the **Arrow** buttons next to the **Account ID** and selecting the account that you want to edit.

4. When you have finished entering all of the accounts, review the Chart of Accounts to make sure you haven't made any errors. If you find any problems, double-click the account in question and correct it. When you are finished, close the Maintain Chart of Accounts window and click the **Next** button.

5. You are now asked if you want to enter the beginning balances. **WARNING**: Begin this process only if you have enough time to enter all the balances. If you are ready to proceed, click **Next**.

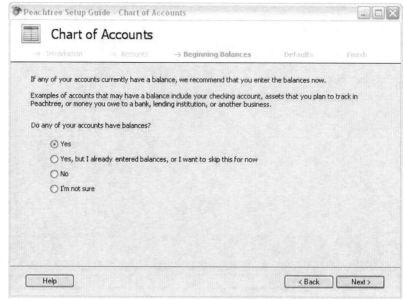

Figure 14

SETTING UP BEGINNING ACCOUNT BALANCES

Requirements

1. To set up your beginning balances, you first need to decide upon the accounting period. Begin by clicking on the **Enter Account Beginning Balances** button.

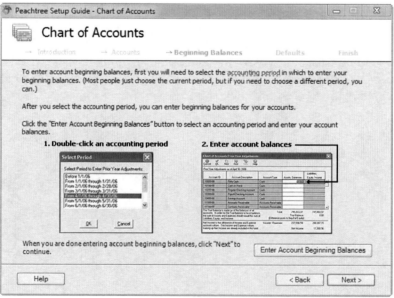

Figure 15

2. Since our books for Chateau Americana begin in the middle of December, we will select the period **From 12/1/XX through 12/31/XX**. Click **OK**.

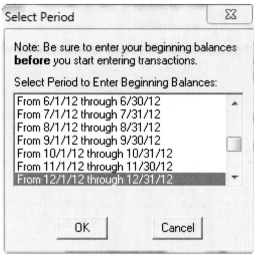

Figure 16

IMPORTANT: When entering beginning balances, Peachtree classifies the balances as either "Assets, Expenses" accounts that have debit balances or "Liabilities, Equities, Income" accounts that have credit balances. Thus, it is imperative that you watch for contra accounts (e.g., allowance for bad debts) and enter them as negative numbers if necessary since, in most instances, Peachtree will not recognize them as contra accounts.

3.   When you are finished entering the beginning balances for all accounts, you should see that the trial balance equals **"0.00"**.

Account ID	Account Description	Account Type	Assets, Expenses	Liabilities, Equity, Income
111000	General Checking Account	Cash	2,222,927.47	
112000	Payroll Checking Account	Cash	1,000.00	
113000	Money Market Account	Cash	782,546.49	
114000	Savings Account	Cash	51,745.56	
119000	Petty Cash	Cash	500.00	
121000	Accounts Receivable	Accounts Receivable	5,366,670.86	
129000	Allowance for Bad Debts	Accounts Receivable	-95,401.58	

The Trial Balance is made up of the balances of all accounts. In order for the Trial Balance to be in balance, the sum of Assets and Expenses should equal the sum of Liabilities, Equity, and Income.

Total: 57,354,948.63   57,354,948.63
Trial Balance: 0.00
(Difference posts to Beg Bal Equity)

Net Income is the difference of Income and Expense account values. The Income and Expense values making up Net Income are already included in the total.

Income - Expenses: 0.00   0.00
Net Income: 0.00

Figure 17

If the sum of Assets and Expenses does not equal the sum of Liabilities, Equity, and Income, Peachtree will create a temporary equity account for any unaccounted for difference. This amount will have to be investigated and adjusted for at a later time. However, the account created (**Beg Bal Equity**) will not go away after the adjustment has been made. It will remain in the Chart of Accounts.

4. Click **OK** once the Trial Balance is equal to 0.00 and click on the **Next** button.

5. There is no need to set up a **Rounding Account**. Click on the **Next** button. You are now finished setting up the Chart of Accounts. Click on the **Next** button.

SETTING UP USER SECURITY

1. Security over a company's financial information is critical. We will now explore the security options available in Peachtree.

2. With the radio button set on **Proceed to User Security Setup**, click on the **Next** button. Click on the **Next** button again to accept **Yes, I want to set up users now**.

3. You must begin by setting up a company or system administrator. This individual has complete access to Peachtree. In addition, this individual will be in charge of adding users and maintaining their passwords. Click now on **Set Up Users** ⟨ Set Up Users ⟩ icon to set up the administrator, as well as other user names and passwords. Note that the **User List** is blank in *Figure 18*.

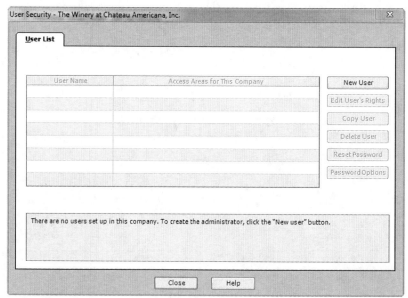

Figure 18

4. Click on the **New User** ⟨ New User ⟩ icon. The default **User Name** is **Admin**. This is the default used by most programs and would be easily hacked. It should be changed to something that is not obvious and a strong password should be chosen. **IMPORTANT**: Keep in mind that once you set a **User Name** and **Password** for the Administrator you will then be

prompted to login whenever you open Peachtree from now on. *REMEMBER IT!!*

5.   Now we will set up another security for another employee. Anna Johnson is the Accounting Supervisor. Her **User Name** is *ajohn* and her **Password** is *password1*. Click on **Selected access** and click **Next**.

Figure 19

6.   Scroll through the categories of access. Think about whether the Accounting Supervisor should have Full Access to each area. Keep in mind that this person is not the same person as the **Administrator** and should not have access to all areas.

7.   Sue Jones is the Payroll Entry Clerk. Her **User Name** is *sjone* and her **Password** is *password2*. Set Sue Jones up so that she only has access to Payroll entry and no access to anything else.

8.   Once you have finished setting up user security for these three individuals, click on the **Close** button and then click on the **Next** button. Leave the radio button on the "**Show me what I might do next**" option and click **Next**.

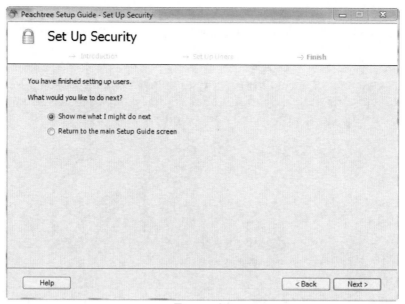

Figure 20

9. Look through the list of Next Steps. We are not ready to perform any of these steps. We can't create invoices, pay vendors or pay employees yet because we have not yet entered any customers, vendors or employees into our system. Click **Close** so we can enter these entities into Peachtree.

Figure 21

SETTING UP ACCOUNTS RECEIVABLE

Requirements

1. Before you begin, make sure that the **Period** in the icons near the top of the page is set to 12/1/XX to 12/31/XX. You also want to change the **System Date** to

12/15/XX. Open the Chateau Americana file if it's not already open. Make sure you are in the **Customers & Sales Task** window.

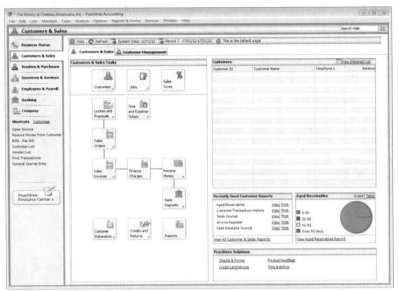

Figure 22

2. Click on **Customers** 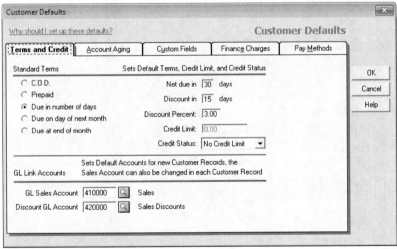. Click on **Set Up Customer Defaults** in the pull-down window. Leave the Standard Terms as "Due in number of days." Remove the Credit Limit since you have not been provided credit limits for any of Chateau Americana's customers. Change the Discount Terms to "3" percent and "15" number of days. Set the defaults for the Sales account and the Sales Discounts account using the pull-down menu. Set the Credit Status to "No Credit Limit."

Figure 23

3. Click on the **Account Aging** tab. Change the aging method to **Invoice date** and click **OK**. There is no need to modify any information on the remaining tabs.

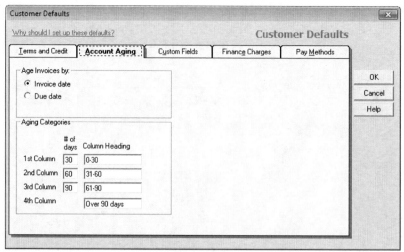

Figure 24

4. Click on **Customers** again but now click on **New Customer**.

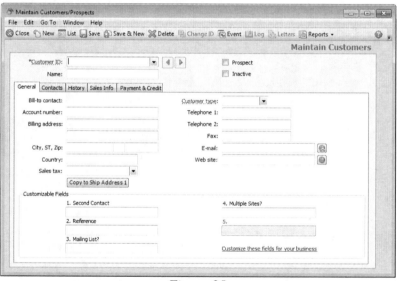

Figure 25

Most of the general information required for each of the customers is self-explanatory and can be found below. You may have to refer to purchase orders for any missing information. (Purchase order documents are found at the back of the Peachtree instructions.) Chateau Americana makes only wholesale sales to distributors. Therefore, no sales tax is applied to any sales transactions. After entering the address, click on **Copy to Ship Address 1**. Be sure to click **Save & New** for each customer as they are entered.

Customer Name	Customer ID	Address/Phone	Terms
Alota Wine Distributors	0509	Pier 32, The Embarcadero San Francisco, CA 94111 Phone: (415) 975-8566	3/15, net 30
Bock Wines and Vines	0501	Pier 19, The Embarcadero San Francisco, CA 94111 Phone: (415) 834-9675	3/15, net 30
California Pacific Wine	0555	Pier 81, The Embarcadero San Francisco, CA 94111 Phone: (415) 827-8455	3/15, net 30
California Premium Beverage	0504	39848 South Street Santa Rosa, CA 95402 Phone: (707) 555-7451 Fax: (707) 555-7452	3/15, net 30
Diversita Wine and Beer Distributors	0511	1328 L Street Sacramento, CA 95814 Phone: (916) 441-5517	3/15, net 30
Pacific Distribution Co.	0505	10034 Westborough Boulevard San Francisco, CA 94080 Phone: (415) 555-1532	3/15, net 30
Seaside Distributors, Inc.	0506	9835 West Hills Road Ukiah, CA 94080 Phone: (707) 555-3102	3/15, net 30
Ukiah Beer, Wines and Vines	0527	782 Talmadge Street Ukiah, CA 95482 Phone: (707) 555-8247	3/15, net 30

5. Using the blue arrow keys next to the **Customer ID** or the pull-down menu, scroll back and click on Alota Wine Distributors and click on the **History** tab**.** Then click on **Customer Beginning Balances**. Enter the beginning balance (as of December 15). You will need to enter an invoice number. For most customers, it will be sufficient to enter Balance Forward as the invoice number. If you are provided with specific information about invoices that are included in the balance forward, however, you can break those amounts out and enter them separately. When you have entered all the beginning balance data, click **Save** and then click **Close**. Continue this process for each of the customer accounts. Note that you can also use the **Customer ID** pull-down menu to find the customer for which you wish to enter data.

Customer Name	Invoice Number	Invoice Date	Amount
Alota Wine Distributors	Bal Forward	12/15/XX	$3,340,283.15
Bock Wines and Vines	Bal Forward	12/15/XX	$39,824.24
California Pacific Wine	Bal Forward	12/15/XX	$47,147.71
California Premium Beverage			
Diversita Wine and Beer Distributors	Bal Forward	12/15/XX	$1,885,031.06
Pacific Distribution Co.	Bal Forward	10/31/XX	$39,153.60
Seaside Distributors, Inc.			
Ukiah Beer, Wines and Vines	Bal Forward	12/15/XX	$15,231.10

6. There is no need to modify any information on the remaining tabs. You are now finished setting up Accounts Receivable. Click **Close** ⊗ Close .

7. You can verify that you have input the correct numbers by clicking on **Forms & Reports** in the top menu of the **Customers & Sales Tasks** screen. Then click on **Accounts Receivable** and open the **Aged Receivables** report. Make a note of the balance at the end of this report. Close the **Aged Receivables** report.

8. Now click on the **General Ledger** at the left side of the **Select a Report or Form** screen and double click **General Ledger.**

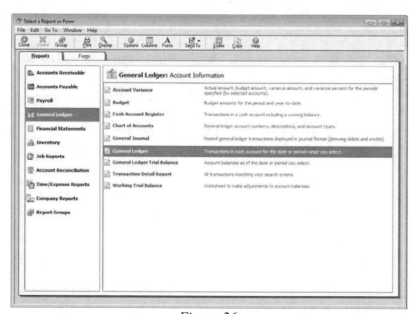

Figure 26

9. Look at the balance under General Ledger account **121000 Accounts Receivable** and compare it to the balance you saw in the **Aged Receivables** report. They should be the same. If they are not, click on **View Detailed List** at the upper right of the **Customers & Sales Tasks** screen and compare the beginning balances to those that were provided to you above. When you find a balance that is incorrect, you can double-click on that customer and it will take you to the **Maintain Customers/Prospects** input screen for the customer in question. You can then click on **History** and then on **Customer Beginning Balances** to correct your mistake.

10. If you wish, you may close the file at this time.

SETTING UP ACCOUNTS PAYABLE

Requirements

1. Open the Chateau Americana file if it's not already open. Click on the **Vendors & Purchases** tab.

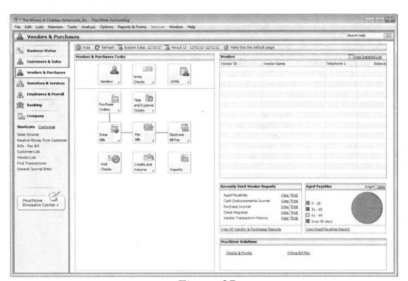

Figure 27

2. Click on **Vendors** and click on **Set Up Vendor Defaults**. Since the terms vary for each vendor, leave the default set to "Due in number of days." Using the pull-down menu, select the Inventory - Production account for the default Expense account. Despite the fact the Inventory – Production is not an Expense account, it is the account that is debited when the company credits most Purchases. The default Discount GL account should also be set to the Inventory - Production account since the company is using the perpetual inventory method. This sets up the debit for purchases to default to Production Inventory and will similarly credit any discounts to Production Inventory. Clear all remaining default values on the **Payment Terms** tab with the exception of the **Net due in** box, which should be left at **30 days** so that the company keeps track of its payables.

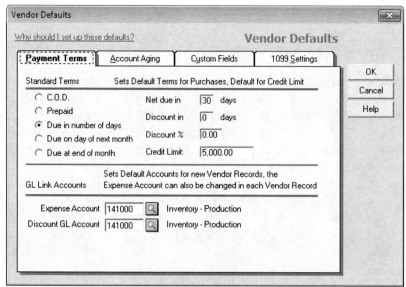

Figure 28

3. Continuing with the vendor defaults menu, click on **Account Aging**. Notice that the default in Peachtree is to age by due date. Change the aging to invoice date and click **OK**.

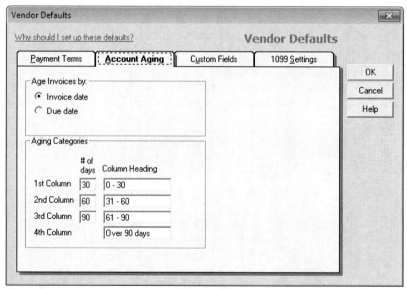

Figure 29

4. Click on **Vendors** again and click on **New Vendor**.

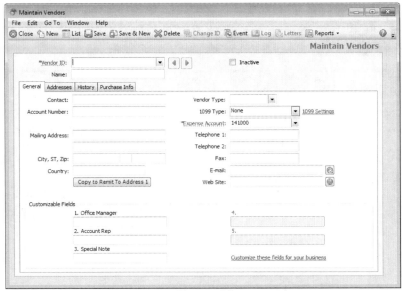

Figure 30

Set up the following five vendor accounts using the following information along with the vendor invoices provided at the end of this module:

Vendor Name	Vendor ID	Address/Phone
Delicio Vineyards	D2538	12701 South Fernwood Livermore, CA 94550 (925)555-1890
Diversi Vineyards	D0999	8713 Montauk Drive Napa, CA 94558 (707)515-8575
Mendocino Vineyards	M0652	8654 Witherspoon Way Hopland, CA 95449 (707)555-1890
Molti Vineyards	M5170	12773 Calma Court Geyersville, CA 95441 (707)956-8626
Pacific Gas & Electric	P0341	P.O. Box 2575 San Francisco, CA 94103 (415)973-8943

The **General** data is self-explanatory. If information is not provided above or on the vendor invoices leave the cell blank. Be sure to click on **Copy to Remit To Address 1** after entering the address for each vendor. Be sure that the correct **Expense Account** (on the right side of the window) has been selected for each vendor before continuing on from this screen. Pull down the menu and you will find the entire Chart of Accounts. For example, Production Inventory is already selected as the default and is valid for the Delicio, Diversi, Mendocino and Molti Vineyards. However, this is not the correct Expense Account for Pacific Gas & Electric.

5. As you did with Customers, click on the **History** tab and click on **Vendor Beginning Balances** to enter the beginning balance.

Vendor Name	Invoice Number	Invoice Date	P.O. Number	Amount
Delicio Vineyards	45354	11/04/XX	9607	$14,563.56
Diversi Vineyards	Bal Forward	12/15/XX		$2,675,814.93
Mendocino Vineyards	Bal Forward	12/15/XX		$28,942.78
Molti Vineyards	Bal Forward	12/15/XX		$2,268,654.52

6. You can check to be sure that you have entered this information correctly, as you did with Accounts Receivable.

7. Click on **Purchase Info** and pull down the **Ship Via** menu. Select "Best Way" for type of shipping for all vendors, except Pacific Gas & Electric. For the vendors with beginning balances, click on the pull-down menu in **Terms and Credit** and select **Customize terms for this vendor**. Click **Use discounts** and change the **Discount in** to **10 days**. Change the **Discount Percent** to **2%**. Remove the credit limit.

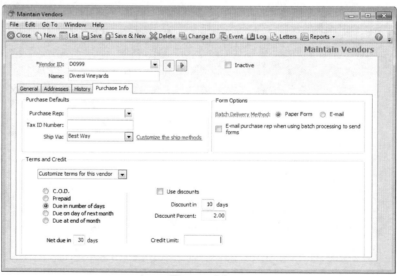

Figure 31

8. Click **Save** after entering each new vendor. Click **Close** .

9. You are now finished setting up Accounts Payable. If you wish, you may close the file at this time.

SETTING UP INVENTORY

Requirements

1. Open the Chateau Americana file. Click **Inventory & Services** and click on the **Inventory Items** [Inventory Items] and select **Set Up Inventory Defaults**. Set the **Item Class** default as Stock item.

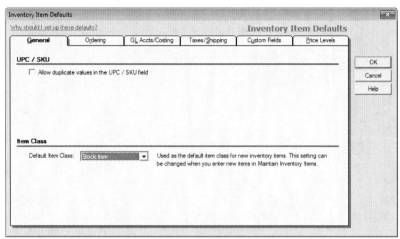

Figure 32

2. Under the **Ordering** tab, change the **Sales Invoice** Out of Stock warning and the **Sales Order** Out of Stock Warning to "**Warn if inventory item is out of stock based on quantity on hand.**" Leave the other defaults in the **Ordering** tab as they are.

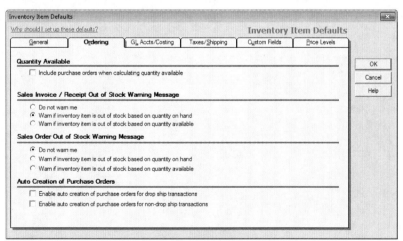

Figure 33

3. Click on the **GL Accts/Costing** tab. Set up the default accounts as follows: GL/Sales Inc should be set to Sales - 410000, GL Invtry/Wage should be set

to Inventory – Finished Goods - 145000, and GL Cost Sales should be set to Cost of Goods Sold – 510000. We need to set up these accounts for stock items only. Change the Costing to LIFO. You will also need to set the GL Freight Account to Cost of Goods Sold - 510000.

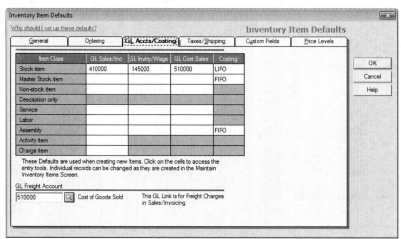

Figure 34

4. Click on **Taxes/Shipping**. Change the **Item Tax Type** to **Exempt**. And the **Ship Method** to **Best Buy**. This is because Chateau Americana typically sells to distributors and, therefore, sales are tax exempt. Click **OK**. You do not need to modify settings on the other tabs.

5. Click on **Inventory Items** again and click on **New Inventory Item**.

   On the **General** tab enter the following information for each inventory item: **Item ID**, **Description**, **Price (Price Level 1)**, **Item Tax Type (select 1 – Regular - Exempt)**, and **Last Unit Cost**. Be sure to save after inputting each inventory item. You do not need to enter any information below the heavy black line.

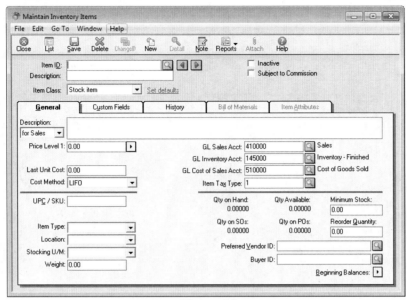

Figure 35

After you have entered the general information for an inventory item, click on **Beginning Balances** in the lower right-hand corner of the window. Click on the item and enter its **Quantity** and **Unit Cost**. Peachtree will automatically calculate the **Total Cost**. Note that when you are through, the **Total Beginning Balances** will not reconcile to the amount that you input into the **General Ledger** when you were setting up the Chart of Accounts for the company. This is a problem with Peachtree. If you were to have put in the **Unit Cost** for each wine that was used previously during the year, that **Unit Cost** would then override the **Last Unit Cost** amount that you entered in the **Maintain Inventory Items** window (see *Figure 35*). The **Unit Cost** fluctuates during the year but Peachtree provides no way to properly represent the previous unit cost without impacting the **Last Unit Cost**. Click **OK** to close the Beginning Balances window.

Figure 36

Be sure you have referred to your instructor to determine which Transaction Set you are to use before you continue to set up inventory!!

Inventory Data

Transaction Set A

Inventory ID	Description	Price	Last Unit Cost	Quantity On Hand	Beginning Balance
R130064	Cabernet Franc	$10.00	$7.50	5,964	$ 26,838.00
R130061	Cabernet Sauvignon	9.50	7.20	65,784	276,292.80
R130056	Merlot	9.00	7.62	83,484	385,696.08
R130072	Shiraz	9.25	7.58	75,888	347,567.04
W120080	Chardonnay	10.00	7.54	420,552	1,909,306.08
W120019	Chenin Blanc	8.25	6.34	44,532	148,736.88
W120015	Riesling	7.85	5.86	118,596	339,184.56
W120016	Sauvignon Blanc	7.85	5.86	93,636	$ 267,798.96
S140000	Sparkling Brut	14.00	10.28	47,064	342,625.91

Transaction Set B

Inventory ID	Description	Price	Last Unit Cost	Quantity On Hand	Beginning Balance
R130064	Cabernet Franc	$12.80	$7.80	5,964	$ 26,838.00
R130061	Cabernet Sauvignon	12.40	7.90	65,784	276,292.80
R130056	Merlot	12.00	8.02	83,484	385,696.08
R130072	Shiraz	12.15	8.14	75,888	347,567.04
W120080	Chardonnay	13.10	7.95	420,552	1,909,306.08
W120019	Chenin Blanc	11.15	6.71	44,532	148,736.88
W120015	Riesling	10.75	6.49	118,596	339,184.56
W120016	Sauvignon Blanc	10.90	6.34	93,636	$ 267,798.96
S140000	Sparkling Brut	16.70	10.48	47,064	342,625.91

Transaction Set C

Inventory ID	Description	Price	Last Unit Cost	Quantity On Hand	Beginning Balance
R130064	Cabernet Franc	$13.40	$9.30	5,964	$ 26,838.00
R130061	Cabernet Sauvignon	14.00	9.40	65,784	276,292.80
R130056	Merlot	13.60	9.52	83,484	385,696.08
R130072	Shiraz	13.75	9.64	75,888	347,567.04
W120080	Chardonnay	14.70	9.45	420,552	1,909,306.08
W120019	Chenin Blanc	12.75	8.31	44,532	148,736.88
W120015	Riesling	12.35	8.09	118,596	339,184.56
W120016	Sauvignon Blanc	12.50	7.94	93,636	$ 267,798.96
S140000	Sparkling Brut	18.30	11.98	47,064	342,625.91

6. Note that you will be typing over the existing information as you enter the next inventory item so it is critical that you click on **Save**.

When you are finished entering all of the inventory items, click **Close**.

SETTING UP PAYROLL

Requirements

1. Open the Chateau Americana file. Click on **the Employees & Payroll** tab.

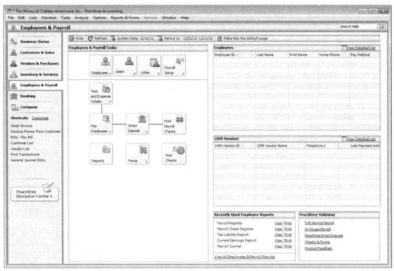

Figure 37

2. Click on the **Employees** 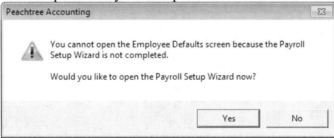 icon. Set up the initial payroll fields by clicking on **Set Up Employee Defaults**. A window pops up asking if you would like to open the Payroll Setup Wizard. Click **Yes**.

Figure 38

3. The first screen describes the various steps in the Payroll Setup Wizard. Click **Next**.

Figure 39

2. The **Payroll Options** window allows you to choose between allowing Peachtree to handle your payroll and allowing the company to handle payroll in-house. Click on **Do It Yourself In-House** and click **Next**.

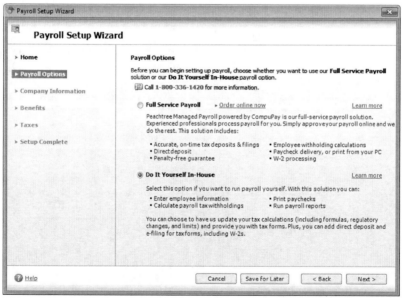

Figure 40

3. The following window asks whether you want to enroll in Peachtree's Tax Update Service. Your corporation would typically want this service so that the administrator and/or accounting clerk would not have the burden of entering all of the tax formulas. However, in order to determine how these formulas actually work, we are going to create them ourselves. Click on **Do It Yourself** and click **Next**.

Figure 41

4. The next window provides additional Payroll options that Peachtree offers. We are not interested in any of these for this assignment so click **Next**.

5. In the next screen, we will leave the Federal Employer ID, State Employer ID and State Unemployment ID blank. Assume the unemployment tax rate is 5.7%. Do not record meals and tips. Click on **Next**.

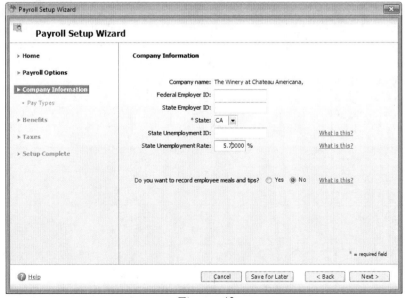

Figure 42

6. You are now prompted to enter the Gross Pay accounts for both Hourly and Salary employees. Chateau Americana has only one expense account for wages and salary. Select the Wages and Salaries Expense account for the

default Gross Pay account. Be sure to include both the **Regular** and **Overtime Pay Type** for **Hourly** employees. Click **Next**.

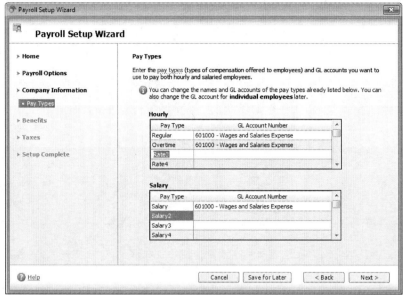

Figure 43

7. The following window asks you to select the benefits that Chateau Americana offers. Obviously, you would typically select several of these benefits but, for the sake of simplicity, we will leave these blank and click on **Next**.

8. You are now prompted to set up the default for Payroll Taxes. Notice that Peachtree allows for only one default account to be chosen for the **Tax liability acct no.** and the **Tax expense acct no.**, despite the fact that companies typically separate the accounts to record a variety of both payroll tax liabilities and expenses. You will, therefore, have to adjust these default accounts later. For now, we will select the most common liability and expense account. Using the pull-down menus, click on the **Federal Income Tax Withheld** account for the **Tax liability acct no.** and the **FICA Tax Expense** account for the **Tax Expense acct no.** Click on **Next**.

Figure 44

9. Click **Finish** in the following window. We now need to adjust the **Employee Defaults**. Click on **Employees** and click on **Set Up Employee Defaults**. Click on the **Employee Fields** tab. When we were in the Payroll Wizard, we set up the G/L Account for the Tax Liability as the Federal Income Tax Withheld account. We now need to adjust the FICA Withheld account and the Medicare Withheld account. In addition, there are two accounts that Peachtree is going to try to use that our company does not need. We will remove those accounts. Use the pull-down menu and enter the proper **G/L Account** code for FICA Withheld (Soc_Sec) and Medicare Withheld (MEDICARE). Remove the checkmarks from the remaining two fields (the fields not being used).

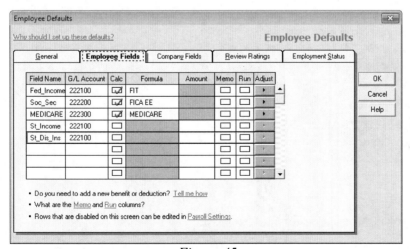

Figure 45

10. Enter the Company payroll information by clicking on **Company Fields**. You will again have to select the proper GL accounts for the employee's

portion of FICA and Medicare or the amounts will not be properly posted to the correct payable accounts. Use the pull-down menu to reference Chateau Americana's general ledger to select the appropriate payroll accounts for the expense accounts and for the payable accounts. Uncheck any remaining fields not being used. Click **OK**.

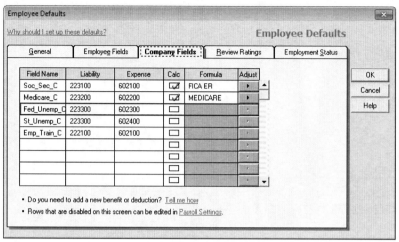

Figure 46

11. Click on **Employees** and click on **New Employee** to enter the individual employee's payroll information. Enter the employee's social security number without hyphens as the "Employee ID."

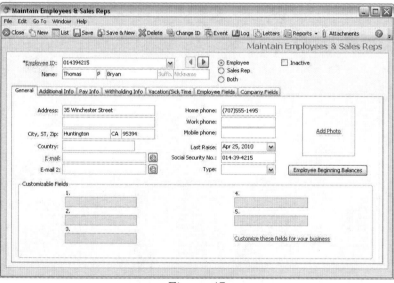

Figure 47

Additional information for each employee can be found below:

Name: Thomas P. Bryan			
Social Security No:	014-39-4215	Pay rate:	$15.00
Address:	35 Winchester Street, Huntington, CA 95394	Pay type:	Hourly
Phone:	(707) 555-1495	Position:	Presses
Date of Birth:	6/14/65	Filing Status:	Single
Date of Employment:	4/25/95	Withholding Allowances	1
Date of Last Raise:	4/25/XX		

Name: Robert T. Hissom			
Social Security No:	349-43-6417	Pay rate:	$14.25
Address:	3187 Heckert Way, Apt. 4A, Huntington, CA 95394	Pay type:	Hourly
Phone:	(707) 555-1219	Position:	Receiving
Date of Birth:	11/9/77	Filing Status:	Single
Date of Employment:	1/4/98	Withholding Allowances	0
Date of Last Raise:	1/4/XX		

Name: Anna C. Johnson			
Social Security No:	296-49-3438	Pay rate:	$1,750
Address:	175 Bunker Hill Lane, Huntington, CA 95394	Pay type:	Salary
Phone:	(707) 555-3856	Position:	Acct Sup
Date of Birth:	9/7/68	Filing Status:	Married
Date of Employment:	2/14/01	Withholding Allowances	3
Date of Last Raise:	2/16/XX		

Name: José G. Rodriquez			
Social Security No:	124-11-7755	Pay rate:	$2,550
Address:	2953 Whistler Hill Lane, Huntington, CA 95394	Pay type:	Salary
Phone:	(707) 555-2024	Position:	Supervisor
Date of Birth:	7/7/71	Filing Status:	Married
Date of Employment:	11/3/93	Withholding Allowances	4
Date of Last Raise:	1/1/XX		

12. Click on the **Pay Info** tab to enter the employee type and pay rate information. The **Pay Method** for the hourly employees is **"Hourly - Time Ticket Hours"** and for salaried employees is "Salary." You will need to enter the Regular Hourly Rate and the Overtime Hourly Rate (1.5 times the regular hourly rate) for hourly employees. All employees are paid on the 15th and the last day of each month.

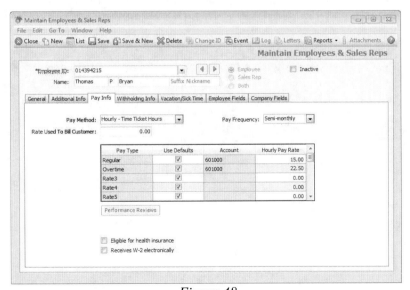

Figure 48

13. Enter the withholding information on the **Withholding Info** tab. Make sure you save each employee as they are entered. Note that you only need to enter the Federal withholding information since state withholdings have not been considered in this exercise.

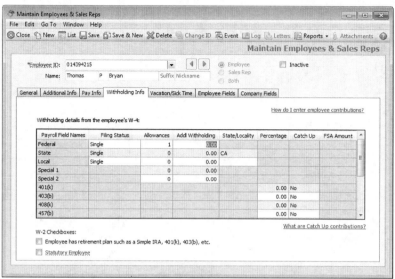

Figure 49

14. Be sure that all fields that are not being used, remain unchecked under the **Employee Fields** and **Company Fields** tabs.

15. When you are finished entering the employee data, go back to the **General** tab, click on **Employee Beginning Balance** and, using the pull-down menu, access each employee to enter the **Employee Beginning Balances** screen. Enter the payroll information for each employee as of December 15, 20XX. You will use the first column only and enter the following year-to-date information (**Hint: You will need to enter those amounts which represent deductions from gross pay as negative amounts.**)

Name	Gross Pay	Federal Income Tax	FICA Withheld	Medicare Withheld	Net Pay
Bryan, T	33,456.21	3,745.42	2,074.29	485.12	27,151.38
Hissom, R	31,751.11	4,035.78	1,968.57	460.40	25,286.35
Johnson, A	38,050.00	2,398.90	2,359.10	551.73	32,740.27
Rodriquez, J	58,650.00	4,612.65	3,636.30	850.43	49,550.62

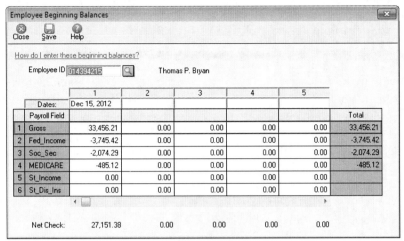

Figure 50

After entering the beginning balances for all employees, click **Close** to return to the **Employee & Payroll Tasks** screen.

SETTING UP PAYROLL FORMULAS

Peachtree uses certain terms and rules for creating formulas that we will define here before proceeding.

- Peachtree allows for multiple equations to appear in a formula and, if a formula has multiple equations, they must be separated by semicolons.

- Constants can appear only on the right side of an equation.

- Variables can appear on either the left side (if you want to set the variable's value) or the right side. The variable **ANSWER** must be in every formula and must be on the left side of the last equation in the formula.

- Peachtree has reserved certain words (found in the Help files) to be used as variables. For example, **ADJUSTED_GROSS** represents an employee's pay, adjusted for those items which are not taxable.

- Peachtree uses standard mathematical operators.

Requirements
1. We now need to set up the payroll formulas to calculate the withholdings and accruals. Click on **Payroll Setup** icon and then click on **Set Up Formulas Manually**.

We will begin by creating a formula for federal income tax withheld for single individuals (see *Figure 48*). In the **Formula ID** field, enter **FITSXX** (fill in the appropriate year using the final two digits in place of the **XX**). We will be using the year 2012 to explain the formula and field names for the remainder of the payroll instruction; therefore, this first formula name will be **FITS12**. This **ID** indicates that we are creating a formula for federal income taxes (**FIT**) for a single individual (**S**) for the tax year 2012 (**12**). The **Name** should be entered as **FIT 12**. (Note that the tax year is dependent upon the tax year which your instructor has already given. It is probably the same year as that in which the transactions are taking place.) Thus, for example, the name for federal income tax withheld for 2012 should be **FIT 12**). The classification (**How do you classify this formula?**) is **Tax** and the **Tax agency** is **Federal**.

The **Effect on gross pay** is **Subtracts from gross**. As stated above, we will begin by calculating **FIT** for individuals claiming their **Filing Status** as **Single**.

We now need to enter a general formula to calculate federal income tax withholdings for all single individuals. Formulas are entered in the **Formula** section of the window. We will use Thomas Bryan's December 31 payroll information to walk through the logic that Peachtree uses for their formulas. The current gross payroll ($1,490.63 for Thomas Bryan) is annualized by multiplying it by 24 (there are 24 pay periods in a semi-monthly payroll method). The number of employee withholding allowances (1) times the annual federal employee allowance ($3,800 for 2012) is subtracted from the annualized gross payroll. Note that the annual federal employee allowance will change if you are completing this assignment for some year other than 2012. You can find this information in IRS Publication 15. The formula then refers to a TABLE to obtain the appropriate amount of tax and it prorates this amount to obtain the amount for the current period.

Thus, the general formula for **FIT is as follows:**

ANSWER = -PRORATE (TABLE (ANNUAL (ADJUSTED_GROSS) - (EMP_FEDERAL_ALLOWANCES * 3800)))

Note that $3,800 is the amount of the annual federal employee allowance regardless of whether the employee is single or married.

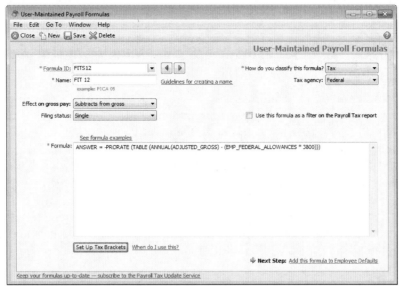

Figure 51

2. Click on **Set Up Tax Brackets** to enter the tax bracket information for **Single** individuals. Refer to Publication 15 for 20XX and enter the tax bracket information from the Annual Payroll Period for Single individuals (Table 7 (a)).

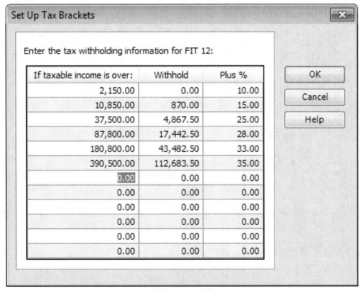

Figure 52

3. Click on **OK** to return to the **User-Maintained Payroll Formulas** and click on **Add this formula to Employee Defaults** in the lower right corner. Click on **OK** when the **Employee Defaults** window pops up.

4. Click on **Save**.

5. Now create the necessary formula for federal income tax withheld for married individuals.

6. The logic behind the formulas for FICA is slightly different in that is uses multiple formulas and more variables. Name the formula **Soc_Sec** and the field **FICA EE XX**. FICA is accrued for both the employee and the employer. As you are undoubtedly aware, FICA is subject to a ceiling; that is, wages are taxable only up to a certain amount. While in 2012, Congress extended the temporary reduction in the percentage withheld on the employee's income, it did not make a similar reduction for the employer's share. Therefore, for the sake of simplicity, we are ignoring the temporary reduction in the rate and say that, for 2012, wages are taxable up to $110,100 and the amount that is withheld is equal to 6.2% of taxable wages. Therefore, we first need to set the limit in the formula box. Then we need to tell Peachtree what the FICA percent is and, finally, we need to define the amount by which we will be multiplying the FICA percentage. Thus, our formula appears as follows:

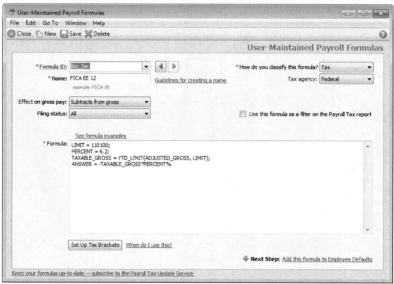

Figure 53

7. Now create formulas for the employer's accrual, as well as for Medicare.

ENTERING TRANSACTIONS

Requirements

1. Open the Chateau Americana file. There are two ways in which you can enter transactions. The first is to click on the Navigation Bar on the left side to open the appropriate window. For example, you would click on **Customers & Sales** to enter credit sales.

2. The listings of the transaction sets begin on page 97. The following, however, provides some detailed instructions and hints on entering those transactions. Using the Transaction Set assigned by your instructor, examine

the first transaction for December 16. The documents supporting the transactions are provided behind each Transaction Set. (**Note: The amounts in the figures that follow do not necessarily agree with those in the Transaction Set assigned to you!!**)

3. The first transaction is a sale to California Premium Beverage. Enter this transaction in Peachtree by clicking on **Customers & Sales**. Click on the **Sales Invoices** icon and select **New Sales Invoice**.

4. Using the **View** button next to the **Customer ID** field, select the customer name. Notice that the Customer ID number appears next to the **View** button and the customer name and address appear in the **Bill To:** and **Ship To:** areas. Enter the transaction **Date** and **Invoice No.**.and complete the remainder of the form. Do not enter the sales account representative since you have not set up these individuals as employees of the company. Do not enter any of the shippers for these transactions. Click **Save** after you have entered all information pertaining to the transaction.

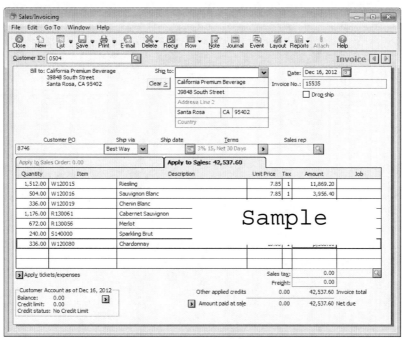

Figure 54

5. Create the **Purchase Order** for the second transaction. Note that when you enter the Item number the field flashes. In addition, you have to manually enter the unit price. When you click on **Save**, an **Invalid ID** window pops up asking if you want to set up the inventory item. Click on **Set Up**.

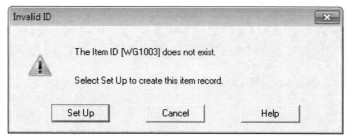

Figure 55

6. Enter the appropriate information. Note that you will need to change the **GL Inventory Acct** to **Inventory – Production**. There is no beginning balance. Click on **Save** and close the window.

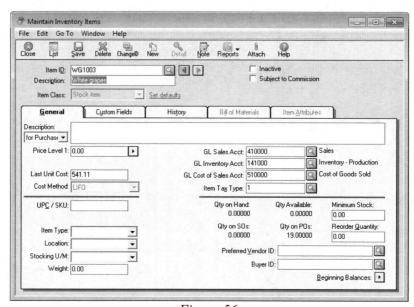

Figure 56

7. Before you **Save** the **Purchase Order**, make sure that all the appropriate information has been entered.

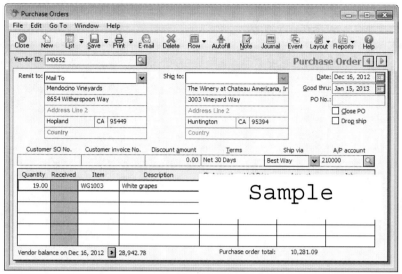

Figure 57

Close the window.

8. The third transaction on December 16th requires you to record the purchase of a truck. When you click on the **Banking** tab, you will notice that there are two ways in which cash disbursements can be handled. You can click on the **Write Checks** icon or **Pay Bills** icon.

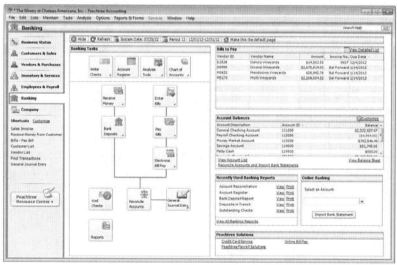

Figure 58

Either selection will allow you to enter the required information for this transaction. If you click on **Pay Bills**, you will notice that the lower part of the window has space to enter a description, along with the ability to change the **GL Account**.

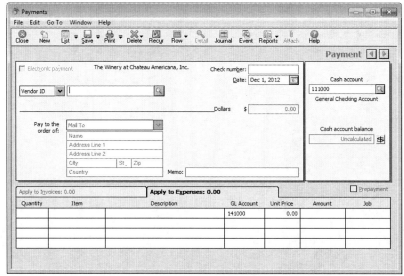

Figure 59

Notice, however, that **Write Checks** does not have any obvious place in which to enter multiple accounts.

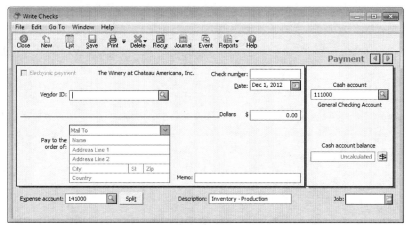

Figure 60

If you choose this option, first fill in all of the appropriate information on the face of the check. Note that there is no Vendor ID for this transaction. You can skip to the vendor Name field. You can then click on the **Split** button Split next to the **Expense account** field to enter all of the accounts involved in this transaction.

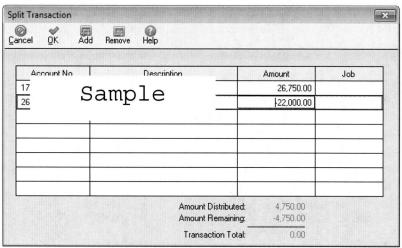

Figure 61

9. For the fourth entry on December 16th, the Board of Directors has declared a cash dividend. This transaction represents a General Journal entry. General Journal entries are recorded by clicking on the **Tasks** button in the main menu and then clicking on **General Journal Entry**. Each General Journal entry should be given its own **Reference** number.

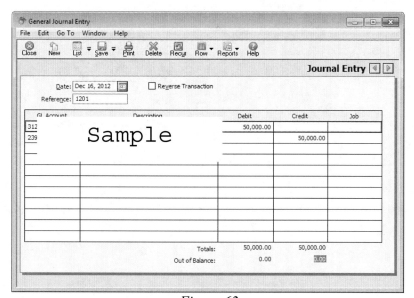

Figure 62

10. Continue working through the transactions from December 17th through the first transaction on December 31st transactions listed below, selecting **Customers & Sales**, **Inventory & Services**, **Employees & Payroll**, or **Banking** as appropriate. Be sure the default accounts being used by the Peachtree Journals are the appropriate accounts for the particular transaction you are entering. You can check the accounts being debited and credited by each transaction by clicking on the **Journal** icon once you have entered the information needed at the top of the transaction screen. If necessary, you can

then change the GL account. However, if the defaults have been set up properly, the Sales Journal will post to Sales and Accounts Receivable; the Cash Receipts Journal will post to Cash, Sales Discounts, and Accounts Receivable.

Remember that not all customers receive credit terms. For those customers who have remitted a check along with their order, you will need to use the **Receive Money** task. If a customer number is not available, tab past the Customer ID field, enter the customer name and address, and enter the details of the sales transaction. You will also use the **Receipts** task for other miscellaneous cash receipts. You can do this either through **Customers & Sales** or through **Banking** by clicking on the **Receive Money** icon. Note, however, that in some cases you will have to click on the **Journal** icon and change the account being credited.

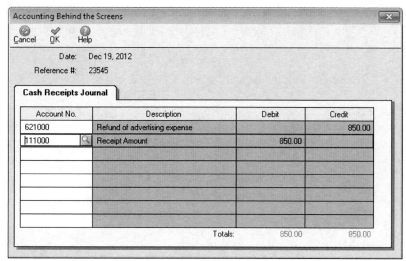

Figure 63

11. For the payroll transactions on December 31, click on **Pay Employees** and then select on **Enter Payroll for Multiple Employees**. A warning pops up saying that your payroll might be calculated incorrectly. Ignore this and close the window.

12. Be sure to enter the appropriate hours for the hourly employees. Think about the Cash Account from which the payroll checks are written. You will need to print a report or the checks in order to record the payroll.

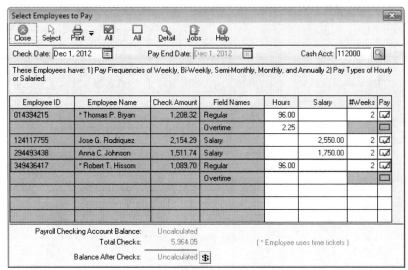

Figure 64

Note that when you enter the payroll data the net pay is slightly different from the net pay you calculated if you prepared the payroll checks in the *CAST Manual AIS Module*. This is because the formulas we created in Peachtree annualize the wages before calculating federal income tax withheld.

TRANSACTION SET A

December	Transaction
16	Receive a purchase order from California Premium Beverage (page 101). Fill and ship the order. Complete Invoice No. 15535.
16	Order 29 tons of white grapes at $541.11 per ton from Mendocino Vineyards. The item number for the white grapes is WG1003. Complete Purchase Order No. 9682.
16	Purchase a 20XW Ford truck for $26,750.00. The terms include a $4,750.00 down payment and a 3-year, 6% promissory note to Ford Credit for the remaining $22,000.00. Principal and interest on the note are due monthly beginning January 4, 20XY. The company expects the truck to have a useful life of 5 years and no salvage value. Prepare Check No. 19257 payable to Potter Valley Ford for the down payment.
16	The Board of Directors of Chateau Americana authorized a $50,000 cash dividend payable on January 20th to the stockholders of record on January 15th. Record the transaction.
17	Receive a phone complaint from Seaside Distributors about a case of Chenin Blanc that was damaged in shipment. The case was part of Invoice No. 15175, dated November 5, 20XX, in the amount of $20,438.40. Seaside paid the invoice on November 19, 20XX and took advantage of the discount (terms 3/15, net 30). Prepare Check No. 19286 to reimburse Seaside for the damaged inventory that was *not* returned to the company.
19	Receive $850 refund from California Wine & Cheese Monthly for overpayment of advertising costs (page 102).
19	Receive payment in full from Pacific Distribution Co. on Invoice No. 15243 dated November 13, 20XX, in the amount of $19,576.80 (page 103). Record the cash receipt.
19	Receive a purchase order (page 104) with payment (page 105) from Sonoma Distributors. Fill and ship the order. Record the sale.
22	Receive 19 tons of red grapes at $703.40 per ton from Mendocino Vineyards. Also received Invoice No. M7634 from Mendocino Vineyards with the shipment (page 106). Terms on the invoice are 2/10, net 30. Record the receipt of inventory.
26	Receive utility bill from Pacific Gas and Electric in the amount of $18,887.62 (page 107). Prepare Check No. 19402.
30	Receive Brokerage Advice from Edwards Jones for purchase of 500 shares of Microsoft at $49.20 per share plus $400 broker's commission (page 108). Prepare Check No. 19468.
30	Prepare Check No. 19473 payable to Mendocino Vineyards for the shipment received on December 22.
31	Receive payment in full for the December 16 purchase from California Premium Beverage (page 109). Record the cash receipt.

December	Transaction
31	Prepare Payroll Checks (Nos. 7111-7114) for Anna Johnson, José Rodriguez, Tom Bryan, and Bob Hissom. Time cards for Tom and Bob are on pages 110-111. Prepare Check No. 19474 to transfer cash from the general cash account to the payroll account.
31	Prepare Check No. 19475 to repay $50,000 of the principal on long-term debt to Bank of Huntington.

MONTH-END PROCEDURES

There are two methods by which you can access the General Journal in Peachtree.

- You can use the menu: **Tasks > General Journal Entry**.
- You can click on the **Company** tab and then click on **General Journal Entry**.

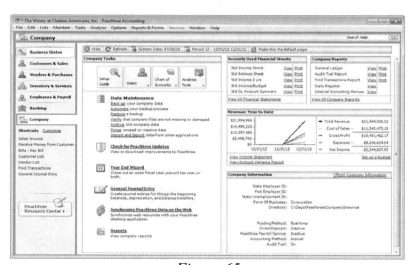

Figure 65

Either method will pull up the **General Journal** window.

1. Calculate monthly accrued interest expense for the installment note to Ford Credit (based on 365 days per year and interest starting to accrue on December 17, 20XX). Make the appropriate adjusting entry. The payable is posted to Other Accrued Expenses Payable.

2. For your convenience, depreciation in the amount of $105,341.50 has been calculated on all assets for the month of December **except** for the Ford Pickup. Calculate the depreciation for the truck and add that amount to the $105,341.50 to determine the total depreciation expense for December. Record the appropriate adjusting entry in the General Journal.

3. The monthly bank statement indicates bank charges of $30, a returned check from Alota Wine Distributors in the amount of $19,475.26, and a check printing fee of $60. Record this in the General Journal.

4. Your account balances can be verified at this time by clicking on **Business Status** and clicking on **View Account List**. You may have to adjust the accounting period first by clicking on **Customize**.

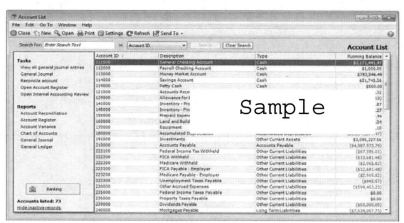

Figure 66

5. The transactions for the Payroll Journal, Accounts Receivable, and Accounts Payable can also be verified through the **Reports** menu under each of the transaction tabs.

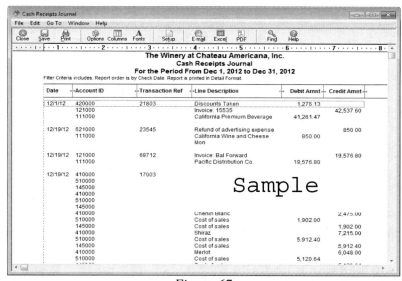

Figure 67

6. Take some time and examine some of the journals provided for you in Peachtree. If you completed the *CAST Manual AIS Module*, think about the similarities and differences of these journals to those you prepared manually. For example, compare and contrast the processes required to create and post a sales entry in Peachtree to those required in the *CAST Manual AIS Module*.

You should observe that the defaults you created during set-up have simplified the posting process, but also have obscured part of the double-entry process.

YEAR-END PROCEDURES

1. Year-end adjusting entries should be recorded in the general journal after reconciling the unadjusted trial balance (the beginning balances in the working trial balance). You **DO NOT** need to close the books for the end of the year. Prepare the following year-end adjusting journal entries:

   a. Calculate the allowance for bad debts using the net sales method. Experience indicates that 0.05% of net sales should be set aside for bad debts. Record the appropriate adjusting entry.

   b. The calculation of federal income tax expense is a year-end adjusting entry but it cannot be made until all other entries have been made and *net income before taxes* has been determined. Therefore, you must first calculate net income before taxes. Then calculate federal income tax expense and record the adjusting entry. **HINT:** The rates can be found in the instructions to Schedule J of Form 1120 (the Federal corporate income tax return) or in a tax textbook that contains corporate tax information.

   Adjusting entries should be verified through the working trial balance as was done previously.

2. Print, and prepare to submit, the financial statements (including the **Balance Sheet**, the **Income Statement**, and the **Statement of Cash Flows**), the **Aged Receivables Report**, the **Aged Payables Report,** and the **Payroll Checks, Register** or **Report** and any other reports or statements that your instructor requests.

California Premium Beverage

PURCHASE ORDER

39848 South Street
Santa Rosa, CA 95402
Phone (707) 555-7451 Fax (707) 555-7452

To:
Chateau Americana
3003 Vineyard Way
Huntington, CA 95394

Ship To:
California Premium Beverage
39848 South Street
Santa Rosa, CA 95402

ABC Permit #: A59782

P.O. DATE	P.O. NUMBER	SHIPPED VIA	F.O.B. POINT	TERMS
12/13/XX	8746	CA Express	Destination	3/15, net 30

ITEM NO	QTY	SIZE	DESCRIPTION	UNIT PRICE	TOTAL
W120015	1512	0.750	Riesling	7.85	11,869.20
W120016	504	0.750	Sauvignon Blanc	7.85	3,956.40
W120019	336	0.750	Chenin Blanc	8.25	2,772.00
R130061	1176	0.750	Cabernet Sauvignon	9.50	11,172.00
R130056	672	0.750	Merlot	9.00	6,048.00
S140000	240	0.750	Sparkling Brut	14.00	3,360.00
W120080	336	0.750	Chardonnay	10.00	3,360.00
				TOTAL	42,537.60

Jorge Gonzalez   *12/13/XX*
————————————————————   ————————————
Authorized by   Date

California Wine and Cheese Monthly	Lone Star Bank	23545
573 Parkins Ave.	Dallas, TX 27540	
Ukiah, CA 95482		

Date ___ 12/15/XX

PAY___ Eight Hundred Fifty and 00/100 Dollars --- $ ___ 850.00 ___

To the
order of

Chateau Americana
3003 Vineyard Way
Huntington, CA 95394

- SAMPLE, DO NOT CASH -

|:000000|: :000000000: 23545

California Wine and Cheese Monthly	23545

Reference	Amount
Overpayment of monthly advertising	$850.00

Pacific Distribution Company   Bank of America   **69712**
10034 Westborough Boulevard   San Francisco, CA 94104
San Francisco, CA 94080

Date ___ 12/16/XX

PAY___ Nineteen Thousand Five Hundred Seventy Six and 80/100 Dollars ----------------- $ ___ 19,576.80

To The   Chateau Americana
Order Of   3003 Vineyard Way
               Huntington, CA 95394

- SAMPLE, DO NOT CASH -

⑈:000000⑈: :000000000: 69712

Pacific Distribution Company   **69712**

Reference	Net Amount
Invoice #15243, customer # 0505	$19,576.80

PURCHASE ORDER

PO Number: 4376
Date: 12/19/XX

To:
Chateau Americana
3003 Vineyard Way
Huntington, CA 95394

Ship To:
SONOMA Distributors
3224 Greenlawn Street
Ukiah, CA 95482
Phone (707) 555-1705 Fax (707) 555-1706

SHIPPED VIA	ABC #	F.O.B. POINT	TERMS
United Express	A557912	Huntington	Cash

ITEM NO	QTY	SIZE	DESCRIPTION	UNIT PRICE	TOTAL
W120015	480	0.750	Riesling	7.85	3,768.00
W120080	468	0.750	Chardonnay	10.00	4,680.00
W120019	300	0.750	Chenin Blanc	8.25	2,475.00
R130072	780	0.750	Shiraz	9.25	7,215.00
R130056	672	0.750	Merlot	8.00	6,048.00
				TOTAL	24,186.00

Chrystal Harrington   *12/19/XX*
Authorized by   Date

Sonoma Distributors
3224 Greenlawn Street
Ukiah, CA 95482

Humboldt Bank
Ukiah, CA 95482

17003

Date ___12/19/XX___

P~AY~___Twenty-four Thousand One Hundred Eighty Six and 00/100 Dollars ----------------- $ ___24,186.00___

To the
order of   Chateau Americana
              3003 Vineyard Way
              Huntington, CA 95394

- SAMPLE, DO NOT CASH -

¦:000000¦: :000000000: 17003

Sonoma Distributors   **17003**

Reference	Discount	Net Amount
Payment for PO 4376		$24,186.00

CUSTOMER INVOICE

Invoice Number   **M7634**

Mendocino Vineyards
8654 Witherspoon Way
Hopland, CA 95449
Phone: (707) 555-1890

Invoice Date   12/20/20XX

Sold To:

Chateau Americana, Inc.
3003 Vineyard Way
Huntington, CA 95394

Credit Terms: 2/10, Net 30

Ship To:

Chateau Americana, Inc.
3003 Vineyard Way
Huntington, CA 95394

Customer I.D	Customer P.O. Number
CHATAM	9660

Description	Product Number	Quantity	Cost	Extended
Cabernet Sauvignon Grapes	CS1250	19 tons	$703.40	$13,364.60

Total Cost: $13,364.60

Comments:

Distribution: Copy 1 — Accounting; Copy 2 – Shipping; Copy 3 – Customer

Payment Coupon

Bill Date: 12/23/20XX

Please Pay by 01/17/20XX
$18,887.62

Amount Enclosed

Account No. 21790-1879

Chateau Americana, Inc.
3003 Vineyard Way
Huntington, CA 95394

Send Payment to:

Pacific Gas and Electric
P.O. Box 2575
San Francisco, CA 94103

- -

Retain bottom portion for your records, detach and return stub with payment.

Service	Chateau Americana, Inc.	Your Account Number	Rate Class	Billing Date
For:	3003 Vineyard Way Huntington, CA 95394	**21790-1879**	**Commercial**	**12/23/20XX**

Meter Number	Service Period	Days	Type of Reading	Multiplier	Units	Meter Readings Current	Meter Readings Past	Usage
68869800	**11/23/XX – 12/23/XX**	**31**	**Actual**	**1**	**KWH**	**1098412**	**1001301**	**97111**

Previous Balance	16,895.53
Payment	16,895.53
Balance Forward	0.00
Current Charges	18,887.62

	Due Date	Total Due
	01/17/20XX	18,887.62

Pacific Gas and Electric

1000 Energy Drive, San Francisco, CA 94103, (415) 973-8943

Edward Jones Financial Services
100 Market Street
San Francisco, CA 94109
(415)504-9000

Customer
Chateau Americana, Inc.
3003 Vineyard Way
Huntington, CA 95394

Account Number
02334-85763

Tax Identification #
23-7788954

SAVE THIS STATEMENT FOR TAX PURPOSES

Date	Description	Symbol	Fees and/or Commissions($)	Net Dollar Amount ($)	Share Price ($)	Transaction Shares
12/30/03	Microsoft Corporation Common Shares	MSFT	400.00	24,600.00	49.20	500.0000

California Premium Beverage
39848 South Street
Santa Rosa, CA 95402

Bay View Bank
Santa Rosa, CA 95407

21803

Date   12/29/XX

PAY   Forty-One Thousand Two Hundred Sixty-One and 47/100 Dollars ------------------ $ 41,261.47

To The
Order Of   Chateau Americana
3003 Vineyard Way
Huntington, CA 95394

- SAMPLE, DO NOT CASH -

⑈000000⑈ ⑆000000000⑆ 21803

California Premium Beverage

21803

Reference	Discount	Net Amount
# 0504 Invoice 15535	$1,276.13	$41,261.47

Period Ending: December 31, 20XX
Employee Name: Thomas P. Bryan
Signature: Tom Bryan
Approved: PJB

	1st Day	2nd Day	3rd Day	4th Day	5th Day	6th Day	7th Day
Out		05:00 PM	04:33 PM	04:02 PM			
In		12:01 PM	11:59 AM	11:58 AM			
Out		11:30 AM	11:30 AM	11:30 AM			
In		07:29 AM	07:31 AM	06:45 AM			
Approved		4	5	4	4.5	4.75	4

Period Ending: December 26, 20XX
Employee Name: Thomas P. Bryan
Signature: Tom Bryan
Approved: PJB

	1st Day	2nd Day	3rd Day	4th Day	5th Day	6th Day	7th Day
Out		04:04 PM	04:00 PM	04:00 PM	Holiday	Holiday	
In		12:02 PM	12:01 PM	12:02 PM			
Out		11:31 AM	11:33 AM	11:30 AM			
In		07:28 AM	07:30 AM	07:29 AM			
Approved		4	4	4	4	4	4

Period Ending: December 19, 20XX
Employee Name: Thomas P. Bryan
Signature: Tom Bryan
Approved: PJB

	1st Day	2nd Day	3rd Day	4th Day	5th Day	6th Day	7th Day
Out		04:03 PM	04:02 PM	04:01 PM	04:00 PM		
In		11:59 AM	11:58 AM	12:00 PM	12:01 PM		
Out		11:30 AM	11:30 AM	11:30 AM	11:30 AM		
In		07:31 AM	07:30 AM	07:29 AM	07:31 AM		
Approved		4	4	4	4	4	4

Period Ending: December 31, 20XX
Employee Name: Robert T. Hissom
Signature: Bob Hissom
Approved: PJB

Day	Out	In	Out	In	Approved
1st Day					
2nd Day	03:57 PM	11:55 AM	11:30 AM	07:26 AM	4
3rd Day	04:01 PM	11:59 AM	11:30 AM	07:30 AM	4
4th Day	04:00 PM	11:58 AM	11:32 AM	07:32 AM	4
5th Day					4
6th Day					4
7th Day					4

Period Ending: December 26, 20XX
Employee Name: Robert T. Hissom
Signature: Bob Hissom
Approved: PJB

Day	Out	In	Out	In	Approved
1st Day					
2nd Day	04:03 PM	12:01 PM	11:31 AM	07:31 AM	4
3rd Day	04:00 PM	12:00 PM	11:33 AM	07:30 AM	4
4th Day	04:03 PM	12:04 PM	11:30 AM	07:29 AM	4
5th Day	Holiday				4
6th Day	Holiday				4
7th Day					4

Period Ending: December 19, 20XX
Employee Name: Robert T. Hissom
Signature: Bob Hissom
Approved: PJB

Day	Out	In	Out	In	Approved
1st Day					
2nd Day					
3rd Day	04:03 PM	12:02 PM	11:34 AM	07:30 AM	4
4th Day	04:00 PM	11:59 AM	11:30 AM	07:31 AM	4
5th Day	03:59 PM	12:02 PM	11:30 AM	07:27 AM	4
6th Day	04:02 PM	12:01 PM	11:30 AM	07:29 AM	4
7th Day					4

TRANSACTION SET B

December	Transaction
16	Receive a purchase order from California Premium Beverage (page 114). Fill and ship the order. Complete Invoice No. 15535.
16	Order 29 tons white grapes at $541.11 per ton from Mendocino Vineyards. The item number for the white grapes is WG1003. Complete Purchase Order No. 9682.
16	Purchase a 2004 Ford truck for $30,250.00. The terms include a $4,750.00 down payment and a 3-year, 6% promissory note to Ford Credit for the remaining $25,500.00. Principal and interest on the note are due monthly beginning January 4, 20XY. The company expects the truck to have a useful life of 5 years and no salvage value. Prepare Check No. 19257 payable to Potter Valley Ford for the down payment.
16	The Board of Directors of Chateau Americana authorized a $50,000 cash dividend payable on December 31st to the stockholders of record on December 26th. Record the transaction. Use Check No. 19476 made payable to 'Stockholders of Record' when paid.
17	Receive a phone complaint from Seaside Distributors about a case of Chenin Blanc that was damaged in shipment. The case was part of Invoice No. 15175, dated November 5, 20XX, in the amount of $20,438.40. Seaside paid the invoice on November 19, 20XX and took advantage of the discount (terms 3/15, net 30). Prepare Check No. 19286 to reimburse Seaside for the damaged inventory that was *not* returned to the company.
19	Receive notification of $850 interest income that was deposited directly into the checking account from a certificate of deposit from State Employees' Credit Union. Record the cash receipt.
19	Receive payment in full from Pacific Distribution Co. on Invoice No. 15243 dated November 13, 20XX, in the amount of $19,576.80 (page 103). Record the cash receipt.
19	Receive a purchase order (page 115) with payment (page 116) from Sonoma Distributors. Fill and ship the order. Record the sale.
22	Receive 19 tons red grapes at $703.40 per ton from Mendocino Vineyards. Also received Invoice No. M7634 from Mendocino Vineyards with the shipment (page 52). Terms on the invoice are 2/10, net 30. Record the receipt of inventory.
26	Receive utility bill from Pacific Gas and Electric in the amount of $18,887.62 (page 107). Prepare Check No. 19402.
30	Receive Brokerage Advice from Edwards Jones for purchase of 500 shares of Microsoft at $49.20 per share plus $400 broker's commission (page 108). Prepare Check No. 19468.
31	Receive payment in full for the December 16 purchase from California Premium Beverage (page 117). Record the cash receipt.
31	Prepare Check No. 19473 payable to Mendocino Vineyards for the shipment received on December 22.

December	Transaction
31	Prepare Payroll Checks (Nos. 7111-7114) for Anna Johnson, José Rodriguez, Tom Bryan, and Bob Hissom. Time cards for Tom and Bob are on pages 110-111. Prepare Check No. 19474 to transfer cash from the general cash account to the payroll account.
31	Prepare Check No. 19475 to repay $50,000 of the principal on long-term debt to Bank of Huntington.

Refer to pages 98-100 for the Month-End and Year-End procedures.

California Premium Beverage

PURCHASE ORDER

39848 South Street
Santa Rosa, CA 95402
Phone (707) 555-7451 Fax (707) 555-7452

To:
Chateau Americana
3003 Vineyard Way
Huntington, CA 95394

Ship To:
California Premium Beverage
39848 South Street
Santa Rosa, CA 95402

ABC Permit #: A59782

P.O. DATE	P.O. NUMBER	SHIPPED VIA	F.O.B. POINT	TERMS
12/13/06	8746	CA Express	Destination	3/15, net 30

ITEM NO	QTY	SIZE	DESCRIPTION	UNIT PRICE	TOTAL
W120015	1512	0.750	Riesling	10.75	16,254.00
W120016	504	0.750	Sauvignon Blanc	10.90	5,493.60
W120019	336	0.750	Chenin Blanc	11.15	3,746.40
R130061	1176	0.750	Cabernet Sauvignon	12.40	14,582.40
R130056	672	0.750	Merlot	12.00	8,064.00
S140000	240	0.750	Sparkling Brut	16.70	4,008.00
W120080	336	0.750	Chardonnay	13.10	4,401.60
				TOTAL	56,550.00

Jorge Gonzalez   *12/13/06*
Authorized by   Date

PURCHASE ORDER

PO Number: 4376
Date: 12/19/XX

To:
Chateau Americana
3003 Vineyard Way
Huntington, CA 95394

Ship To:

SONOMA DISTRIBUTORS

3224 Greenlawn Street
Ukiah, CA 95482
Phone (707) 555-1705 Fax (707) 555-1706

SHIPPED VIA	ABC #	F.O.B. POINT	TERMS
United Express	A557912	Huntington	Cash

ITEM NO	QTY	SIZE	DESCRIPTION	UNIT PRICE	TOTAL
W120015	480	0.750	Riesling	10.75	5,160.00
W120080	468	0.750	Chardonnay	13.10	6,130.80
W120019	300	0.750	Chenin Blanc	11.15	3,345.00
R130072	780	0.750	Shiraz	12.15	9,477.00
R130056	672	0.750	Merlot	12.00	8,064.00
				TOTAL	32,176.80

Chrystal Harrington   *12/19/XX*

Authorized by   Date

Sonoma Distributors
3224 Greenlawn Street
Ukiah, CA 95482

Humboldt Bank
Ukiah, CA 95482

17003

Date ___12/19/XX___

PAY ___Thirty-Two Thousand One Hundred Seventy-Six and 80/100 Dollars ---------------- $ ___32,176.80___

To the
order of

Chateau Americana
3003 Vineyard Way
Huntington, CA 95394

- SAMPLE, DO NOT CASH -

⑆000000⑆⑈000000000⑈ 17003

- -
- - - - - - - - - - - - - - - - -

Sonoma Distributors		**17003**
Reference	Discount	Net Amount
Payment for PO 4376		$32,176.80

California Premium Beverage	Bay View Bank	21803
39848 South Street	Santa Rosa, CA 95407	
Santa Rosa, CA 95402		

Date ___12/29/XX___

PAY___Fifty-Four Thousand Eight Hundred Fifty-Three and 50/100 Dollars ------------------ $ ___54,853.50___

To The
Order Of
Chateau Americana
3003 Vineyard Way
Huntington, CA 95394

- SAMPLE, DO NOT CASH -

⑂:000000⑂: :000000000: 21803

California Premium Beverage		21803

Reference	Discount	Net Amount
# 0504 Invoice 15535	1,696.50	$54,853.50

TRANSACTION SET C

December	Transaction
16	Receive a purchase order from California Premium Beverage (page 120). Fill and ship the order. Complete Invoice No. 15535.
16	Order 31 tons white grapes at $591.11 per ton from Mendocino Vineyards. The item number for the white grapes is WG1003. Complete Purchase Order No. 9682.
16	Purchase a 2004 Ford truck for $32,750.00. The terms include a $4,750.00 down payment and a 3-year, 6% promissory note to Ford Credit for the remaining $28,000.00. Principal and interest on the note are due monthly beginning January 4, 20XY. The company expects the truck to have a useful life of 5 years and no salvage value. Prepare Check No. 19257 payable to Potter Valley Ford for the down payment.
16	Receive Check No. 10375 in the amount of $19,250.00 (see page 121) from Castle Vineyards for the sale of the Fork Lift that was purchased on December 23, 20XW. The Fork Lift originally cost $18,881.00 and was being depreciated over 10 years. To record this transaction, you will need to calculate the depreciation that was taken on the Fork Lift. Depreciation for December was calculated and included in the total depreciation given to you in the Month-End entries before the sale took place and depreciation for the year needs to be adjusted. Record the transaction.
17	Receive a phone complaint from Seaside Distributors about a case of Chenin Blanc that was damaged in shipment. The case was part of Invoice No. 15175, dated November 5, 20XX, in the amount of $20,438.40. Seaside paid the invoice on November 19, 20XX and took advantage of the discount (terms 3/15, net 30). Prepare Check No. 19286 to reimburse Seaside for the damaged inventory that was *not* returned to the company.
19	Receive notification of $850 interest income that was deposited directly into the checking account from a certificate of deposit from State Employees' Credit Union. Record the cash receipt.
19	Receive payment in full from Pacific Distribution Co. on Invoice No. 15243 dated November 13, 20XX, in the amount of $20,164.30 (page 122). Record the cash receipt.
19	Receive a purchase order (page 123) with payment (page 124) from Sonoma Distributors. Fill and ship the order. Record the sale.
22	Receive 21 tons red grapes at $718.63 per ton from Mendocino Vineyards. Also received Invoice No. M7634 from Mendocino Vineyards with the shipment (page 125). Terms on the invoice are 2/10, net 30. Record the receipt of inventory.
26	Receive utility bill from Pacific Gas and Electric in the amount of $19,271.12 (page 126). Prepare Check No. 19402.
30	Receive Brokerage Advice from Edwards Jones for purchase of 500 shares of Microsoft at $49.20 per share plus $400 broker's commission (page 108). Prepare Check No. 19468.
31	Receive payment in full for the December 16 purchase from California Premium Beverage (page 127). Enter the cash receipt.

December	Transaction
31	Prepare Check No. 19473 payable to Mendocino Vineyards for the shipment received on December 22.
31	Prepare Payroll Checks (Nos. 7111-7114) for Anna Johnson, José Rodriguez, Tom Bryan, and Bob Hissom. Time cards for Tom and Bob are on pages 110-111. Prepare Check No. 19474 to transfer cash from the general cash account to the payroll account. Record the payroll transactions and all appropriate *accruals*.
31	Prepare Check No. 19475 to repay $80,000 of the principal on long-term debt to Bank of Huntington.

Refer to pages 98-100 for the Month-End and Year-End procedures.

California Premium Beverage

PURCHASE ORDER

39848 South Street
Santa Rosa, CA 95402
Phone (707) 555-7451 Fax (707) 555-7452

To:
Chateau Americana
3003 Vineyard Way
Huntington, CA 95394

Ship To:
California Premium Beverage
39848 South Street
Santa Rosa, CA 95402

ABC Permit #: A59782

P.O. DATE	P.O. NUMBER	SHIPPED VIA	F.O.B. POINT	TERMS
12/13/06	8746	CA Express	Destination	3/15, net 30

ITEM NO	QTY	SIZE	DESCRIPTION	UNIT PRICE	TOTAL
W120015	1512	0.750	Riesling	12.35	18.673.20
W120016	504	0.750	Sauvignon Blanc	12.50	6,300.00
W120019	336	0.750	Chenin Blanc	12.75	4,284.00
R130061	1176	0.750	Cabernet Sauvignon	14.00	16,464.00
R130056	672	0.750	Merlot	13.60	9,139.20
S140000	240	0.750	Sparkling Brut	18.30	4,392.00
W120080	336	0.750	Chardonnay	14.70	4,939.20
				TOTAL	64,191.60

Jorge Gonzalez   _12/13/06_
Authorized by   Date

Castle Vineyards
3224 Castle Way
Ukiah, CA 95482

Humboldt Bank
Ukiah, CA 95482

17003

Date _____ 12/16/XX _____

PAY ___ Nineteen Thousand Two Hundred Fifty and 00/100 Dollars ----------------- $ _____ 19,250.00 _____

To the
order of

Chateau Americana
3003 Vineyard Way
Huntington, CA 95394

- SAMPLE, DO NOT CASH -

⦙:000000⦙: :000000000: 17003

Sonoma Distributors

17003

Reference	Discount	Net Amount
Payment for Fork Lift		$19,250.00

Pacific Distribution Company   Bank of America   **69712**
10034 Westborough Boulevard   San Francisco, CA 94104
San Francisco, CA 94080

Date ___12/16/XX___

PAY___Twenty Thousand One Hundred Sixty Four and 30/100 Dollars ----------------- $ ___20,164.30___

To The   Chateau Americana
Order Of   3003 Vineyard Way
                  Huntington, CA 95394
                                                      - SAMPLE, DO NOT CASH -

|:000000|: :000000000: 69712

Pacific Distribution Company   **69712**

Reference	Net Amount
Invoice #15243, customer # 0505	$20,164.30

PURCHASE ORDER

PO Number: 4376
Date: 12/19/XX

To:
Chateau Americana
3003 Vineyard Way
Huntington, CA 95394

Ship To:
SONOMA Distributors
3224 Greenlawn Street
Ukiah, CA 95482
Phone (707) 555-1705 Fax (707) 555-1706

SHIPPED VIA	ABC #	F.O.B. POINT	TERMS
United Express	A557912	Huntington	Cash

ITEM NO	QTY	SIZE	DESCRIPTION	UNIT PRICE	TOTAL
W120015	480	0.750	Riesling	12.35	5,928.00
W120080	468	0.750	Chardonnay	14.70	6,879.60
W120019	300	0.750	Chenin Blanc	12.75	3,825.00
R130072	780	0.750	Shiraz	13.75	10,725.00
R130056	672	0.750	Merlot	13.60	9,139.20
				TOTAL	36,496.80

Chrystal Harrington   *12/19/XX*
Authorized by   Date

Sonoma Distributors	Humboldt Bank	**17003**
3224 Greenlawn Street	Ukiah, CA 95482	
Ukiah, CA 95482		

Date ___12/19/XX___

PAY___Thirty-Six Thousand Four Hundred Ninety-Six and 80/100 Dollars ------------------ $ ___36,496.80___

To the   Chateau Americana
order of   3003 Vineyard Way
               Huntington, CA 95394

- SAMPLE, DO NOT CASH -

⑈:000000⑈: :000000000: 17003

Sonoma Distributors		**17003**
Reference	Discount	Net Amount
Payment for PO 4376		$36,496.60

CUSTOMER INVOICE

Mendocino Vineyards
8654 Witherspoon Way
Hopland, CA 95449
Phone: (707) 555-1890

Invoice Number	**M7634**
Invoice Date	12/20/20XX

Sold To:

Chateau Americana, Inc.
3003 Vineyard Way
Huntington, CA 95394

Credit Terms: 2/10, Net 30

Ship To:

Chateau Americana, Inc.
3003 Vineyard Way
Huntington, CA 95394

Customer I.D	Customer P.O. Number
CHATAM	9660

Description	Product Number	Quantity	Cost	Extended
Cabernet Sauvignon Grapes	CS1250	21 tons	$718.63	$15,091.23

Total Cost: $15,091.23

Comments:

Distribution: Copy 1 — Accounting; Copy 2 – Shipping; Copy 3 – Customer

Payment Coupon

Bill Date: 12/23/20XX

Please Pay by 01/17/20XX
$18,851.58

Amount Enclosed

Account No. 21790-1879

Chateau Americana, Inc.
3003 Vineyard Way
Huntington, CA 95394

Send Payment to:

Pacific Gas and Electric
P.O. Box 2575
San Francisco, CA 94103

- -

Retain bottom portion for your records, detach and return stub with payment.

Service	Chateau Americana, Inc.	Your Account Number	Rate Class	Billing Date
For:	3003 Vineyard Way	**21790-1879**	**Commercial**	**12/23/20XX**
	Huntington, CA 95394			

Meter Number	Service Period	Days	Type of Reading	Multiplier	Units	Meter Readings Current	Past	Usage
68869800	**11/23/XX – 12/23/XX**	**31**	**Actual**	**1**	**KWH**	**1098412**	**1001301**	**97111**
Previous Balance								16,895.53
Payment								16,895.53
Balance Forward								0.00
Current Charges								19,271.12

	Due Date	Total Due
	01/17/20XX	19,271.12

Pacific Gas and Electric

1000 Energy Drive, San Francisco, CA 94103, (415) 973-8943

California Premium Beverage

Bay View Bank
Santa Rosa, CA 95407

21803

39848 South Street
Santa Rosa, CA 95402

Date ___12/29/XX___

PAY___Sixty-Two Thousand Two Hundred Sixty-Five and 85/100 Dollars ------------------ $ ___62,265.85___

To The
Order Of

Chateau Americana
3003 Vineyard Way
Huntington, CA 95394

- SAMPLE, DO NOT CASH -

⑆000000⑆ ⑈000000000⑈ 21803

California Premium Beverage

21803

Reference	Discount	Net Amount
# 0504 Invoice 15535	1,925.75	$62,265.85

DATABASE APPLICATIONS USING MICROSOFT® ACCESS 2010: The Winery at Chateau Americana

LEARNING OBJECTIVES

After completing and discussing this material, you should be able to:

- Recognize and explain the purpose of the elements of a relational database
- Build selected elements of a database management system
- Recognize and evaluate the strengths and weaknesses of the controls embedded in a database management system
- Compare and contrast a database package with a general ledger package and with a manual accounting information system

BACKGROUND

Before you begin the database assignments, it is important to understand a little about a database management system and its terminology and to understand the scope of these assignments. A database management system (DBMS) is based on a logical data model. The majority of DBMSs in existence today (*Access*, *MySQL*, *Oracle*, *FoxPro*, etc.) are based on the relational data model. A relational database (which will be the only type of database to which we refer) represents all of the data about the entity in a collection of tables. The following exercises are specific to *Microsoft® Access 2010*, but the theory discussed herein applies to any relational database.

The structures and methods used to manage the data are called objects. There are seven types of objects in *Access*. They are tables, queries, forms, reports, pages, macros, and modules.

Tables are the fundamental storage entity of a relational database. Therefore, all database data is stored in one or more tables comprised of rows and columns. A row, or **record**, contains all the data about a specific instance, or item, in the table.

A column, or **field**, in a table represents characteristics or attributes of the data. Most tables will contain one field that represents the **primary key** (i.e., a value that uniquely identifies each record). In *Figure 1* below, CustomerNo is the primary key. Each field can contain only one data type. Data types constrain the type of data that can be entered into a field (e.g., text, number, counter, currency, date/time).

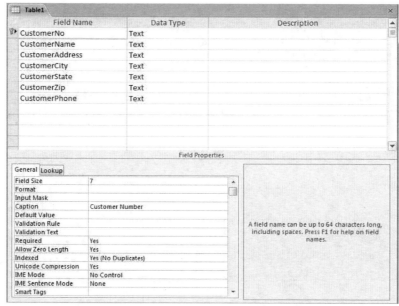

Figure 1

A record's fields contain individual values for each attribute that characterizes that particular record, as shown in *Table 1*.

CustomerNo	CustomerName	CustomerAddress	CustomerCity
WD564	Wine Distributors, Inc.	1285 Napa Ave.	Mendocino

Table 1

Queries are used for asking questions about the data in one or more tables in a database. Queries can be used to locate and display a subset of the records of a table (the **select query**), or modify data (using one of four types of **action queries**) such as combining information from several tables into a single result (the **append query**), changing the values in one or more records (the **update query**), selecting one or more records and creating a new table for them (the **make-table query**), or deleting one or more records (the **delete query**).

Queries can be created in *Access* using SQL (structured query language), a text-based query language. Syntax is very important and very specific in creating SQL statements. The SQL in *Figure 2* uses a field (SupplierNo) common to two tables that might exist in an organization's database (i.e., a Purchase Order table and a Supplier table) to present several fields from the two tables in one form.

Figure 2

Queries can also be created in *Access* using QBE (query by example), a graphical database query interface in which the user selects one or more tables to query and then selects the columns which should be included in the query response. Since it is a graphical interface, QBE is typically the technique of choice because it is easier to use. QBE allows the user to place values or expressions, called selection criteria, below particular field names, thereby limiting the records that are retrieved. Thus, queries are used to reduce the amount of displayed information, summarizing it, and giving it meaning. *Figure 3* presents the same query using the QBE technique as was described in *Figure 2*.

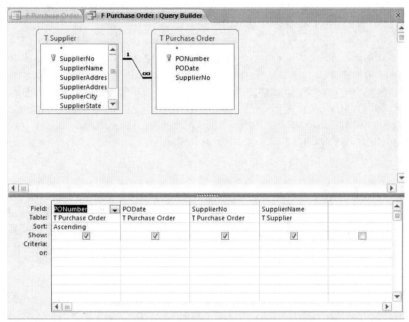

Figure 3

Forms allow the user to see data from tables in a more convenient and attractive format. Forms can be customized so that they precisely match an existing paper form, making it easier to move from hard copy to soft copy. Therefore, with the use of forms, the user can easily view or change the information that is contained in a table.

Forms contain **labels** and **controls**. **Controls** display data, perform actions, or make forms easier to read. Text boxes are examples of bound controls. A bound control is one that obtains its data from a field in an underlying table or query. An unbound control is not connected to a field. Lines, shapes, and instructions regarding the use of a form are examples of unbound controls. **Labels** can be attached to controls, in which case they are pre-specified by the **Caption**, or they can be stand-alone, in which case they are created using the **Label** icon in the Menu. (Both of these will be discussed later). Forms can also include other forms, or subforms, to allow data entry into more than one table at a time.

Embedded aids and prompts are other useful tools that aid in the creation of forms. Some of these can be created by the database designer and some of them are provided by the program itself. For example, **Form Navigation** buttons, located at the bottom of the screen, enable the user to move to another record by moving up or down one record at a time, selecting a particular record number, or moving to the first or last record in the table.

Reports utilize data from one table or several tables linked together to provide the user with meaningful information. Reports allow the user to decide where that information should appear on a printed page. In other words, the user can specify how information will be grouped, sorted and formatted for the printer. Reports can be used to sort, group, and summarize data in almost limitless ways. As a result, reports can appear as invoices, purchase orders, sales summaries, or financial statements. However, whereas the user can enter, edit, and interact with the data in a **Form**, he or she cannot interact with the data in a **Report**.

Macros are more advanced *Access* objects. Macros are mini-programs that contain sets of instructions that automate frequently performed tasks, such as opening a form, printing a report, or processing an order. They can also be used to automate custom tasks and are a relatively easy way to achieve custom results in a database without having programming knowledge. Finally, they can also assist in the creation of turnkey applications that anyone can use, whether or not they have experience with *Access*.

Modules are even more advanced *Access* objects than macros. They are similar to macros in that they allow for automation and customization. However, these tools require knowledge of *Visual Basic* programming and give the user more precise control over the actions taken.

REQUIREMENTS

These assignments will be limited to familiarizing you with tables, queries, forms, and reports. We leave the development of macros and modules for more advanced database design classes. The objective of this assignment is *not* to provide you with expertise in the development of a database, but to provide you with an initiation to and an appreciation of both the complexity and the power of a database when used to create an accounting information system.

Good programming procedures require a certain amount of structure or standardization. For example, when saving tables, queries, forms, and reports created in a database, it is often useful to use a naming convention (i.e., a method which names the objects in a way that will let the user know to which classification the object belongs). This assists the designer and the user alike in navigating throughout the database. Therefore, the naming convention indicated in *Table 2* will be used throughout this assignment:

Table	T *tablename*
Queries	Q *queryname*
Forms	F *formname*
Reports	R *reportname*

Table 2

Please read the following sections carefully. They are intended to be tutorial in nature as well as providing you with the information necessary to complete your *Access* assignments. In some instances, the assignment provides you with explicit instructions about creating the necessary tables, forms, queries and reports. However, in other instances, the assignment allows you to make choices about design considerations such as form style, size, font size, etc. Therefore, it is imperative to follow the directions carefully **AND** to critique the forms and reports you create from a user's perspective.

Finally, as always, it is important to **back your work up frequently**!

CREATING A NEW DATABASE AND NEW TABLE

Requirements

1. Create a new database by launching *Access*. On the right hand side of your screen, notice that there is an area under **File Name** that says **Database1.accdb**. Check with your instructor to determine his or her required file naming convention for the assignment and change the name accordingly. Now click on **Create** under **Blank Database**.

Figure 4

You are now ready to design the database. As discussed previously, tables are the fundamental storage entity of a relational database so we will begin there.

2. When your newly created database opens, it automatically creates a table for you. See *Figure 5*.

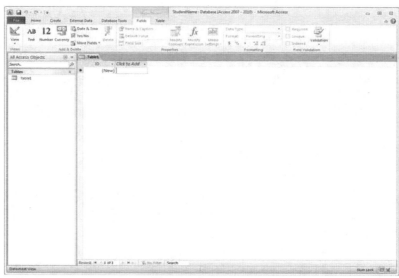

Figure 5

We will make some adjustments to this table. Notice that the table has one field whose field name is "ID." This field name is rather generic and would not be specific to any table that you would create. It certainly isn't very descriptive. Therefore, begin by renaming this field. Right-click on **ID** and select **Rename Column**. Type **SupplierNo** in place of **ID**.

> *At this point, it is very important that you check your work. Before you tab out of the Field Name, make it a habit to check your spelling. Field Names are recorded in the **data dictionary**. The data dictionary contains information about the entire structure of the database. Thus, for each data element, the data dictionary might include the data element name, its description, the records in which it is contained, its source, its field length and type, the program in which it is used, the outputs in which it is contained, and its authorized users.*
>
> *It is often very difficult to remove data elements from the data dictionary. Therefore, it is critical that you check your work very carefully when you are creating fields in tables.*

Now you can change the **View** of the table. To do this, click on **View** >

Design View in the **Views** section [Views] of the **Fields** tab. *Access* prompts you to save the table and ask for the table name. Save the table as **T Supplier**. Notice the changes in the **Design View** (*Figure 6*).

Figure 6

The **Table** window that is displayed now contains three columns: **Field Name, Data Type,** and **Description**. You may move among these columns by either clicking in various fields with the mouse or by clicking in a field and then using the **Tab** key.

Field Names can include almost any combination of letters, numbers, spaces, and special characters. **Field Names** may not include a period, an exclamation point, a backquote character, or brackets. In addition, a **Field Name** cannot contain leading spaces. When the cursor is in the **Data Type** column, you will see a button to pull down a menu. This button allows you to select the **Data Type** for the given **Field Name**. Take some time to explore the various data types. The **Description** property is optional and is used to provide useful information about the table or query and its fields. Check with your instructor to determine whether you are to complete the description field for this assignment.

3. Notice that *Access* has automatically made **SupplierNo** the primary key. You can tell this because the field has the **Primary Key** icon next to it now.

    As we discussed earlier, a primary key is a value that uniquely identifies each record. By defining a primary key, Access does three things:
    a. *It insures that no two records in that table will have the same value in the primary key field.*
    b. *It keeps records sorted according to the primary key field.*
    c. *It speeds up processing.*

4. Notice that *Access* has also automatically set the **Data Type** for **SupplierNo** to **AutoNumber**. This is not what you want since Chateau Americana uses a combination of letters and numbers to identify their suppliers. Change the **Data Type** to **Text** using the pull-down menu.

You can toggle to the **Field Properties** pane at the bottom of the window by pressing **F6** or you can move to the **Field Properties** pane by moving your mouse to the desired field. This pane allows the user to specify the properties for the chosen field and type. *Table 3* describes some of the most important field properties.

Field Property	Description
Field Size	Sets the maximum size for data stored in a Text, Number or AutoNumber field. In a text field, the size may range from 1 to 255. The default is 255 and, therefore, should be set to something reasonable to fit the field. In Number fields, the default is set to Long Integer.
Format	Specifies how data is to be displayed in a field. It is particularly useful in specifying the format for numbers, currency, dates, and times.
Decimal Places	Specifies the number of digits to the right of the decimal point. "**Auto**" allows the Format property to determine the number of decimal places automatically.
Input Mask	Makes data entry easier by adjusting the data entered so that it conforms to the standard set in the Input Mask. It is also used to control the values users can enter.
Caption	Specifies the text for labels attached to controls created by dragging a field from the field list and serves as the heading for the field when the table or query is in Datasheet view.
Default Value	Specifies a default value for a field (e.g., Napa can be set as the Default Value for a City field; the user then has the option of accepting the Default Value or inputting different data).
Validation Rule	Specifies the requirements for data entry. For example, you can create a rule that specifies that all entries must contain five numeric characters as might be the case with zip codes.
Validation Text	Text input in the Validation Text property specifies the message to be displayed to the user when the Validation Rule is violated. For example, when a record is added for a new employee, you can create a Validate Rule requiring that the entry in the **Start Date** field fall between the company's founding date and the current date. If the date entered is not in this range, you can enter text into the Validation Text property so that it will display a message such as, "**Start date is incorrect.**"

Field Property	Description
Allow Zero Length	Indicates whether an empty string (i.e., a string containing no characters) is a valid entry. If **Yes**, the field will accept an empty string even when the Required property is set to **Yes**.
Indexed	Sets a single-field index (i.e., a feature which speeds the sorting and searching of a table). The primary key is always indexed. When a record is indexed, it is also necessary to specify whether duplicates will be allowed. For example, when creating a purchase order table, the primary key might be "PO #" and you would not want to allow duplicates. However, when creating a table to add the inventory purchased on a particular purchase order, you might still want to be able to sort and search based upon the PO # (which would require that field to be indexed), but you would expect that a particular purchase order might have several items of inventory. Therefore, duplicates would be allowed.

Table 3

5. Press **F6** to switch to the **Field Properties** pane of the **Table** window and establish the following properties for **SupplierNo** (no entries are required for any other properties for **SupplierNo.**):

Field Size	**5**
Caption	**Supplier Number**
Validation Rule	**Like "?####"** (Note: Include quotation marks)
Validation Text	**Invalid entry. The Supplier Number must consist of one letter and four numbers.**
Required	**Yes**
Indexed	**Yes (No duplicates)**

Table 4

6. All Data Types for all subsequent fields in this table should be set to **Text**. The second Field Name should be **SupplierName**, the Field Size is **35**, and the Caption should be **Supplier Name**. The third Field Name should be **SupplierAddress1**, the Field Size is **35**, and the Caption should be **Supplier Address**. The fourth Field Name should be **SupplierAddress2** and the field size is **35**. There is no caption for this field. The fifth Field Name should be **SupplierCity** with a Field Size of **25** and an appropriate Caption.

7. The sixth Field Name should be **SupplierState**. The Field Size is **2**. Set the Input Mask property for the **SupplierState** field by typing **>LL** and use an appropriate Caption. The > symbol will cause all characters that follow to be converted to uppercase. The two L's mean that the input requires two letters. No other characters are allowed and there must be two letters.

8. The seventh Field Name should be **SupplierZip**. Set the Field Size to **10.** Activate the **Input Mask Wizard** (the button with three small dots located in the Input Mask Property) to aid in making a template for the Zip Code. You will have to save the table before proceeding. Select **Zip Code** from the menu (see *Figure 7*).

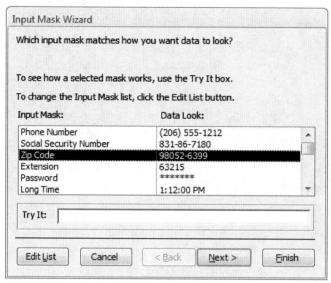

Figure 7

9. Click **Next** twice, and choose to store the Zip Code with the hyphen. Click on **Finish.** Select an appropriate Caption.

10. The last field name is **SupplierTelephone**. Set the Field Size to **14**. Use the Input Mask Wizard to set the Input Mask property to the pre-defined Phone Number setting. Use an appropriate Caption.

11. You are now finished with the table.

Figure 8

12. When you close this object and all objects in the future, use the **X** in the upper right hand corner of the screen to save and close the object. By doing this, you will avoid having to provide names to queries that are underlying the database that should not appear in the Query window, thus limiting the possibility that users may gain unauthorized access.

13. If you wish to quit *Access* at this time, simply close the program and your database will be saved with the name you used to create it.

CREATING A FORM

Although data can be entered from the **Datasheet** view of a table, this would be similar to entering data in a spreadsheet. It is not very easy to do this if the spreadsheet is large, with many columns and many rows. The utilization of forms makes data entry easier and the database more user friendly. A form can display data in almost any format. A very simple form can be designed to display one record at a time. More complex forms can be created as 'fill-in-the-blanks' forms that resemble paper documents used within a company.

Requirements

1. Open your database. You will now enter relevant data into the Supplier Table (i.e., T Supplier) after you create a form utilizing the **Form Wizard**.

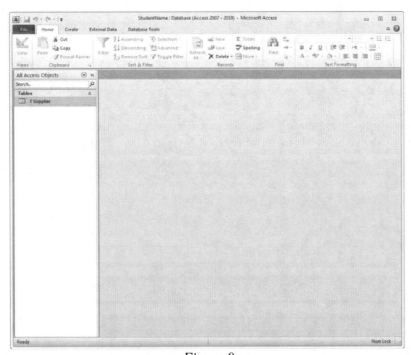

Figure 9

2. Select the **Create** tab in your **Database** window and click on the **Form Wizard** 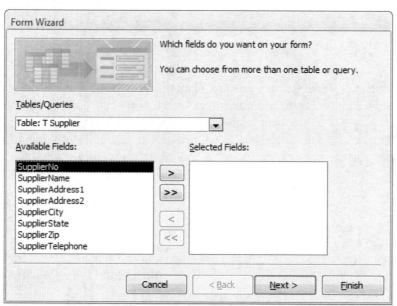 icon. Be sure that **T Supplier** appears in the **Tables/Queries** box.

3. Select all the fields you created in the table for inclusion in the new form by clicking on the >> button in the middle of the window and click on **Next**. See *Figure 10*.

Figure 10

4. The next window allows you to choose a layout. Take some time to view each of the various layouts and then select the **Columnar** format. Click **Next**.

5. Recalling the naming convention discussed earlier, entitle the form **F Supplier**. Select **Modify the form's design**. Click **Finish**.

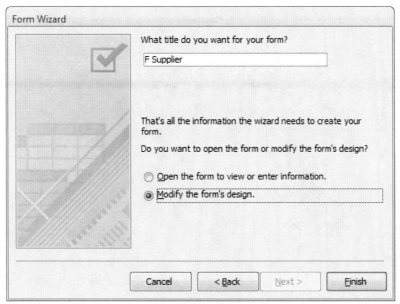

Figure 11

6. First, notice that when the form is created, the fields are different sizes. This relates to the varying sizes that we specified when we created the table. This format is the default format for the Form Wizard in Office 2010. We will still want to make some adjustments to the field sizes, however, as well as to the form in general.

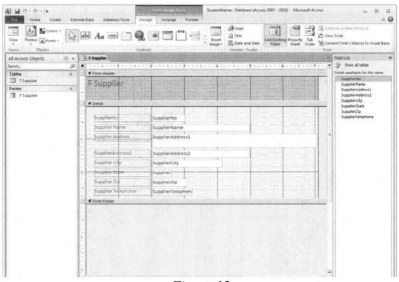

Figure 12

7. Click on the Design tab. Click on the box that contains the label "**F Supplier**" in the **Form Header** section and change this to "**Supplier Form**." Be sure to stretch the length of the box out so that the words appear on one line. You can do this by clicking outside the label lines and then clicking on the edge of the label box once again. Drag the right edge of the box to the right to increase the width. While the box is highlighted, click on the **Home**

tab. Format the label using a **bold font of your choosing with a font size of 20**.

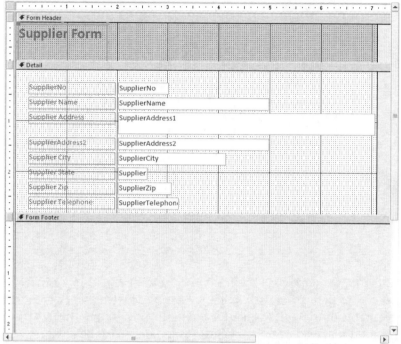

Figure 13

8. Shrink the height and length of the **Supplier Address** field, if necessary. Move the remaining fields up to maintain the proper spacing between the fields.

9. Shrink the **Supplier State** field.

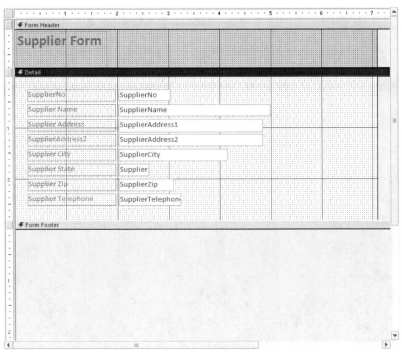

Figure 14

10. Close the form and select **Yes** to save it.

11. Now you are ready to begin entering data using your newly created Supplier form. Open the Supplier Form by double clicking on **F Supplier** in the **Database** window. Enter data for each of Chateau Americana's suppliers listed below:

Supplier Name	Supplier Number	Supplier Address	Supplier Phone
Delicio Vineyards	D2538	12701 South Fernwood Livermore, CA 94550	(925)555-2967
Mendocino Vineyards	M0652	8654 Witherspoon Way Hopland, CA 95449	(707)555-1890

As you enter the supplier information, pay attention to the size of the fields. You can adjust the size by toggling back to the **Design View**. Click on **Views** icon (at the upper left-hand side of the Home section of the toolbar) and stretch or shrink the desired field and then toggle back to the **Form View** by clicking on the **Views** icon again. After you have entered the first supplier's information press the **Enter** key to input the next supplier's information.

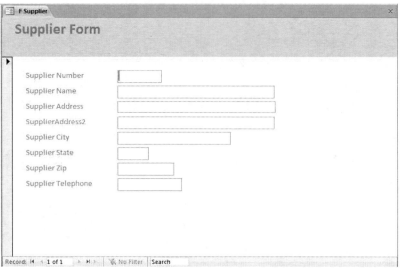

Figure 15

12. Close the form by clicking on the **X** in the upper right hand corner of the form.

13. If you wish to quit *Access* at this time, simply close the program and your database will be saved with the name you used to create it.

ENSURING SEQUENTIAL INTEGRITY

Completeness is an important aspect of internal control. Completeness suggests not only that all data in a transaction are captured, but also that all transactions **are** recorded. Therefore, it is important to ensure that no documents are lost or misplaced. One way to accomplish this is to pre-number documents and verify the sequential integrity of the completed documents.

Requirements

1. Open your *Access* database used for the previous assignments and create a new table by clicking on the **Create** tab and then clicking on the **Table Design** icon.

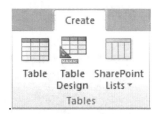

Figure 16

2. The first Field Name in this new table is **PONumber**. Choose **AutoNumber** as the Data Type and enter **PO #** as the Caption. Do not change any other default values for this or other Field Names in the **Field Properties** pane unless instructed to do so.

3. The second Field Name is **PODate**. The Data type is **Date/Time**. Use the Input Mask Wizard to create the Input Mask property. You will have to save the table before proceeding. Save the table as **T Purchase Order**. *NOTE: A primary key is not to be designated at this time. When asked if a primary key should be created, click **NO**. If a primary key was created automatically, remove it. You will set the primary key later.* Choose **Short Date** for the Input Mask. Click on **Next** twice and then click **Finish**. The Caption should be **PO Date**.

4. The third Field Name is **SupplierNo**. The Data Type should be set to **Text**. Set the Field Size to **5** and enter the Caption as **Supplier Number**. Close the **T Purchase Order** table.

   *Notice that you have already used the Field Name "**SupplierNo.**" It was the primary key in the T Supplier table. When a field name appears in one table that is a primary key in another table, it is called a **Foreign Key**. Foreign keys are used to link tables together.*

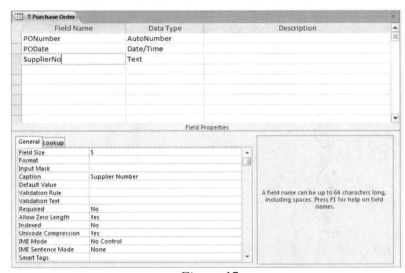

Figure 17

5. Create another new table using the **Table Design** icon.

6. The only field in this table is **PONumber**. The Data Type should be **Number** and the Field Size property should be set to **Long Integer**.

7. Save the table as **T TempPONo**. When asked if a primary key should be created, click **NO**.

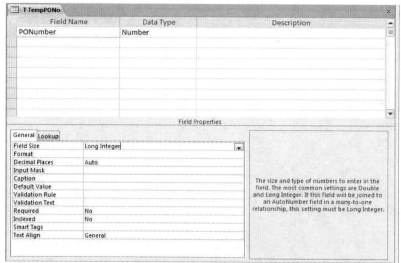

Figure 18

8. Open **T TempPONo** by double clicking the table name in the **All Tables** window.

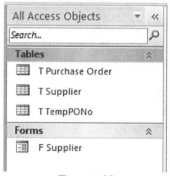

Figure 19

9. Set the value of the **PONumber** to **9681**. Close the table.

Figure 20

10. Click on the **Create** tab and click on **New** and then click **Query Design**.

Figure 21

11. Double click on **T TempPONo** from the **Show Table** dialogue window and close the dialogue window.

12. Click on the **Append** icon in the **Query Type** section. The **Append Query** copies some or all of the records from one table (e.g., the **T TempPONo**) to another table (e.g., the **T Purchase Order**). To begin the prenumbering of the purchase orders with 9682, the number you just entered in the **T TempPONo** table must be appended (added) to the **T Purchase Order** table. To do this, select **T Purchase Order** in the **Table Name** pull-down menu in the **Append** window. Be sure that **Current Database** is selected and click **OK**.

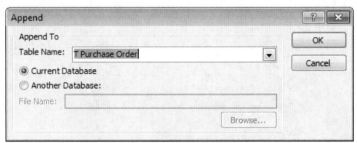

Figure 22

13. Click on **PONumber** in the **T TempPONo** window and drag it to the Append To: field in the Design Grid in the lower half of the window.

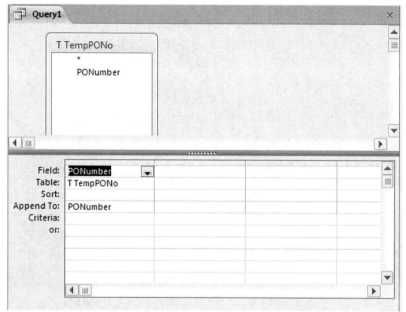

Figure 23

14. Now, click on the **Run** ⚡ Run icon in the **Results** section. A dialog window will then appear stating "You are about to append 1 row(s). Click on **Yes** to append the row of data from the T TempPONo table to the T Purchase Order table.

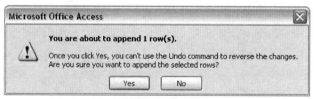

Figure 24

15. Double-click on the **T Purchase Order** table. You will notice that the first PO # in this table is now 9681. Therefore, when you begin to enter data the next purchase order entered will be PO # 9682. Change the view to the **Design** view and designate **PONumber** as the primary key by highlighting the PONumber field and clicking on the Primary Key [⚷ Primary Key] icon in the **Tools** section. Close and save the table.

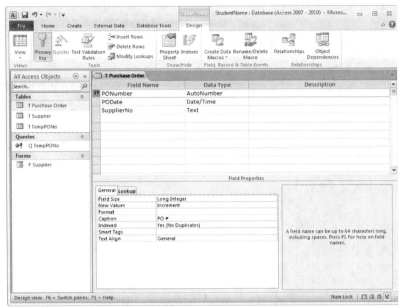

Figure 25

16. Finally, delete **T TempPONo**.

17. If you wish to quit *Access* at this time, simply close the program and your database will be saved with the name you used to create it.

CREATING RELATIONS

As stated previously, *Access* is a relational database. This implies that associations or relationships are created between common fields (i.e., columns) in two tables to link the data from one table to another. For example, one-to-one (1:1) relationships occur when a record (i.e., row) in a table relates to a record in another table once and only once. One-to-many (1:N) relationships occur when a record in a table relates to several records in another table. Many-to-many (N:N) relationships occur when several records in a table relate to several records in another table.

For example, there should be a one-to-many relationship established between the **Supplier** table and the **Purchase Order** table so that data regarding suppliers does not have to be duplicated on the purchase orders. In this section, you will set up these other tables for the expenditure cycle and create relations among them. The following instructions will aid in setting up a relationship linking the **Purchase Order** table to the **Supplier** table.

Requirements

1. Open your previously created database. Open the Relationships window by clicking on the **Relationships** Relationships icon in the **Database Tools** tab.

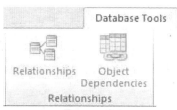

Figure 26

2. Add both the **T Supplier** and **T Purchase Order**. Close the **Show Table** dialogue window.

Figure 27

3. Click and drag the **SupplierNo** field in **T Supplier** to the **SupplierNo** field in the **T Purchase Order**.

4. Click the **Enforce Referential Integrity** check box. Referential integrity ensures that records referenced by a foreign key cannot be deleted unless the record containing the foreign key is first removed. Thus, in this case, a supplier cannot be deleted from the database if there is an outstanding purchase order for that supplier.

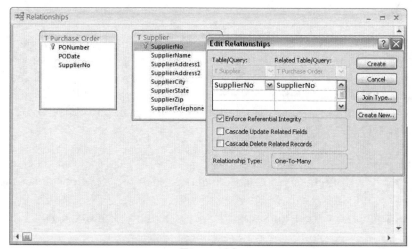

Figure 28

5. Click on the **Create** button.

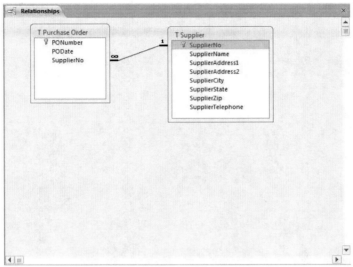

Figure 29

6. Save and close the relationship.

7. If you wish to quit *Access* at this time, simply close the program and your database will be saved with the name you used to create it.

INTEGRATING FORMS WITHIN FORMS

There are times when you may want to show data from tables that are linked with a one-to-many relationship. To do this, we can insert one form within another. That is, we can create a subform within the main form. For example, we might want to insert inventory data into a purchase order form. The following instructions will assist you in doing this.

Requirements

1. Open your *Access* database used for the previous assignments and create a new table.

2. The first Field Name is **InvCode**. Set the Data Type to **Text** and the Field Size to **7**. Enter the Caption as **Inventory Code**. Set this field as the table's primary key. Since this is the primary key, make sure that you make it a Required field. Other than that, do not change any other default values for this or other Field Names in the **Field Properties** pane unless instructed to do so.

3. The second Field Name is **InvDescription**. Set Data Type to **Text**, the Field Size to **35**, and enter the Caption as **Description**.

4. The third Field Name is **InvCost**. Set Data Type to **Currency** and enter the Caption as **Cost**.

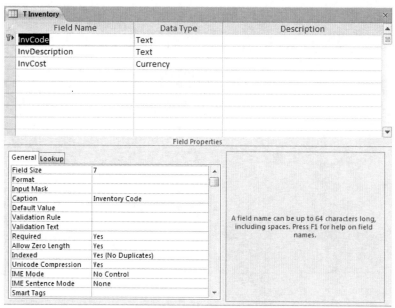

Figure 30

5. Save the table as **T Inventory** and close the table.

6. Select the **Create** tab in your **Database** window and click on the **Form Wizard** 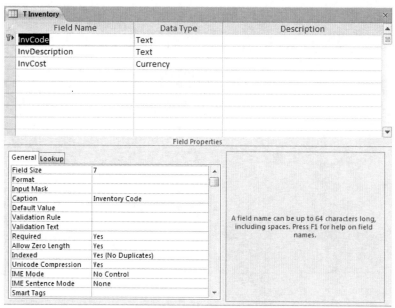 Form Wizard icon. Be sure that **T Inventory** is highlighted in the **Tables/Queries** box.

7. Select all of the available fields from **T Inventory** for inclusion in your new form using the >> icon. Click on **Next**. Choose a **Tabular** format and click on **Next**. Now, choose a backdrop for the form and click on **Next**. The form's title should be **F Inventory.** Be sure to select the radio button that allows you to modify the form design. Click on **Finish**.

8. Click on the Design tab. Click on the box that contains the label "F Inventory" and change this to "**Inventory**." Click outside the label once and then click on the edge of the label box once again. Notice that the **Formatting** toolbar is enabled. Format the label using a **bold font of your choosing with a font size of 20.** Adjust the height of label text box as needed so that it does not overlap with the other labels in the **Form Header** section.

9. You now need to resize the remaining labels and controls as you did for the **Supplier Form.** Left align the label for **Cost**. Shrink the width of the label and the control box since these are more than wide enough for any potential entries.

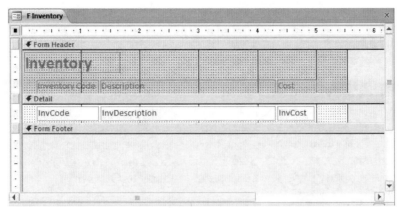

Figure 31

10. Review *Figure 31*. Notice that there is very little empty space below the control boxes in the **Detail** section and the **Form Footer**. This is because the **Detail** section represents one record. Therefore, any space that is left in the **Detail** section will be included as space between each record (i.e., space between each line of inventory in our Inventory form).

11. Close and save the form. Open the **Inventory** Form and enter all inventory data from Chateau Americana's Inventory Price List found below. Close the form after all data is entered.

Inventory Code	Description	Cost
CK30110	1 ¾ US Cork	0.25
CK30120	2 US Cork	0.34
CP30130	Crème Caps Wine	0.11
CP30140	Black Caps Wine	0.09
BT30010	750 Green Bottle	0.99
BT30020	750 Brown Bottle	0.60
LB30210	Crème Wine Bottle Labels	0.18
RM10005	Red Merlot Grapes	691.30
WC20004	White Chardonnay Grapes	732.50

12. Now you need to create the table that will store the inventory data so that it can be linked to the **Purchase Order** table and the **Inventory** table. Create a new table.

13. The first Field Name is **PONumber**. Set the field's Data Type to **Number**. Enter the Caption as **PO #**. Change the Required property to **Yes**. Set the Indexed property to **Yes (Duplicates OK)**. Do not change any other default values for this or other Field Names in the **Field Properties** pane unless instructed to do so.

14. Enter **InvCode** in the next field and set the field's Data Type to **Text**. Set Field Size to **7** and enter the Caption as **Inventory Code**. Set the Required property to **Yes**. Set the Indexed property to **Yes (Duplicates OK)**.

15. While holding down the **Control** key, select the **PONumber** and **InvCode** fields by clicking on their row selectors.

16. Click on the **Primary Key** icon. This will allow both fields to be the primary key.

17. Enter **POInvQuantity** in the third field name and set its Data Type to **Number**. Set the Field Size property to **Long Integer** and the Decimal Places property to **0**. Set the Caption property to **Quantity**.

18. Enter **InvCost** in the last field name and set its Data Type to **Currency**. Set the Caption property to **Cost**.

19. Save the table as **T Purchase Order Sub** and close.

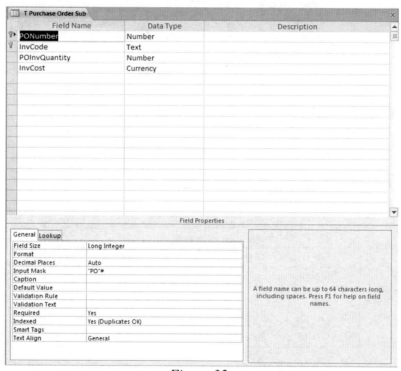

Figure 32

20. Click on the **Relationships** icon Relationships in the **Database Tools** tab again.

Click on the **Show Table** icon Show Table . Add **T Inventory** and **T Purchase Order Sub**. Create a link between the two tables that is based on **InvCode**. Be sure to click the **Enforce Referential Integrity** check box. Also create a link between **T Purchase Order Sub** and **T Purchase Order** and click on **Enforce Referential Integrity**. Close the **Relationships** window and save the new relationships.

21. We will now create the **Purchase Order** form using the **Form Wizard** 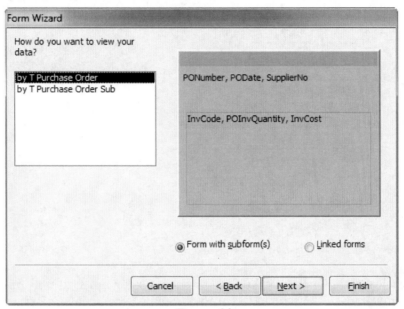 . Click on **T Purchase Order in the** Tables/Queries box and include all of the fields in the form. Then click on the **T Purchase Order Sub** table in the Tables/Queries box. Double click on **InvCode**, **POInvQuantity**, and **InvCost**. Click on **Next**. The **Form Wizard** should appear as shown in *Figure 33*.

Figure 33

22. Click **Next**. Accept **Datasheet for** the layout by clicking **Next** in the following screen. Change the form titles to **F Purchase Order and F Purchase Order Sub Subform**. Click the radio button that allows you to modify the form's design.

23. Highlight the **F Purchase Order Sub** label. Delete the label.

24. Slide the **F Purchase Order Sub Subform** to the left and expand the subform as shown in *Figure 34*.

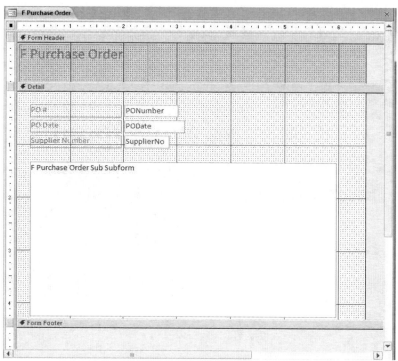

Figure 34

25. Change the form a heading to **Purchase Order Form** using similar size and font as those used in the form headings you created for suppliers and inventory.

26. Close the form and reopen it in Design View to obtain the design view of the subform. See *Figure 35*.

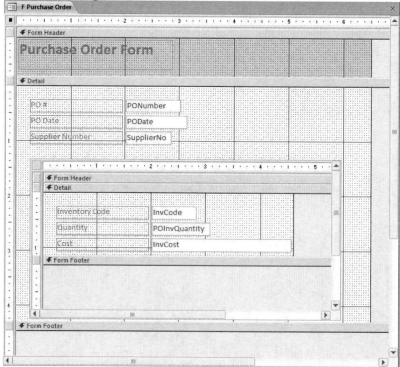

Figure 35

27. Highlight the **F Purchase Order Sub Subform**. Click on the **Design** tab and click on the **Property Sheet** icon in the **Tools** section. Be sure there is a black box in the upper left corner of the subform and that the **Record Source** under the **Data** tab on the **Property Sheet** is set to **T Purchase Order Sub**. The **Record Source** property specifies the source of the data for a form or a report. It can be a Table name, a Query name, or an SQL statement.

28. Click on the **Build** button next to the **Record Source**. Click **Yes** in response to the question "Do you want to create a query based on the table?"

29. Click on the **Show Table** icon under the **Query Setup** section and add the **T Inventory** table. Close the **Show Table** window.

30. Click and drag the **PONumber** field from **T Purchase Order Sub** to the first field cell in the QBE grid, then set its Sort order to **Ascending**.

31. Click and drag the **POInvQuantity** field from **T Purchase Order Sub** to the second field cell in the QBE grid. Click and drag the **InvCode** and the **InvCost** fields from **T Purchase Order Sub** to the third and fourth field cells, respectively.

32. Click and drag the **asterisk** row from **T Inventory** to the fifth field cell in the QBE grid. Note that **T Inventory*** appears in the cell. Selecting the **asterisk** captures all fields from that table. See *Figure 36*.

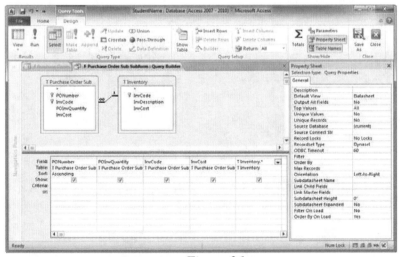

Figure 36

33. Click **Run** under the **Results** section of the **Design** tab of the menu bar. Close the **Query Builder** window by clicking on the **X** in the upper right-

hand corner and **Yes** in response to the question as to whether you want to save the changes made and return to the design view.

34. Right click on the **InvCode** control box in the **Detail** section and select **Properties** from the pull-down menu. Make sure the **Control Source** property (**Data** tab) is not set to **T Inventory.InvCode**. If it is, use the **Control Source** pull-down menu and change it so that it is bound to **T Purchase Order Sub.InvCode**. The **Control Source** property specifies what data is to appear in the control. As stated before, a control can be bound to a table, query, or SQL statement. It can also be the result of an expression (i.e., a combination of field names, controls, constants, functions, operators, etc.). Now think about how these principles apply to the **Inventory Cost** field.

35. Shrink the size of the labels and move the controls over so that they are still close to the labels

36. Drag down the **Form Footer.** Drag down both the label and the control for the **InvCost** field.

37. Click on the **Add Existing Fields** icon in the **Design** tab. Drag **InvDescription** to the space created between **POInvQuantity** and **InvCost**. Align the label and control so that they are in line with the other labels and controls. Lengthen the width of the **InvDescription** control. See *Figure 37.*

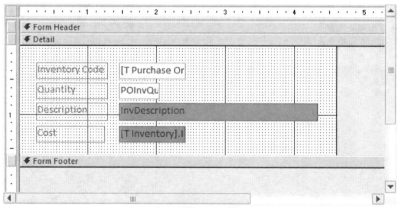

Figure 37

38. Click on the **Form View** to see how the form will appear to users. Notice that the **Cost** field appears before the **Description** field. In addition, the labels for the fields are truncated.

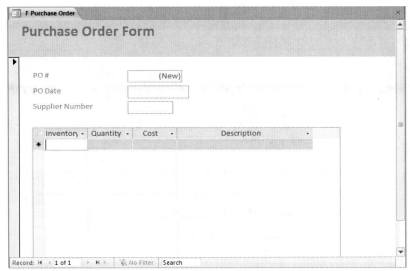

Figure 38

39. Click back on the **Design View**. Click on the **Tab Order** icon to move the **Description** field above the **Cost** field.

Figure 39

40. Drag the width of the fields in the **F Purchase Order Sub Subform** so that you can clearly see all of the labels and so there will be enough room for the inventory description.

41. In the **Design View**, click on the **Design** tab. Right click on the **Description** control box and select **Properties** from the pull down menu. Click on the

Data tab and, from the pull-down menu in the **Control Source** property, set the new text box to **InvDescription**.

42. Highlight both the **InvDescription** and **InvCost** control boxes. Click on the **Property Sheet** icon. Note that the Selection type in the **Property Sheet** window now indicates that there is a "**Multiple Selection**". Thus, when you make changes, you are doing so for both **InvDescription** and **InvCost**. Change the controls as follows:

- Click on the **Data** tab and change the **Enabled** property to **No**. The Enabled property specifies whether the field can receive user input.
- While still in the **Data** tab, change the **Locked** property to **Yes**. The Locked property specifies whether the field can be edited by the user in the Form view.

    Note that setting these two properties in this fashion embeds internal controls in the database. This prevents unauthorized editing of the data.

- Click on the **Other** tab and change the **Tab Stop** property to **No**. The Tab Stop specifies whether the cursor will stop in a particular field when the tab or enter key is hit.
- Click on the **Format** tab and change the **Back Color** property to "**Background Light**" (or choose gray from the color palette). The Back Color property specifies the color in the interior of a control box.
- While still in the the **Format** tab, change the **Border Style** property to **Transparent**. The Border Style property specifies the type of border surrounding a control box.

    Note that setting these three properties in this fashion facilitates form design and user-friendliness. They signal to the user that no input is intended in these fields.

43. Now select the main **Purchase Order** form by right clicking on square between the two rulers on the **Purchase Order** form. The square will now have a black box in it.

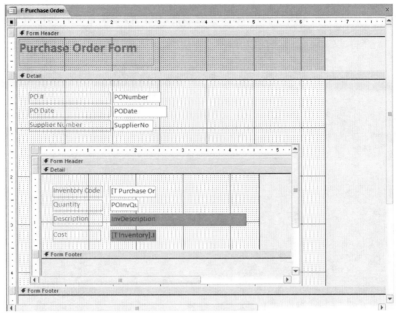

Figure 40

44. Right click on the black square and select **Properties** from the menu. Then select the **Record Source** property (**Data** tab) and click on the **Build** button ![...]. Click **Yes** in the dialogue box that appears to open the form's **Query Builder** window.

45. Click on the **Show Table** icon in the **Query Setup** section of the **Design** tab of the menu bar. Add **T Supplier** and close the **Show Table** window.

46. Click and drag the **PONumber** field from **T Purchase Order** to the first field cell in the QBE grid and then designate **Sort** as ascending.

47. Click and drag the remaining two fields from **T Purchase Order** to the second and third QBE grid field cells.

48. Click and drag the **SupplierName** field from the **T Supplier** to the fourth QBE grid field cell.

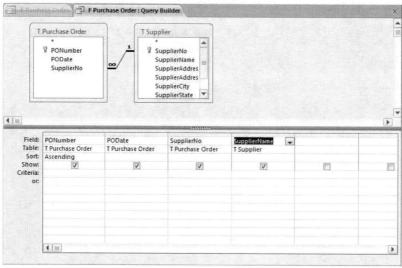

Figure 41

49. Now, select **Run** Run under the **Results** section of the **Design** tab of the menu bar. Save and close the query to return to the form in the **Design View**. Close the form **Properties** window.

50. Click on the **Design** tab and click on the **Add Existing Fields** icon. Drag **SupplierName** next to **SupplierNumber** and delete the label. Right click on the control box and click on **Properties** to pull up the **Property Sheet**. Set the **Enabled** property (**Data** tab) to **No**, the **Locked** property (**Data** tab) to **Yes**, and the **Tab Stop** property (**Other** tab) to **No**. Set the **Font Size** (**Format** tab) to 10 and make the **Font Weight** property (**Format** tab) to bold. Set the **Back Color** property (**Format** tab) to **#D8D8D8** (or grey from the color palette), and the **Border Style** property (**Format** tab) to **Transparent**. Close the **Properties** window and save the form as **F Purchase Order**.

51. Open the **Purchase Order** form and create Purchase Order No. 9682 for the following transaction:

On December 16, 2012, Franz Bieler (CA Buyer) ordered 29 tons of white chardonnay grapes (inventory code: WC20004) at $732.50 per ton from Mendocino Vineyards (Supplier #: M0652).

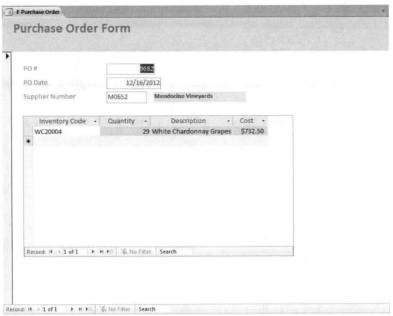

Figure 42

52. If you wish to quit *Access* at this time, simply close the program and your database will be saved with the name you used to create it.

CREATING A QUERY

Recall that queries can be used to ask questions about data or to perform actions on data. As you will now see, they can also be used as the basis for a report. You will need to create a purchase order to send to the supplier to order the inventory required by Chateau Americana. To do this, you will have to build a query that will obtain data from fields in several different tables. In this query, you will create a field that will calculate totals by extending unit prices and quantities ordered and a field that combines several address fields into a single address field.

Requirements

1. Open your *Access* database **Create** tab. Click on the **Query Design** icon

   in the **Queries** section.

2. Highlight all four previously created tables (T Inventory, T Purchase Order, T Purchase Order Sub, and T Supplier) in the **Show Table** window by clicking on each while holding down the **Shift** key, and click on **Add**. Close the **Show Table** window.

3. Drag and click the fields from the tables listed below to the design grid Field cells:

T Purchase Order fields:
- **PONumber**
- **PODate**
- **SupplierNo**

T Inventory fields:
- **InvCode**
- **InvDescription**
- **InvCost**

T Supplier fields:
- **SupplierName**
- **SupplierAddress1**
- **SupplierAddress2**
- **SupplierCity**
- **SupplierState**
- **SupplierZip**

T Purchase Order Sub field:
- **POInvQuantity**

4. Set the **Sort** property for **PONumber** from **T Purchase Order** and **InvCode** from **T Inventory** to **Ascending**.

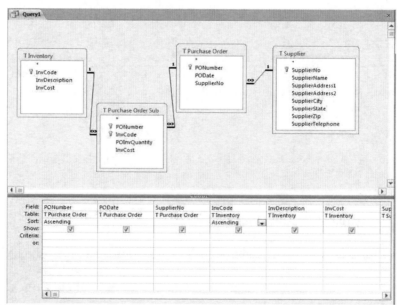

Figure 43

5. For mailing purposes, it is necessary to concatenate (i.e., link together) the city, state, and zip code fields. This is done by creating an additional field in the next open Field cell in the grid. Click on the next open Field cell and then click on the **Builder** 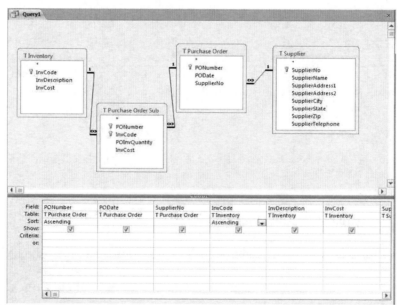 icon in the **Query Setup** section under the **Design** tab to bring up the **Expression Builder** window. In the **Expression**

Elements pane located in the lower left portion of the **Expression Builder** window, click on the + symbol next to the database file that refers to your database. Then click on **Tables** and click **T Supplier**. Note that the fields in the **T Supplier** table now appear in the **Expression Categories** pane located in the lower middle section of the **Expression Builder**.

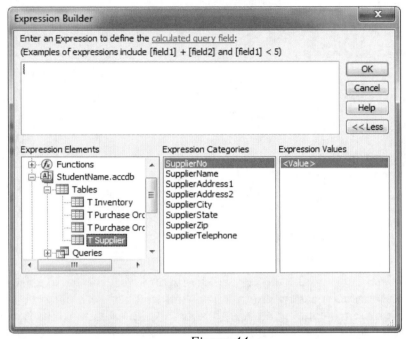

Figure 44

IMPORTANT NOTE: In the following instructions, the symbol ^ represents a space.

6. In the upper pane of the **Expression Builder** window, type **SupplierAddressComp:^**

7. In the **Expression Categories** pane of the Expression Builder window, double-click on **SupplierCity**. Notice that when you did this the field name appeared in the upper portion of the window **BUT** some unwanted text also appeared that you will need to remove. Before the field name, <<Expr>> appears. Before we remove this, let's finish the expression.

8. Type **& ", ^" &** (with quotation marks) then double-click on **SupplierState**, type **& " ^^^" &** (with quotation marks) and double-click on **SupplierZip**. Now we will go back and remove the unwanted text. Scroll back to the beginning of the field name. As we previously noted, when you double-clicked on **SupplierCity**, *Access* inserted "«Expr»" into the expression just after the field name **SupplierAddressComp**. Highlight this and hit the **Delete** key so that your syntax will be correct. Next click **OK.**

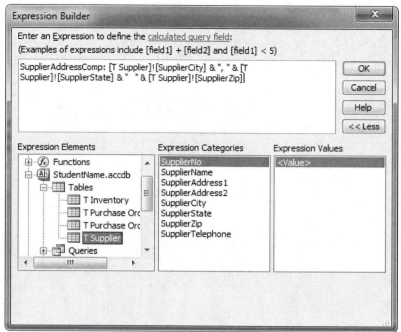

Figure 45

9. The next open grid Field cell will be used to calculate the extension for the cost times the quantity ordered. The **Builder** button can again be utilized to obtain help in entering the text for this field. Enter **Extension: [T Purchase Order Sub]![POInvQuantity]*[T Inventory]![InvCost]**. Next click **OK**.

10. Click on the **Run** icon to test the query. The result should include each of the fields listed above as well as the two new fields created in steps 6 through 9. Close and save this query as **Q Purchase Order**.

11. If you wish to quit *Access* at this time, simply close the program and your database will be saved with the name you used to create it.

CREATING A REPORT

The purchase order form you previously created is an internal form. Its intent was to provide a convenient, user-friendly form for employees, but it is not in a format that provides all the information needed by suppliers. Therefore, it will be necessary to create a **report** (using *Access* terminology) that can be sent to suppliers when Chateau Americana wants to make a purchase. You will use the query that you just created to build this report.

Requirements

1. Open your *Access* database and click on the **Report Design** icon in the **Reports** section under the **Create** tab. Click on the **Property Sheet** icon in the **Tools** section under the **Design** tab. Click on the pull-down menu in the **Record Source** field and select **Q Purchase Order**.

2. Click and drag the right edge of the report to the 6-inch mark on the top ruler. Click and drag the **Page Footer** and **Page Header** area edges up to reduce the height of each to zero. **NOTE: You will not enter anything into these sections!!!**

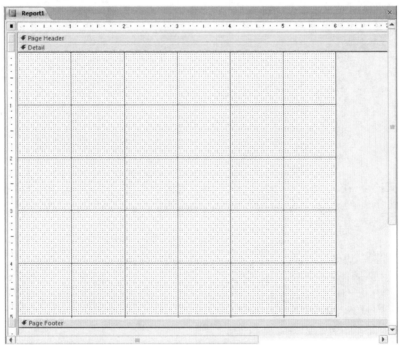

Figure 46

3. Click on the **Group & Sort** icon in the **Grouping & Totals** section under the **Design** tab. Then click on **Add a group** in the **Group, Sort, and Total** window. Select **PONumber** as the first field to group on in the **Group, Sort, and Total** window.

4. Click on the **More** button to expand the options. Change "**without a footer section**" to "**with a footer section.**" Change the option "**do not keep group together on one page**" to "**keep whole group together on one page.**"

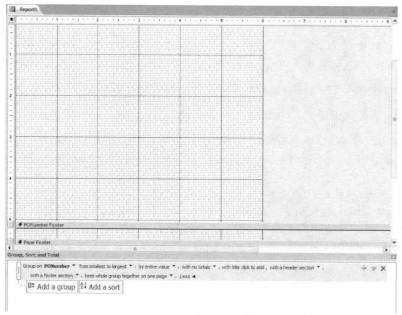

Figure 47

5. Click on the X on the **Group, Sort, and Total** menu line to close the **Grouping Dialogue Box**.

6. Click on the **Add Existing Fields** icon from the **Tools** section under the **Design** tab. Then click and drag the following fields to the **Detail** section.

   - **InvCode**
   - **InvDescription**
   - **InvCost**
   - **POInvQuantity**
   - **Extension**

   Each field will become a control on the report. Close the **Field List** window.

7. Click on the **Inventory Code** label (**NOT** the control box, just the label) and press Ctrl-X. This will cut the label away from the control box. Click on the **PONumber Header** bar, then press Ctrl-V to place the label in that section. Do the same for the remaining labels. Line the labels up horizontally just above the **Detail** bar line in the order above. Line up the control boxes just below their related labels.

8. Enlarge the **Header** section by dragging the **Detail** bar downward. Bring down the labels for the **Detail** section also.

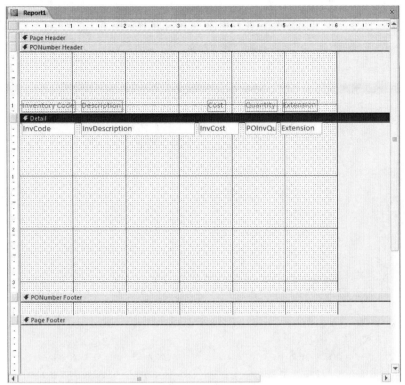

Figure 48

9. Using the **Field List** again, click and drag the following fields to the PONumber Header section:

- **PONumber**
- **PODate**
- **SupplierNo**
- **SupplierName**
- **SupplierAddress1**
- **SupplierAddress2**
- **SupplierAddressComp**

Delete the labels for everything but the purchase order number. Arrange the control boxes using good form design principles. Close the **Field List** window. Enlarge the **PONumber Header**.

10. Pull-down the **Controls** menu (found in the **Controls** section of the **Design** toolbar) and click on the **Label** icon. Create a label for Chateau Americana's name, address and telephone number at the top of the purchase order by drawing rectangles with the **Label** tool. Use an appropriate font size (found in the **Home** tab) so that the supplier will know immediately who the buyer is.

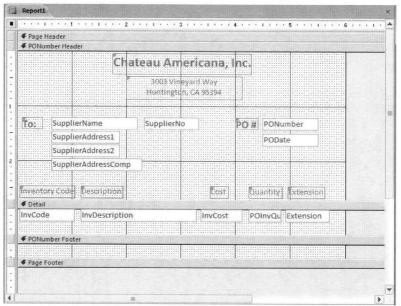

Figure 49

11. A **Control** box must be made to calculate the total of the extension amounts for each line of the purchase order. Pull down the menu for the **Controls** icon again and click on the **Text Box** tool to create a control in the **PONumber Footer** section. Position the control box just below the **Extension** control box in the **Detail** section. Highlight the newly created control and click on **Property Sheet**. Set its **Control Source** property to **=Sum([Extension])** (found under the **Data** tab) and its format to **Currency** (found in the pull-down menu for **Format** under the **Format** tab).

12. Double click on the attached label and change the caption to **Total**.

13. Look at the report you have just created by clicking on the **View** icon in the **Views** section under the **Design** tab and select **Report View**. Feel free to change the formatting (e.g., font sizes, bolding, italics, spacing, etc.) for any field you desire. The key is to utilize good form design principles to enhance the user's understanding of the purchase order.

14. Close and save the report as **R Purchase Order.**

15. You have now completed the *Access* assignment. Simply close the program and your database will be saved with the name you used to create it.

SUMMARY

In the preceding exercises, you have explored some of the power behind a database management system. You have created *Access* tables. You have learned the importance of primary keys and foreign keys. You have created queries to create composite fields and to combine fields from multiple tables into a single form or report. You have designed forms to display the information in a more user-friendly, intuitive manner and you have entered the data into those forms to see how they work. Finally, you have designed a report using the data from multiple tables. But this is just the beginning. There is much more to learn about database systems!

CLIENT ACCEPTANCE:
The Winery At Chateau Americana

LEARNING OBJECTIVES

After completing and discussing this case, you should be able to:

- Understand types of information used to evaluate a prospective audit client
- Evaluate background information about an entity and key members of management
- Perform and evaluate preliminary analytical procedures
- Make and justify a client acceptance decision
- Describe matters that should be included in an engagement letter

INTRODUCTION

Since its founding in 1980, Chateau Americana (CA) has cultivated a reputation as one of America's finest wineries. The small, family-owned winery has an impressive vineyard whose 125 acres yields a variety of grapes including Cabernet Sauvignon, Cabernet Franc, Chardonnay and Riesling. In the last several years, CA's wines have received accolades at several highly regarded wine competitions which have dramatically increased the demand for its wines. This recent growth, along with the accompanying challenges and opportunities, has caused the winery's management to have doubts as to whether their current accounting firm is prepared to provide the advice and services required by a growing company.

Claire Helton, a partner with your accounting firm (Boston & Greer, LLP) recently met with the winery's president and chief financial officer (CFO) about the company's present and future needs. After several follow-up meetings, the winery's CFO contacted Claire to notify her that CA would like to have your firm submit a proposal to perform the company's financial statement audit. You have been asked by Claire to assist her in the evaluation of CA as a potential audit client and to assist with the preparation of the engagement proposal.

BACKGROUND INFORMATION

CA, owned by the Summerfield family, is a relatively modest winery with an annual production of approximately 385,000 cases of wine. Several years of sales growth have enabled the company to reinvest in its operations while simultaneously reducing its debts. Encouraged by its success and growing acclaim, management is contemplating an initial public offering within the next several years.

Overview of the Wine Industry

The domestic wine industry is comprised of almost 1,800 wineries. California is home to more than 800 of these wineries, almost half of the nation's wineries. More impressive still, California wineries account for more than 90 percent of the annual domestic wine production (565 million gallons) and approximately 70 percent of the nation's $19 billion in sales. An understanding of California's wineries is instructive because it is a "snapshot" of the domestic wine industry. The wine industry is highly concentrated with the five largest US winemakers accounting for 55 percent of domestic wine production.

Several of the world's largest winemakers are located in California. Ernest & Julio Gallo, one of the largest winemakers in the world, is privately owned and is estimated to have annual sales in the billions of dollars. Another large winemaker, one that is publicly-owned, is Constellation Brands. The company has seen its annual sales vary between $2.9 and $4.8 billion. Although there are several other large California wineries, they are much smaller than Gallo and Constellation with annual sales that are generally less than $200 million. In addition, many small California wineries specialize in the production of particular varieties of grapes and generate much lower sales.

Wine reaches the consumer through a variety of distribution channels. More than 43 percent of wine sales occur through supermarket chains. Specialty shops and mass merchandisers account for 24 percent and 19 percent of sales, respectively. The remainder is accounted for by restaurants, small convenience stores, and other outlets. Internet sales and distribution are relatively small primarily because of financial security concerns and interstate alcohol shipping regulations.

The wine industry appears to have a bright future. Wine consumption is directly related to household income, with higher income families consuming more wine than lower income families. Consumption is highest among adults between the ages of 35 and 64 because of higher disposable income. An aging and prosperous baby boom generation is expected to increase wine consumption and support premium priced wines. Consolidation within the industry is likely to continue as wineries search for economies of scale in production and advertising and interest in product expansion (i.e., grape varieties and brand names) broadens.

Overview of Chateau Americana

CA has experienced significant sales growth in recent years and expects to report record sales of almost $22 million for the year ending December 31, 20XX. Audited sales for the two prior years totaled $20.2 and $18.2 million, respectively. Over the same three year period, the company's asset base has also grown, increasing by more than 15 percent from $36.4 to $42 million. CA has been a profitable winery for a number of years and expects to report profits of approximately $2 million for the current year. Much of CA's growth has been fueled through the company's policy of reinvestment. To this end, retained earnings have increased approximately $3.7 million over the last three years, while total liabilities have increased $1.9 million. The winery's CFO provided the balance sheets and income statements for the current and two preceding years which are presented at the end of this narrative.

The winery's crown jewel is its 125-acre vineyard which yields a harvest of some fifteen varieties of grapes. Each year the vineyard provides approximately 800 tons of grapes, or one-fourth of the winery's production requirement. The remaining grapes are purchased from other vineyards, most of which are in California. CA is particularly proud of its production process - a blend of traditional techniques and state-of-the-art technology – which produces widely acclaimed red and white wines.

The company primarily sells its wines to distributors and retail shops. CA has developed several exclusive distribution agreements which have significantly increased its presence in several large metropolitan areas. The company is seeking similar opportunities in other areas.

The Company's Management

CA has a management team that is widely respected in the industry. The winery's owners have invested considerable time and energies in hiring individuals whom they believe are competent and trustworthy. Several members of the Summerfield family occupy key management positions.

- Edward Summerfield is the family's patriarch and president of the company. He has received several entrepreneurship awards and is generally perceived as an astute business person.
- Taylor Summerfield is vice president of marketing for the company. Prior to assuming this position, she had a successful career in sales and marketing. Taylor is well-educated and earned an MBA from an Ivy League school.
- Jacques Dupuis, Edward's son-in-law, is vice-president of winery operations. He has an extensive background in viticulture (i.e., grape growing) and vinification (i.e., wine making).
- Rob Breeden, the company's CFO, is the sole individual to hold a key management position who is not a member of the Summerfield family. He has substantial financial experience and was previously employed in public accounting for nine years and served as controller and CFO for another winery in California. Rob holds undergraduate and graduate degrees in accounting and is a CPA.

Edward and other members of management have taken considerable steps to ensure the stability of the winery's management team. To this end, management members have an open door policy that encourages a free exchange of ideas and concerns. In addition, Edward has instituted a compensation plan that provides substantial bonuses to all employees, including members of management, who meet performance goals. He believes that his policies and approach to business are the reasons that CA has had very low employee turnover. In fact, Rob is the newest member of management with just over two years of service to the company. He replaced the former CFO who resigned from the company after more than 15 years. According to Edward, the former CFO resigned because he wanted to spend more time with his wife who was suffering from a serious illness.

Client Background Investigation

Your firm customarily has a background investigation conducted prior to accepting a new audit client. The investigation of CA included the winery's corporate history and the background of each member of management. Two issues arose during the investigation. First, the company's credit history indicates that the company was delinquent on several obligations that were referred to collection agencies six years ago. Recent credit history is much more favorable and no problems of ongoing significance were found. The second issue relates to criminal charges filed against Jacques Dupuis while living in France. According to public records and news sources, Jacques and several other employees were accused of stealing trade secrets from a former employer – a French winery. Although charges were eventually dropped because of insufficient evidence, many in France still believe Jacques was guilty of stealing trade secrets.

The Company's Information System

The winery employs a fully integrated information system (IS) to collect, store and share data among its employees. The present system has been operational for approximately 14 months. Although employees are generally satisfied with the system, some complain that the transition from the previous system occurred too quickly and without adequate planning and training. Although the company has been computerized for more than 10 years, its former system was a combination of manual and computerized processes. Consequently, the new system represents a significant change in the company's IS.

Management believes the new system is the best on the market. After having been through a similar IS conversion process at his former employer, Rob Breeden insisted that the company investigate the prospects of developing an integrated IS using database technology. Following his detailed evaluation of the potential for in-house development of the system, Rob advised Edward that the system could be developed by the company's employees. Internal memos obtained from the company indicate that Edward deferred to Rob's judgment in making the decision to proceed with the in-house development process.

The current system is based on a relational database. The IS modules include purchasing and accounts payable, sales and accounts receivable, production and inventory, payroll, and the general ledger. Each of these modules provides data that are critical to the company's continued growth and success. Internal memos indicate that the company has experienced some employee turnover because of continuing problems with the accounts payable and accounts receivable modules. In fact, there are rumors that the former CFO resigned over disagreements with Edward about the need for a new IS.

Discussions with the Predecessor Auditor

As required by auditing standards, your firm asked for and received permission from management to contact the company's former auditor. Several phone calls were required before you were able to speak with the former partner-in-charge of the CA audit, Harry Lawson. At first, Harry was hesitant to talk with you about his firm's past relationship with CA. He said he needed to speak with Rob Breeden before you and he could have any substantive conversation.

You met with Harry at his office a few days later to learn more about his firm's relationship with the winery's management and recent audits. Harry was very complementary of the Summerfield family, describing Edward as a man of great integrity and business savvy. He stated that he was very impressed by the company's strong professional environment and complete lack of nepotism. Harry did express concerns about the winery's new CFO. He felt that Rob was too eager to "make his mark" on the company as evidenced by the implementation of the company's new IS. According to Harry, Rob believed the winery's old IS was limiting CA's future because of its inability to provide accurate data in a timely manner and was insistent that a new system be implemented. Several of the winery's internal memos reviewed by you indicated that Rob was the real force behind the new system.

You asked Harry if there were any disagreements with management about either accounting principles or his firm's audit procedures. He quickly mentioned that his firm had always enjoyed a very good relationship with CA until Rob became CFO. When you asked him to explain further, Harry said that Rob is very knowledgeable, but also more aggressive than CA's former CFO. He specifically mentioned that last year's audit team noted policy changes related to Accounts Receivable and Accounts Payable. With respect to receivables, the company instituted more aggressive collection procedures and reduced the Allowance for Bad Debts by more than $100,000 from the previous year. The company also implemented a practice of paying vendors who offer discounts within that discount period, but simultaneously delayed payments to vendors who offer no discounts by 10 to 15 days beyond the indicated terms. Notwithstanding these changes, Harry said that he was unaware of any significant negative reaction by customers or vendors.

Finally, you asked Harry to explain his understanding of why CA had decided to change audit firms. After a brief silence, he said that Edward and Rob had told him that they believed the company needed a "fresh perspective" and was concerned that his firm would not be able to provide the services required as their company continued its growth.

Financial Statements

Financial statements for the current and preceding two years were provided by Rob Breeden and are included at the end of this narrative. Harry Lawson's firm issued an unqualified audit opinion on the company's financial statements for each of the preceding two years.

REQUIREMENTS

Client acceptance is a challenging process that requires considerable professional judgment. Although such decisions are typically made by highly experienced auditors, you have so impressed the managers and partners in your office that you have been asked to assist with the client acceptance procedures for Chateau Americana.

Before you perform the remaining audit procedures listed on the audit program, identify four to six procedures auditors may perform as part of the client acceptance process. Are any of the procedures identified by you required by generally accepted auditing standards?

Now you are ready to assist the engagement partner, Claire Helton, by completing all open audit procedures on the audit program. Document your work on the provided audit schedules that follow Chateau Americana's financial statements. You should assume that audit schedules CA-104 and CA-105 were properly prepared and have already been included with other relevant audit documentation.

The Winery at Chateau Americana
Audit Program for Client Acceptance

For the Year Ended December 31, 20XX

Reference:	CA-100
Prepared by:	CH
Date:	11/14/XX
Reviewed by:	

Audit Procedures	Initial	Date	A/S Ref.
1. Obtain an overview of the client's operations by interviewing client personnel and touring the facilities.	CH	11/16/XX	CA-104
2. Obtain permission from the potential client to communicate with the predecessor auditor. Contact the predecessor and request relevant information regarding the client.	CH	11/5/XX	CA-105
3. Brainstorm about and briefly describe financial and non-financial factors that are relevant to the decision to accept the potential client.			CA-106
4. Perform preliminary analytical procedures using the financial statements provided by the client. Calculate ratios for comparison to the industry averages provided.			CA-107
5. Discuss the overall results of the preliminary analytical procedures. Identify relationships or areas that may be of concern during the audit.			CA-108
6. Based on the information obtained do you recommend that the firm accept or not accept the potential client? Briefly explain the basis for your recommendation.			CA-109
7. Identify matters that should be included in an engagement letter for this client.			CA-110

The Winery at Chateau Americana, Inc.
Balance Sheets as of December 31, 20XX – 20XV
(In Thousands)

ASSETS

	(Unaudited) 20XX	20XW	20XV
CURRENT ASSETS			
Cash	$ 3,005	$ 2,992	$ 3,281
Accounts receivable (net of allowance)	5,241	4,816	3,703
Investments	3,095	2,081	2,294
Production inventories	11,578	10,407	9,107
Finished goods inventories	4,015	3,902	3,567
Prepaid expenses	142	85	69
Total Current Assets	27,076	$ 24,283	$ 22,021
PROPERTY, PLANT & EQUIPMENT	30,230	28,135	27,612
Less accumulated depreciation	15,277	14,096	13,185
Net Property, Plant & Equipment	14,953	14,039	14,427
TOTAL ASSETS	$ 42,029	$ 38,322	$ 36,448

LIABILITIES AND SHAREHOLDERS' EQUITY

	20XX	20XW	20XV
CURRENT LIABILITIES			
Accounts payable	$ 4,988	$ 3,683	$ 2,221
Accrued expenses	599	569	640
Notes payable	813	654	891
Current portion of long term debt	410	525	464
Payroll taxes withheld and payable	100	95	96
Federal income tax payable	172	157	134
Total Current Liabilities	7,082	5,683	4,446
LONG TERM DEBT	7,229	6,918	7,983
TOTAL LIABILITIES	14,311	12,601	12,429
SHAREHOLDERS' EQUITY			
Common stock (No par value, 5,000,000 shares authorized, 45,000 shares issued)	90	90	90
Additional paid-in capital	3,567	3,567	3,567
Retained earnings	24,061	22,064	20,362
Total Shareholders' Equity	27,718	25,721	24,019
TOTAL LIABILITIES AND SHAREHOLDERS' EQUITY	$ 42,029	$ 38,322	$ 36,448

The Winery at Chateau Americana, Inc.
Statements of Income for Years Ended December 31, 20XX – 20XV
(In Thousands)

	(Projected) 20XX	20XW	20XV
Sales	$ 21,945	$ 20,189	$ 18,170
Cost of goods sold	11,543	10,525	9,777
Gross profit	10,402	9,664	8,393
Selling, general and administrative expenses	7,017	6,824	6,218
Operating income	3,386	2,840	2,175
Interest expense	360	211	257
Provision for income taxes	1,028	927	483
Net income	$ 1,997	$ 1,702	$ 1,435

Selected Industry Ratios

	20XX	20XW
Current Ratio	4.9	4.7
Accounts Receivable Turnover	4.42	4.30
Average Days to Collect Accounts Receivable	82.58	84.88
Inventory Turnover	0.67	0.80
Days in Inventory	545	456
Assets to Equity	1.99	2.14
Debt to Equity Ratio	0.99	1.14
Times Interest Earned	6.91	7.29
Return on Assets	5.56 %	7.61 %
Return on Equity	5.92 %	10.76 %

The Winery at Chateau Americana
Evaluation of Financial and Non-financial Factors

For the Year Ended December 31, 20XX

Reference: *CA-106*
Prepared by:
Date:
Reviewed by:

Financial factors:

Non-financial factors:

The Winery at Chateau Americana
Preliminary Analytical Procedures

Reference: _CA-107_
Prepared by: _____
Date: _____
Reviewed by: _____

For the Year Ended December 31, 20XX

Ratio	Industry Ratios 20XX	Industry Ratios 20XW	Chateau Americana 20XX	Notes
Current Ratio	4.9	4.7		
Accounts Receivable Turnover	4.42	4.30		
Average Days to Collect A/R	82.58	84.88		
Inventory Turnover	0.67	0.80		
Days in Inventory	545	456		
Assets to Equity	1.99	2.14		
Debt to Equity Ratio	0.99	1.14		
Times Interest Earned	6.91	7.29		
Return on Assets	5.56%	7.61%		
Return on Equity	5.92%	10.76%		

The Winery at Chateau Americana
Summary of Preliminary Analytical Procedures

For the Year Ended December 31, 20XX

Reference: *CA-108*
Prepared by:
Date:
Reviewed by:

The Winery at Chateau Americana
Client Acceptance Recommendation
For the Year Ended December 31, 20XX

Reference: _CA-109_

Prepared by: _____

Date: _____

Reviewed by: _____

Recommendation:

_____ Accept the potential client

_____ Do not accept the potential client

Basis for above recommendation:

The Winery at Chateau Americana
Establishing an Understanding with the Client
For the Year Ended December 31, 20XX

Reference: _CA-110_
Prepared by: _____
Date: _____
Reviewed by: _____

Matters to include in an engagement letter:

UNDERSTANDING THE BUSINESS ENVIRONMENT:
The Winery At Chateau Americana

LEARNING OBJECTIVES

After completing and discussing this case, you should be able to:

- Describe and document information related to the evaluation of a client's business environment
- Describe sources of business risks and understand the relationship between business risk and the risk of material misstatements in the financial statements
- Describe the types of information that should be used in assessing the risk of material misstatements in the financial statements
- Articulate the types of questions that may be used to conduct interviews of client personnel

INTRODUCTION

Chateau Americana (CA) recently hired your accounting firm to perform an audit of its financial statements for the year ended December 31, 20XX. Your partner, Claire Helton, approached you several days ago with a request for help in planning this year's audit engagement. She asked for assistance in three specific areas: understanding the winery's business environment, assessing business risks, and identifying and assessing factors relevant to the risk of material misstatements in CA's financial statements. As you work to develop an understanding of the business environment, Claire asked that you specifically consider factors related to business operations, management and corporate governance, business objectives and strategies, and performance measurement.

Claire invited you to accompany her on a recent visit to the winery during which she interviewed CA's president Edward Summerfield, vice-president of marketing Taylor Summerfield, chief financial officer Rob Breeden, and the vice-president of winery operations Jacques Dupuis. The following transcripts were taken from those interviews. At the end of the transcripts, you will also find excerpts from various trade publications which will help you learn more about the wine industry.

INTERVIEW TRANSCRIPTS

Claire: Edward, thank you for meeting with us today. We're here to learn more about the winery's history and your vision of the company's future.

Edward: Well Claire, we're thrilled to have you and the rest of your team working with us. I believe Chateau Americana has an amazing future. Many fine people have worked hard to make this company great and we've endured our share of bumps along the way, but I think most of us would agree that we've learned a great deal over the years and have a stronger company as a consequence.

Let me give you a bit of background about us. After spending more than 20 years working for other companies in the wine industry, I decided to start my own company. Although my family was a bit skeptical at first, they were and continue to be supportive. The winery has become the typical family business with a good deal of family involvement. My daughter is vice president of marketing, my son-in-law is vice president of winery operations, and several of my grandchildren have worked for us during their summer breaks. In all, we have approximately 250 permanent employees and we hire an additional 30 to 40 seasonal employees for harvest. Many of our employees have been with us for a number of years and we have been fortunate to have very little employee turnover.

Our current production is approximately 385,000 cases with capacity for an additional 80,000 cases. Our intention is to grow our business to a sustained level between 410,000 and 450,000 cases. We expect to achieve this level within the next three to five years. Our wines are sold in more than 20 states and we have exclusive distribution agreements with several small wine distributors in a few states. We have a sales force of highly motivated and experienced individuals. We plan to add several new sales positions in the coming months.

The wine business is highly competitive and because we're one of almost 1,800 wineries, we have to remain vigilant if we want to continue to thrive. Our geographic location assists us in staying abreast of industry trends. Almost half of all domestic wineries are in California, so there's a concentration of talent here that's nowhere else in the U.S.

Claire: I've read about the trend toward consolidation in the industry. How will this trend affect your company?

Edward: Well, that's a great question. As I mentioned a minute ago, this is a family business and we have no interest in being taken over by a bigger winery. My family and I have had a number of discussions about this and we all agree that this company is our family's future.

I'm certain that we will need to be vigilant as we move forward, and I believe that our people are committed to being as efficient and innovative as possible while maintaining our winery's commitment to its small business values.

Claire: What kinds of innovations have been made recently?

Edward: We have adopted new technologies in our winemaking process and even more recently in our accounting information system. I understand that you plan to talk with Rob later today. I would suggest you speak to him about the details.

We have adopted new technologies in our winemaking process and even more recently in our accounting information system. I understand that you plan to talk with Rob later today. I would suggest you speak to him about the details.

However, I can give you my perspective on our new accounting information system. When we first started our company, we were very small and primarily relied on a paper trail to document our business. We had numerous journals and ledgers and were constantly relying on information that was outdated. Over the last ten years, we've become much more reliant on technology and until about 18 months ago we were using a combination of software programs to maintain our records. I became convinced several years ago that we needed to move to a more integrated system that would grow with us and provide more current information. Rob was instrumental in helping us make the transition to the new system.

Claire: How have your employees reacted to the new information system? Have you had any turnover related to the system change?

Edward: Like any change, some employees have been unhappy with the new system, but they'll become accustomed to it. We've had some turnover in accounting, but I don't know the details. You'll have to ask Rob about that.

Claire: Okay, I have questions on two additional matters before we meet with Rob. First, how would you describe the management group's operating style and philosophy? Second, could you describe how the board of directors functions?

Edward: Well, as I've mentioned before, this is a family company. All of us place a great deal of value on integrity and hard work. I, along with the rest of management, support open communications and encourage employees to approach any member of management with suggestions and concerns. Since we started our business in 1980, we have been focused on producing excellent wines and establishing a solid reputation. I believe that we've stayed true to our mission and I feel strongly that we have employees that are committed to the same values.

Our board of directors is comprised of three employees and four non-employees. I serve as chairman of the board. The other employee board members are my daughter Taylor and Rob Breeden, our CFO. The four non-employee board members are my wife Charlotte, Bill Jameson, and Susan Martinez, and Terrence Dillard. Bill and Susan are local business owners and have a great deal of experience with family-owned businesses. Terrence is an attorney with whom I have a longstanding personal relationship. Like me, my wife worked in the wine industry before we started Chateau Americana. I wanted our company to benefit from her work experience, so she agreed to serve on our board.

Claire: How often does the board meet and generally how long are the meetings?

Edward: The length of the meetings varies quite a bit, but a typical meeting lasts for two to three hours. We generally meet four times a year, but we can meet as often as our operations necessitate.

Claire: Do you have either an audit committee or a compensation committee?

Edward: No. Our company is so small that no one on the board has ever felt it necessary to establish such committees. Everyone is on the same page regarding our company and its future, so we always discuss and resolve any differences that may arise during our meetings.

Claire: Those are all of my questions for now. Thanks very much for taking the time to meet with us. We'll let you know if we have other questions.

◆◆◆

After meeting with Edward, you met with Taylor Summerfield, the company's vice president of marketing.

Claire: Taylor, it's great to see you again. We wanted to meet with you so we could learn about the winery's marketing strategy and how the company is positioning itself in the industry.

Taylor: The wine industry is very competitive. Most consumers choose wine based on just three factors: price, brand, or variety. In addition, consumers tend to buy wines only for special occasions. Domestic consumers have a long way to go before they purchase and consume wines in the same patterns as Europeans.

In the past, we've relied on a product differentiation strategy. That is, we have not competed on price, but have focused our energies and resources on appealing to a certain set of wine drinkers. For instance, several of our wines have won highly coveted awards which we have tried to leverage into targeted advertising campaigns aimed at consumers who are willing to spend $10 to $30 for a good bottle of wine. We've found that many of these consumers are baby boomers.

Claire: How are other demographic groups addressed by your marketing strategy?

Taylor: Although baby boomers purchase a significant percentage of our wines, we are making inroads with younger consumers. There are a significant number of individuals between the ages of 35 and 64 who have sufficient disposable income and the desire to purchase better table wines. We are currently discussing some new strategies targeted at that segment of the population. We have discussed the possibility of sponsoring or co-sponsoring certain events such as arts festivals, golf tournaments, and various charity functions.

Claire: What is your advertising budget?

Taylor: Approximately $750,000.

Claire: Is this sufficient?

Taylor: I would like to devote more of our resources to advertising and marketing, but I'm also aware of some of our other needs. My father and I meet frequently about the company's marketing strategy and we both agree that we need to increase the advertising budget. I expect that we will increase our budget by 10 to 20 percent in the next couple of years.

Claire: Turning to your customer base, do you have any *key* customers?

Taylor: We've specifically tried to avoid over reliance on a single customer or a small number of customers. However, we have developed close relationships with several reasonably large distributors. We monitor sales and collections activity with these customers to limit our exposure. I should tell you that no single customer accounts for more than five percent of our annual sales.

Claire: One last question if I may. How large is your sales force?

Taylor: Currently, we have 20 sales people. We intend to add several sales positions in the near future to help with our projected sales growth. Our goal is to increase sales by eight to ten percent per year.

Claire: Is that a realistic goal?

Taylor: I think so. Our sales growth has averaged approximately nine percent over the last several years. I feel confident that a bigger sales force will allow us to easily increase our sales.

Claire: Great, thanks for meeting with us. We'll be in touch if we have any other questions.

♦♦♦

Following the meeting with Taylor, you made your way to Rob Breeden's office. Rob is the company's chief financial officer.

Claire: Rob, thank you for meeting with us this afternoon. We wanted to talk about several issues. Let's start with the company's accounting department. Can you describe the personnel and the general operations of the department?

Rob: Sure, we have a great group of folks in accounting. With the exception of two individuals who left within the last several months we've had very little turnover. We only use full-time employees in the department. Each employee reports directly to me and has very clearly defined responsibilities.

Edward is very concerned about employee training and so everyone is encouraged to maintain their education. In fact, the company reimburses employees for the cost of courses taken at the local university. We've been very pleased at the employee response to the policy. I believe it helps us retain our people.

Claire: Next, can you tell us about the new accounting information system. Can you give us a brief overview of the system and explain why you chose it?

Rob: The system is the result of an intense in-house development process. During my tenure with my former employer we developed a similar system using database technology. Here we based our system on Access. The software is really quite powerful and it allowed us to develop all of the modules that we need to have updated and accurate information.

In addition, the new system will easily accommodate our needs for the foreseeable future. Integration was also important to us as our previous system was not well integrated. With this system, all of our functional areas are linked so that employees have access to the same updated information. The integration has dramatically improved our operations in areas such as purchasing, shipping, and cash management.

Claire: I understand there has been some employee turnover as a consequence of frustrations with the new system.

Rob: We've had a few employees to leave in recent months, but I'm not sure that I would agree with the contention that they left because of frustration with the system. We have made every effort to train our people and to address their concerns, but I recognize that some individuals may still not be happy with changes that I've made.

Claire: You mentioned cash management – I noticed the company generally maintains a healthy cash balance.

Rob: Yes, we've really improved our cash management in the last 12 to 18 months. There are several reasons for the improvement. First, we've instituted a new disbursements policy that allows us to take advantage of any early payment discounts. This policy alone has saved us quite a bit of money. We continually monitor our cash collections and credit granting practices to avoid excessive write-offs. In fact, one of my concerns when I started working with the winery was the company's potential exposure to several large customers. Since my arrival, we've dramatically cut our reliance on certain customers. Finally, our new AIS has enabled us to monitor our cash position more closely than ever before.

Claire: So, I take it that you're comfortable with the reliability of the financial reports that are generated?

Rob: Absolutely. I was less comfortable with the old system because of the lack of integration. In addition, I've encouraged Edward and the Board to be more active in reviewing our monthly financials. My sense is that they were less involved in the financial aspect of the business prior to my arrival because of their relationship with the former CFO.

Claire: Have they become more involved?

Rob: Yes, Edward and I meet regularly to review the financial statements and I make a presentation to the board at every meeting.

Claire: How is the company financed?

Rob: Like many similar companies, the winery is financed through a combination of the owners' personal wealth and debt. The Summerfield family invested in the company many years ago and they have been rewarded handsomely. The company does have a modest amount of long-term debt, but we are reducing that debt as our operations allow. We plan to eliminate most of the outstanding long-term debt within the next three to five years.

Claire: Does the company have ready access to a line of credit?

Rob: Yes. Edward has developed very strong relationships with several local banks. We currently have a line of credit at Bank of Huntington.

Claire: With respect to the company's equity - are there any non-family stockholders?

Rob: No. Although we've discussed plans about a future IPO, Edward and the family have been reluctant to issue shares to anyone outside of the family. Their view is that non-family ownership may complicate operations in an unnecessary way.

Claire: Do you agree with them?

Rob: Yes. I don't see any value in diluting the family's ownership of the company given our current financial position.

Claire: Are there any related party transactions?

Rob: None to speak of really. Edward personally owns some of the equipment that we use in the winery, but there are no other significant transactions. We pay him approximately $9,000 each month.

Claire: Okay, we'll need to get a copy of that lease agreement. Let's move on to compensation matters. Give us an overview of the company's compensation philosophy.

Rob: Edward is a self-made man. He expects employees to work hard and believes the company should pay them well. Given our status as a family-owned business, employees are viewed as more than labor.

Claire: Are there any incentive compensation plans?

Rob: Our salespeople are paid a base salary plus a commission. All other employees receive annual bonuses based on the company's overall performance.

Claire: Does management participate in this annual bonus plan?

Rob: Yes. Everyone has the potential to receive a bonus.

Claire: What is the typical bonus?

Rob: The average bonus is approximately 10 percent of an employee's annual salary, but we've had bonuses as high as 30 percent.

Claire: What basis is used to calculate the bonuses?

Rob: Our bonus plan emphasizes operating efficiency and effectiveness. We consider factors such as employee performance evaluations, production efficiencies and innovations, sales, and profits.

Claire: So, you would say that there is a strong link between performance and compensation.

Rob: Yes, this is not a company that tolerates lazy employees or lackluster performance.

Claire: I'm certain it's not. You have been really helpful this afternoon. Thank you for your time Rob.

◆◆

Your final meeting of the day was with Jacques Dupuis, vice-president of winery operations.

Claire: Good afternoon Jacques. We appreciate your time this afternoon. We have just a few questions for you. How would you characterize the winery's manufacturing facilities?

Jacques: Absolutely. The winery has world-class manufacturing facilities. Edward has built a company that nicely blends the best of traditional winemaking with modern technology. I have no doubt that we have the equipment, experience and capacity to produce world-class wines.

Claire: What is the winery's average current production? Do you have any concerns about meeting production goals?

Jacques: We typically produce 380,000 to 390,000 cases of wine per year. We are close to capacity. I would estimate that we could produce an additional 20,000 to 30,000 cases without sacrificing quality. So long as our goals don't surpass 420,000 cases we have adequate production capacity.

Claire: Are there plans to increase production capacity?

Jacques: I don't believe so.

Claire: Alright. Do you have an adequate work force to manage production needs?

Jacques: Generally we are able to hire as many workers as necessary. However, we have had some difficulties in finding good, solid workers recently. It's as if people just don't want to work hard anymore.

Claire: I understand. You've been very helpful this afternoon. Thank you for your time. We may want to speak with you again if you don't mind.

Jacques: I'm glad to help. Just let me know if you have other questions.

◆◆

You returned to the office following your meeting with Rob to find that Claire had asked one of the firm's assistants to gather information to help in your understanding of the wine industry. The assistant prepared the following summary observations based on her readings of various trade publications.

- The wine industry spent slightly more than $100 million on marketing activities in the U.S. in 20XU.

- U.S. wine consumers are more brand-oriented than consumers in other countries.

- There has been an increase in non-traditional wine marketing including direct mail, offbeat advertising and such Internet sites as Wine.com.

- The U.S. wine market is characterized by a large number of wineries producing a wide variety of products, most with a small market share.

- In the fragmented wine market, the middle tier of medium-sized wine producers is expected to fall prey to merger and acquisition activity over the next few years. Smaller niche producers will need to specialize if they are to survive.

- Supermarkets dominate off-premises sales of wine. Their distribution strategy focuses on improved merchandising, stocking larger bottle sizes and strong price promotions.

- Significant demand for wines during the late 1990s led to rising prices, resulting in faster growth in sales value than in sales volume.

- Wine consumption is directly related to income. High income families are much more likely to consume wine than lower income families.

- Prosperous baby boomers are expected to increase their wine consumption in the future, especially of premium wines.

- The trend towards consolidation is expected to continue as companies search for strategies to benefit from economies of scale in production and distribution.

REQUIREMENTS

Claire Helton, the partner in charge of the Chateau Americana audit engagement, has asked that you complete select audit procedures relevant to understanding the company's business environment. Document your work on the audit schedules that follow the audit program.

The Winery at Chateau Americana
Audit Program for Understanding
    the Business Environment
For the Year Ended December 31, 20XX

Reference: *UB-200*
Prepared by:
Date:
Reviewed by:

Audit Procedures	Initial	Date	A/S Ref.
1. Document your assessment of Chateau Americana on each of the following criteria: a. industry, regulatory and other external factors, b. nature of the entity, c. objectives and strategies, d. measurement and review of the entity's financial performance.			*UB-201*
2. Document your assessment of Chateau Americana's control environment.			*UB-202* *UB-203*
3. Identify and discuss factors affecting Chateau Americana's business risk. For each of the factors, indicate the client's business objective that is put at risk.			*UB-204*
4. Based on your knowledge of Chateau Americana, what accounts are likely to have a lower risk of material misstatement and what accounts are likely to have higher risk of material misstatement? Briefly describe the basis for each account's assessment.			*UB-205*

The Winery at Chateau Americana
Evaluation of the Entity and its Environment

Reference: _UB-201_
Prepared by: _____
Date: _____

For the Year Ended December 31, 20XX

Reviewed by: _____

Industry, regulatory and other external factors:

Nature of the entity:

Objectives and strategies:

Measurement and review of the entity's financial performance:

The Winery at Chateau Americana
Assessment of Control Environment

Reference: _UB-202_
Prepared by: _____
Date: _____

For the Year Ended December 31, 20XX

Reviewed by: _____

Communication and enforcement of integrity and ethical values:

Commitment to competence:

Participation of those charged with governance:

Management's philosophy and operating style:

The Winery at Chateau Americana
Assessment of Control Environment

For the Year Ended December 31, 20XX

Reference: *UB-203*
Prepared by: _____
Date: _____
Reviewed by: _____

Organizational structure:

Assignment of authority and responsibility:

Human resource policies and practices:

Overall Assessment: Summarize your overall assessment of Chateau Americana's control environment by selecting from among the following statements:

_____   The overall control environment is weak.
_____   The overall control environment is moderately weak.
_____   The overall control environment is neither weak nor strong.
_____   The overall control environment is moderately strong.
_____   The overall control environment is strong.

The Winery at Chateau Americana
Business Risks and At-risk Objectives

For the Year Ended December 31, 20XX

Reference: _UB-204_
Prepared by: _____
Date: _____
Reviewed by: _____

Factors affecting business risks:

Business objectives that are put at risk:

The Winery at Chateau Americana
Evaluation of Potential Misstatements

For the Year Ended December 31, 20XX

Reference: _UB-205_
Prepared by: _____
Date: _____
Reviewed by: _____

Accounts likely to have a lower risk of material misstatement:

Accounts like to have a higher risk of material misstatement:

IDENTIFICATION OF AUDIT TESTS FOR THE EXPENDITURE CYCLE (ACQUISITIONS AND CASH DISBURSEMENTS):
The Winery at Chateau Americana

LEARNING OBJECTIVES

After completing and discussing this case, you should be able to:

- Recognize common business documents used with purchases and cash disbursements
- Recognize common control activities used to process purchases and cash disbursements
- Identify control activities that reduce the likelihood of material misstatements and link the activities to management assertions
- Design tests of controls for control activities related to purchases and cash disbursements
- Design substantive tests of transactions to detect material misstatements for non-payroll accounts in the expenditure cycle
- Design analytical tests to detect potential material misstatements for non-payroll accounts in the expenditure cycle
- Design substantive tests of balances to detect material misstatements for accounts payable
- Link tests of controls and substantive tests to management assertions related to purchases, cash payments, and accounts payable
- Identify significant deficiencies and material weaknesses for non-payroll expenditure cycle accounts

INTRODUCTION

Chateau Americana (CA) has an annual production of approximately 385,000 cases of wine. Production of the 385,000 cases of wine requires roughly 3,200 tons of grapes. One-fourth of the needed grapes are harvested from CA's 125-acre vineyard, the remaining grapes are predominantly purchased from California vineyards. Other purchases associated with the production of wine include oak barrels, bottles, cork, neck wrappers, and labels. CA also has non-payroll administrative, marketing, and maintenance expenditures associated with its wine operations. Marketing expenditures such as priority distribution, special promotions, and print advertising have substantially increased in the past year to improve CA's market penetration.

BACKGROUND INFORMATION ABOUT THE AUDIT

CA has the following general ledger accounts related to purchasing and cash disbursement activities:

- Inventory – Production
- Prepaid Expenses
- Accounts Payable
- Accrued Expenses
- Cost of Goods Sold
- Occupancy Expense
- Marketing Expense
- Communications Expense
- Professional Services Expense
- Supplies Expense
- Data Processing Expense
- Travel and Entertainment Expense
- Insurance Expense
- Dues and Subscriptions Expense
- Tax Expense
- Maintenance Expense
- Automobile Expense
- Lease Expense
- Other Operating Expense
- Miscellaneous Expense

In accordance with professional standards, Mikel Frucella, audit manager, reviewed CA's control environment, risk assessment policies, and monitoring system and has assessed them as strong. Julia Granger, staff auditor, reviewed CA's information system and control activities related to purchases and cash disbursements and prepared the enclosed flowcharts (referenced in the top right hand corner as *E-110, E-111,*and *E-112*). Mikel has decided there is no need to document the company's policies nor perform tests of controls for purchase returns and allowances as the number and size of purchase returns and allowances is relatively small.

As the audit senior, you have been assigned responsibility for (1) identifying internal control activities that assure that non-payroll purchase and cash disbursement transactions are properly stated in all material respects, (2) developing tests of controls that test the design and operating effectiveness of identified internal control activities, and (3) identifying substantive tests to detect material misstatements related to non-payroll expenditure cycle accounts. You have conducted some preliminary discussions with client personnel and noted the following

- Purchase returns and allowances transactions are recorded in the purchases journal
- Purchase discounts are recorded in the cash disbursements journal
- Adjustments to expenditure cycle accounts are recorded in the general journal and require preparation of a prenumbered adjustment memo

REQUIREMENTS

Complete steps 5 through 8 in the Expenditure Cycle Planning Audit Program (audit schedule *E-100*) and document your work on audit schedules *E-100, E-120, E-121, E-130, E-140, E-141, E-150, E-151, E-160, E-161, E-170,* and *E-171*. Julia Granger has already completed steps 1 through 4 and has documented the results of her work on audit schedules *E-100, E-110, E-111,* and *E-112*. Assume that the client performs the control activities identified in the flowcharts.

Ingraham / Jenkins

The Winery at Chateau Americana
Expenditure Cycle Planning Audit Program

For the Year Ended: December 31, 20XX

Reference: _E-100_
Prepared by: _JG_
Date: _11/12/XX_
Reviewed by: ___

Audit Procedures	Initial	Date	A/S Ref.
1. Obtain and study a copy of the client's policies and procedures manuals related to purchases and cash disbursements.	JG	11/12/XX	N/A
2. Discuss with and observe client personnel performing control activities related to purchases and cash disbursements.	JG	11/12/XX	N/A
3. Perform a walk-through of the client's polices and procedures related to purchases and cash disbursements.	JG	11/12/XX	N/A
4. Obtain or prepare a flowchart for purchases and cash disbursements showing control activities, document flows, and records.	JG	11/12/XX	E-110 E-111 E-112
5. Document client control activities that reduce the likelihood of material misstatements for management assertions related to purchases and cash disbursements.			E-120 E-121
6. Document potential internal control deficiencies.			E-130
7. Use the planning audit test matrices to list potential tests of controls related to purchases and cash disbursements.			E-140 E-141
8. Use the planning audit test matrices to identify potential			
a. Substantive tests of transactions,			E-150 E-151
b. Analytical tests, and			E-160 E-161
c. Tests of balances related to non-payroll expenditure cycle accounts.			E-170 E-171

Assurance - 34

The Winery at Chateau Americana
Expenditure Cycle - Purchases Flowchart

For the Year Ended December 31, 20XX

Reference: *E-110*
Prepared by: *Client/JG*
Date: *11/12/XX*
Reviewed by: _____

Purchasing

Legend:
NUM - filed numerically by Purchase Order number
A - off-page connector
B - off-page connector
C - off-page connector

The Winery at Chateau Americana
Expenditure Cycle - Purchases Flowchart

For the Year Ended December 31, 20XX

Reference:	*E-111*
Prepared by:	*Client/JG*
Date:	*11/12/XX*
Reviewed by:	

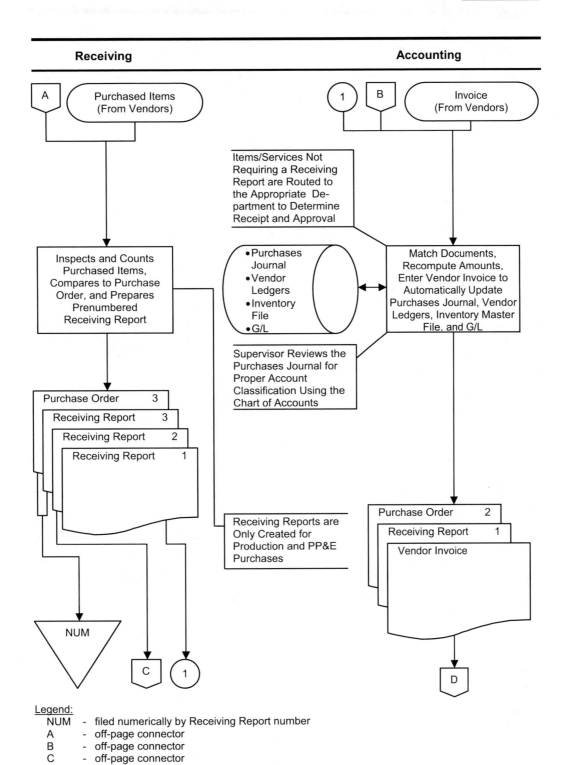

Receiving

Accounting

A — Purchased Items (From Vendors)

1 — B — Invoice (From Vendors)

Items/Services Not Requiring a Receiving Report are Routed to the Appropriate Department to Determine Receipt and Approval

Inspects and Counts Purchased Items, Compares to Purchase Order, and Prepares Prenumbered Receiving Report

- Purchases Journal
- Vendor Ledgers
- Inventory File
- G/L

Match Documents, Recompute Amounts, Enter Vendor Invoice to Automatically Update Purchases Journal, Vendor Ledgers, Inventory Master File, and G/L

Supervisor Reviews the Purchases Journal for Proper Account Classification Using the Chart of Accounts

Purchase Order 3
Receiving Report 3
Receiving Report 2
Receiving Report 1

Receiving Reports are Only Created for Production and PP&E Purchases

Purchase Order 2
Receiving Report 1
Vendor Invoice

NUM

C

1

D

Legend:
NUM - filed numerically by Receiving Report number
A - off-page connector
B - off-page connector
C - off-page connector
D - off-page connector

The Winery at Chateau Americana
Expenditure Cycle - Cash Disbursement Flowchart

For the Year Ended December 31, 20XX

Reference:	*E-112*
Prepared by:	*Client/JG*
Date:	*11/12/XX*
Reviewed by:	

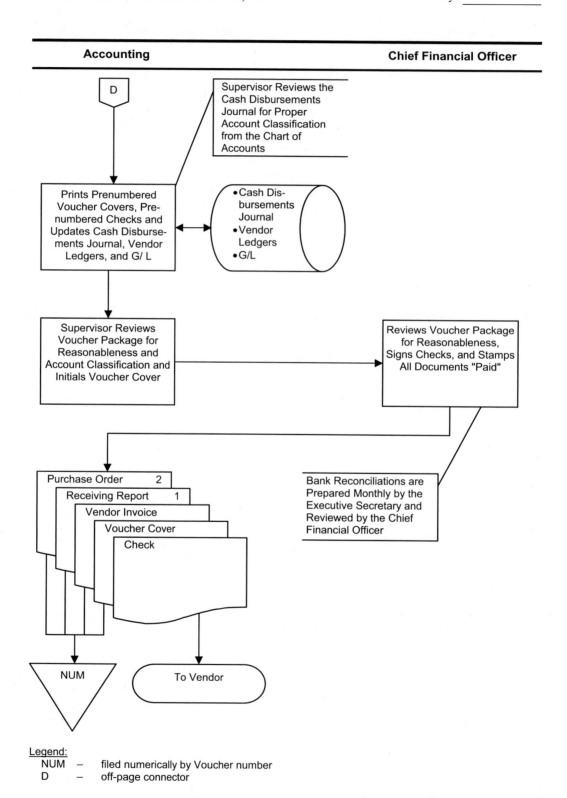

Legend:
NUM – filed numerically by Voucher number
D – off-page connector

The Winery at Chateau Americana
Expenditure Cycle – Purchases Control Activities
   Matrix
For the Year Ended December 31, 20XX

Reference: _E-120_
Prepared by: _____
Date: _____
Reviewed by: _____

Control Activities	Existence	Rights and Obligations	Valuation	Presentation and Disclosure	Completeness
1) Purchasing supervisor reviews and signs all purchase orders.	X	X			
Identify the management assertion(s) each control activity affects with an "X."					

The Winery at Chateau Americana
Expenditure Cycle – Cash Disbursements Control
   Activities Matrix
For the Year Ended December 31, 20XX

Reference: _E-121_
Prepared by: _____
Date: _____
Reviewed by: _____

Control Activities	Existence	Rights and Obligations	Valuation	Presentation and Disclosure	Completeness
Identify the management assertion(s) each control activity affects with an "X."					

The Winery at Chateau Americana
Expenditure Cycle – Internal Control Deficiencies

For the Year Ended December 31, 20XX

Reference: _E-130_
Prepared by:
Date:
Reviewed by:

Internal Control Deficiencies	Client Personnel Discussed With	SD	MW
1) The client does not internally account for all used receiving reports.		Yes	No

Legend:
SD – Significant Deficiency (Yes or No)
MW – Material Weakness (Yes or No)

The Winery at Chateau Americana

Expenditure Cycle - Tests of Controls Planning Matrix

For the Year Ended December 31, 20XX

Reference: *E-140*

Prepared by:

Date:

Reviewed by:

Tests of Controls	Purchases					Cash Disbursements					Accounts Payable				
	Existence	Rights/Obligations	Valuation	Presentation/Disclosure	Completeness	Existence	Rights/Obligations	Valuation	Presentation/Disclosure	Completeness	Existence	Rights/Obligations	Valuation	Presentation/Disclosure	Completeness
TC1) Inquire and observe the purchasing supervisor reviewing and signing purchase orders.	W										W	W			

Indicate whether the test provides Strong (S), Moderate (M), or Weak (W) evidence for the specific management assertion.

The Winery at Chateau Americana
Expenditure Cycle - Tests of Controls Planning Matrix

Reference: *E-141*
Prepared by: _____
Date: _____

For the Year Ended December 31, 20XX

Reviewed by: _____

Tests of Controls	Purchases					Cash Disbursements					Accounts Payable				
	Existence	Rights/Obligations	Valuation	Presentation/Disclosure	Completeness	Existence	Rights/Obligations	Valuation	Presentation/Disclosure	Completeness	Existence	Rights/Obligations	Valuation	Presentation/Disclosure	Completeness

Indicate whether the test provides Strong (S), Moderate (M), or Weak (W) evidence for the specific management assertion.

The Winery at Chateau Americana
Expenditure Cycle - Substantive Tests of Transactions
  Planning Matrix
For the Year Ended December 31, 20XX

Reference: _E-150_
Prepared by: _____
Date: _____
Reviewed by: _____

Substantive Tests of Transactions	Purchases					Cash Disbursements					Accounts Payable				
	Existence	Rights/Obligations	Valuation	Presentation/Disclosure	Completeness	Existence	Rights/Obligations	Valuation	Presentation/Disclosure	Completeness	Existence	Rights/Obligations	Valuation	Presentation/Disclosure	Completeness
TT1) Vouch purchase transactions recorded in the purchases journal to supporting documents.	M		M	M							M		M	M	

Indicate whether the test provides Strong (S), Moderate (M), or Weak (W) evidence for the specific management assertion.

The Winery at Chateau Americana
Expenditure Cycle - Substantive Tests of Transactions
   Planning Matrix
For the Year Ended December 31, 20XX

Reference: *E-151*
Prepared by: _____
Date: _____
Reviewed by: _____

Substantive Tests of Transactions	Purchases					Cash Disbursements					Accounts Payable				
	Existence	Rights/Obligations	Valuation	Presentation/Disclosure	Completeness	Existence	Rights/Obligations	Valuation	Presentation/Disclosure	Completeness	Existence	Rights/Obligations	Valuation	Presentation/Disclosure	Completeness

Indicate whether the test provides Strong (S), Moderate (M), or Weak (W) evidence for the specific management assertion.

The Winery at Chateau Americana
Expenditure Cycle – Analytical Tests Planning Matrix

For the Year Ended December 31, 20XX

Reference: *E-160*
Prepared by:
Date:
Reviewed by:

Analytical Tests	Purchases					Cash Disbursements					Accounts Payable				
	Existence	Rights/Obligations	Valuation	Presentation/Disclosure	Completeness	Existence	Rights/Obligations	Valuation	Presentation/Disclosure	Completeness	Existence	Rights/Obligations	Valuation	Presentation/Disclosure	Completeness
AT1) Scan the year-end vendor ledgers for large, unusual, related party or debit balances and perform follow-up procedures for each one identified.	M		M	M				M	M	M	M	M	M	M	

Indicate whether the test provides Strong (S), Moderate (M), or Weak (W) evidence for the specific management assertion.

The Winery at Chateau Americana
Expenditure Cycle - Analytical Tests Planning Matrix

For the Year Ended December 31, 20XX

Reference: *E-161*
Prepared by:
Date:
Reviewed by:

Analytical Tests	Purchases					Cash Disbursements					Accounts Payable				
	Existence	Rights/Obligations	Valuation	Presentation/Disclosure	Completeness	Existence	Rights/Obligations	Valuation	Presentation/Disclosure	Completeness	Existence	Rights/Obligations	Valuation	Presentation/Disclosure	Completeness

Indicate whether the test provides Strong (S), Moderate (M), or Weak (W) evidence for the specific management assertion.

The Winery at Chateau Americana
Expenditure Cycle - Tests of Balances Planning Matrix

For the Year Ended December 31, 20XX

Reference: *E-170*
Prepared by:
Date:
Reviewed by:

Tests of Balances	Purchases					Cash Disbursements					Accounts Payable				
	Existence	Rights/Obligations	Valuation	Presentation/Disclosure	Completeness	Existence	Rights/Obligations	Valuation	Presentation/Disclosure	Completeness	Existence	Rights/Obligations	Valuation	Presentation/Disclosure	Completeness
TB1) Obtain the last five receiving reports issued before year-end and determine if they were properly included in the purchases journal and year-end vendor ledgers.			W		M								W		M

Indicate whether the test provides Strong (S), Moderate (M), or Weak (W) evidence for the specific management assertion.

The Winery at Chateau Americana
Expenditure Cycle - Tests of Balances Planning Matrix

Reference: *E-171*
Prepared by:
Date:

For the Year Ended December 31, 20XX

Reviewed by:

Tests of Balances	Purchases					Cash Disbursements					Accounts Payable				
	Existence	Rights/Obligations	Valuation	Presentation/Disclosure	Completeness	Existence	Rights/Obligations	Valuation	Presentation/Disclosure	Completeness	Existence	Rights/Obligations	Valuation	Presentation/Disclosure	Completeness

Indicate whether the test provides Strong (S), Moderate (M), or Weak (W) evidence for the specific management assertion.

SELECTION OF AUDIT TESTS AND RISK ASSESSMENT FOR THE EXPENDITURE CYCLE (ACQUISITIONS AND CASH DISBURSEMENTS):
The Winery at Chateau Americana

LEARNING OBJECTIVES

After completing and discussing this case, you should be able to:

- Select appropriate planned tests of controls, substantive tests of transactions, analytical tests, and tests of balances for non-payroll expenditure cycle accounts
- Assess planned control risk for the non-payroll expenditure cycle based on planned tests of controls
- Assess planned detection risk for the non-payroll expenditure cycle based on planned substantive tests

INTRODUCTION

Chateau Americana (CA) has an annual production of approximately 385,000 cases of wine. Production of the 385,000 cases of wine requires roughly 3,200 tons of grapes. One-fourth of the needed grapes are harvested from CA's 125-acre vineyard, the remaining grapes are predominantly purchased from California vineyards. Other purchases associated with the production of wine include oak barrels, bottles, cork, neck wrappers, and labels. CA also has non-payroll administrative, marketing, and maintenance expenditures associated with its wine operations. Marketing expenditures such as priority distribution, special promotions, and print advertising have substantially increased in the past year to improve CA's market penetration.

BACKGROUND INFORMATION ABOUT THE AUDIT

CA has the following general ledger accounts related to purchasing and cash disbursement activities:

- Inventory – Production
- Prepaid Expenses
- Accounts Payable
- Accrued Expenses

- Travel and Entertainment Expense
- Insurance Expense
- Dues and Subscriptions Expense

- Cost of Goods Sold
- Occupancy Expense
- Marketing Expense
- Communications Expense
- Professional Services Expense
- Supplies Expense
- Data Processing Expense

- Tax Expense
- Maintenance Expense
- Automobile Expense
- Lease Expense
- Other Operating Expense
- Miscellaneous Expense

In accordance with professional standards, Mikel Frucella, audit manager, reviewed CA's control environment, risk assessment policies, and monitoring system and has assessed them as strong. Additionally, Mikel determined that tolerable misstatement should be $40,000 for the non-payroll expenditure cycle and that acceptable audit risk should be low. Julia Granger, staff auditor, assessed inherent risk related to purchases, non-payroll cash payments, and accounts payable and prepared the enclosed audit risk matrix (referenced in the top right hand corner as *E-180* and *E-181*). As the audit senior, you have been assigned responsibility for selecting audit procedures to perform for the expenditure cycle that will achieve the desired acceptable audit risk at the lowest possible cost.

REQUIREMENTS

This assignment cannot be completed until the previous CA audit planning assignment is completed. Review the materials in the previous assignment plus the materials in this assignment. Complete audit steps 3 and 4 in the Expenditure Cycle Planning Audit Program – Risk Assessment and Selection of Audit Tests (audit schedule *E-101*) and document your work in audit schedules *E-101, E-140, E-141, E-150, E-151, E-160, E-161, E-170, E-171, E-180, E-182,* and *E-183*. Julia Granger has already completed steps 1 and 2 and has documented the results of her work in audit schedules *E-101, E-180,* and *E-181*.

The Winery at Chateau Americana
Expenditure Cycle Planning Audit Program –
    Risk Assessment and Selection of Audit Tests
Year Ended: December 31, 20XX

Reference: _E-101_
Prepared by: _JG_
Date: _11/13/XX_
Reviewed by: _____

Audit Procedures	Initial	Date	A/S Ref.
1. Complete the acceptable audit risk section of the expenditure cycle "Planning Audit Risk Matrix" by obtaining the acceptable audit risk from the general planning audit schedules.	JG	11/13/XX	E-180
2. Form an initial assessment of inherent risk related to non-payroll expenditure cycle accounts and complete the initial inherent risk assessment section of the "Planning Audit Risk Matrix."	JG	11/13/XX	E-180 E-181
3. Select audit tests to perform by circling the procedure number on the audit tests planning matrices (note: audit tests should be selected such that the combination of inherent risk, control risk, and detection risk for each management assertion related to non-payroll expenditure cycle accounts is reduced to the appropriate level).			E-140 E-141 E-150 E-151 E-160 E-161 E-170 E-171
4. Based on the procedures selected in audit step 3, complete the planned control risk and detection risk sections of the expenditure cycle "Planning Audit Risk Matrix."			E-180 E-182 E-183

The Winery at Chateau Americana
Expenditure Cycle - Planning Audit Risk Matrix
For the Year Ended December 31, 20XX

Reference: _E-180_
Prepared by: _JG_
Date: _11/13/XX_
Reviewed by: _____

Tolerable Misstatement: *$40,000, G6*	Reference	Existence*	Rights /Obligations	Valuation	Presentation/Disclosure	Completeness**
Acceptable Audit Risk	G-10	L	L	L	L	L
Initial Inherent Risk – Purchases	E-181	M		M	M	H
Initial Inherent Risk – Cash Payments		M		M	L	M
Initial Inherent Risk – Accounts Payable		L	M	L	L	H
Planned Control Risk – Purchases	E-182					
Planned Control Risk – Cash Payments						
Planned Control Risk – Accounts Payable						
Planned Detection Risk – Purchases	E-183					
Planned Detection Risk – Cash Payments						
Planned Detection Risk – Accounts Payable						

Planned Inherent Risk should be assessed as:
  High (H) unless the combination of inherent risk factors present justify a lower assessment.
  Moderate (M) if the combination of inherent risk factors present justify this assessment.
  Low (L) if the combination of inherent risk factors present justify this assessment.
Factors justifying a lower inherent risk assessment are:
  High management integrity, Low motivation to materially misstate for external parties,
  Repeat engagement, No material prior year misstatements, No related party transactions,
  Routine transactions, Limited judgement required to correctly record transactions, Low
  susceptibility to defalcation, Stable business environment.

Planned Control Risk should be assessed as:
  Low (L) if control activity(ies) reduces the likelihood of a material misstatement to a
    negligible level and persuasive tests of controls are planned.
  Moderate (M) if control activity(ies) reduces the likelihood of a material misstatement to a
    negligible level and moderately persuasive tests of controls are planned or control
    activity(ies) reduces the likelihood of a material misstatement to a moderate level and
    persuasive tests of controls are planned.
  High (H) if control activity(ies) does not reduce the likelihood of a material misstatement to
    a reasonable level or no tests of controls are planned.

Planned Detection Risk should be assessed as:
  Low (L) if persuasive substantive tests are planned.
  Moderate (M) if moderately persuasive substantive tests are planned.
  High (H) if minimal substantive tests are planned.

Note: * completeness for cash payments, ** existence for cash payments

The Winery at Chateau Americana
Expenditure Cycle - Comments Planned Inherent
   Risk Assessment
For the Year Ended December 31, 20XX

Reference:	*E-181*
Prepared by:	*JG*
Date:	*11/13/XX*
Reviewed by:	

Comments:

The inherent risk assessment for the existence, valuation, and presentation and disclosure assertions for purchases is set at a moderate level even though no misstatements were identified in prior year audit schedules because of the high volume and variable nature of purchased items and this is a first time engagement.

The inherent risk assessment for the completeness assertion for purchases is set at a high level even though no misstatements were identified in prior year audit schedules because of the external incentives for management to understate this account and this is a first time engagement.

The inherent risk assessment for the existence, valuation, and completeness assertion for cash payments is set at a moderate level even though no misstatements were identified in prior year audit schedules because of the high volume of transactions and this is a first time engagement.

The inherent risk assessment for the presentation and disclosure for cash payments is set at a low level as no misstatements were identified in prior year audit schedules and the recording of cash payments is routine and straight forward.

The inherent risk assessment for the existence, valuation, and presentation and disclosure for accounts payable is set at a low level as no misstatements were identified in prior year audit schedules and the recording of accounts payable transactions is routine and straight forward.

The inherent risk assessment for the rights and obligations for accounts payable is set at a moderate level even though no misstatements were identified in prior year audit schedules because of the motivation for employees to purchase items for their own personal use and this is a first time engagement.

The inherent risk assessment for the completeness for accounts payable is set at a high level even though not misstatements were identified in prior year audit schedules due to the external incentive for management to understate this account and this is a first time engagement.

The Winery at Chateau Americana
Expenditure Cycle - Comments Planned Control
  Risk Assessment
For the Year Ended December 31, 20XX

Reference: *E-182*
Prepared by: _____
Date: _____
Reviewed by: _____

Comments:

The Winery at Chateau Americana
Expenditure Cycle - Comments Planned Detection
    Risk Assessment
For the Year Ended December 31, 20XX

Reference: _E-183_
Prepared by: _____
Date: _____
Reviewed by: _____

Comments:

PERFORMANCE OF AUDIT TESTS FOR THE REVENUE CYCLE (SALES AND CASH COLLECTIONS): The Winery At Chateau Americana

LEARNING OBJECTIVES

After completing and discussing this case, you should be able to:

- Recognize common documents and records used with sales and cash collections
- Recognize common control activities used to process sales and cash collection transactions
- Link client control activities, tests of controls, and substantive tests to management assertions for sales, cash collections, and accounts receivable
- Link client control activities, tests of controls, and substantive tests to risk assessments for sales, cash collections, and accounts receivable
- Perform tests of controls and substantive tests for revenue cycle accounts
- Evaluate the results of tests of controls and substantive tests related to revenue cycle accounts using a non-statistical approach

INTRODUCTION

Chateau Americana (CA) produces and sells premium wines targeted to upscale wine drinkers with retail prices ranging from $10 to $35 per bottle of wine. This year CA sold approximately 385,000 cases of wines. The direct sale and distribution of wine to end consumers is generally not permitted by state regulations. Therefore, CA relies on a network of distributors to sell its wines to consumers. CA currently has agreements with distributors to sell its wines in over 20 state jurisdictions. Most agreements are with small to midsize distributors with a few agreements with large distributors. At the moment, CA does not have any sales agreements with large supermarket chains. No distributor accounts for more than five percent of CA's total sales. Last year, CA had net sales of approximately $22 million.

BACKGROUND INFORMATION ABOUT THE AUDIT

CA has the following general ledger accounts related to sales and cash collection activities

- Sales
- Sales Discounts
- Sales Returns and Allowances
- Bad Debt Expense
- Accounts Receivable
- Allowance for Bad Debts

Julia Granger, audit staff, reviewed CA's policies and procedures related to sales and cash collection activities and prepared the enclosed flowcharts (referenced in the top right hand corner as *R-110, R-111, R-112,* and *R-113*) and planned control risk matrix (audit schedule *R-180*). As a result of this process, Julia developed the enclosed audit program (audit schedules *R-101, R-102, R-103, R-104*). The audit program was approved by Mikel Frucella, audit manager, and Claire Helton, audit partner. The two staff auditors assigned to this engagement are Julia Granger and you. Together, you and Julia are responsible for performing the tests of transactions and test of balances outlined in the revenue cycle audit program (audit schedules *R-101, R-102, R-103,* and *R-104*).

Julia Grainger has already selected the audit samples for the tests of transactions and tests of balances and completed audit procedures 2 through 13 and 15 through 17. Her work is documented on various audit schedules provided in this case.

REQUIREMENTS

You have been assigned responsibility for completing audit steps 1a-b, 14a-b, and 18 listed on audit program *R-101, R-103,* and *R-104*. You will want to review the flowcharts on audit schedules *R-110, R-111, R-112,* and *R-113* to become familiar with the accounting documents and records used with sales and cash collections. Assume you have tested 25 of the 30 sample items selected for audit steps 1a-b. Also assume you have tested 15 of the 20 sample items selected for audit steps 14a-b. No deviations or misstatements were observed for these sample items. The accounting documents and records related to the remaining five sample items for audit steps 1a-c and 14a-b are provided behind the audit schedules. The audit firm has a policy of using the same audit sample for planned tests of controls and substantive tests of transactions (dual-purpose tests) whenever possible to maximize audit efficiency. Thus, the results of the test-of-controls aspect of audit steps 1a-c should be documented on audit schedule *R-410*, whereas the substantive test aspect should be documented on audit schedule *R-440*. The results of the test of balances should be documented on audit schedule *R-520*. Adjusting entries should be proposed on schedule *R-210* for any observed misstatements. You should assume that there was no systematic pattern or intent to commit a fraud based on a review and discussion with client personnel concerning observed deviations and misstatements. Finally, you may want to review the audit schedules already completed by Julia Grainger to have an idea of how each audit step is to be documented.

The Winery at Chateau Americana
Revenue Cycle Audit Program

For the Year Ended December 31, 20XX

Reference: *R-101*
Prepared by: *JG*
Date: *2/18/XY*
Reviewed by: _____

Audit Procedures	Initial	Date	A/S Ref.
1. Select a sample of 30 transactions recorded in the sales register throughout the year and perform the following:	JG	2/16/XY	R-310
a. Examine purchase orders, shipping documents, and sales invoices for authenticity and reasonableness.			R-410 R-440
b. Determine if the sales register amounts were correct based on the sales invoice and shipping document.			R-410 R-440
c. Determine if the sales amounts were posted to the correct customer's accounts receivable master file.	JG	2/17/XY	R-410 R-440
2. Reconcile sales recorded in the sales register to sales and accounts receivable recorded in the general ledger for the month of November.	JG	2/17/XY	R-420
3. Scan the monthly sales registers for large, unusual, or related party transactions and perform follow-up procedures for each one identified.	JG	2/17/XY	R-430
4. Select a sample of 30 shipping documents issued throughout the year and perform the following:	JG	2/16/XY	R-311
a. Obtain the related sales invoice and customer purchase order and determine if shipping document was properly accounted for in the sales register.	JG	2/17/XY	R-411 R-440
5. Inquire and observe the office receptionist open mail in the presence of one other CA employee.	JG	2/18/XY	R-400
6. Inquire and observe the office receptionist prepare a cash summary in the presence of one other CA employee.	JG	2/18/XY	R-400

Ingraham / Jenkins

The Winery at Chateau Americana
Revenue Cycle Audit Program

For the Year Ended December 31, 20XX

Reference: _R-102_
Prepared by: _JG_
Date: _2/19/XY_
Reviewed by: _____

Audit Procedures	Initial	Date	A/S Ref.
7. Select a sample of 30 transactions recorded in the cash receipts journal throughout the year and perform the following:	JG	2/16/XY	R-312
a. Examine validated bank deposit slip and cash receipt summary for authenticity and reasonableness.	JG	2/18/XY	R-412 R-441
b. Determine if the cash receipts journal amounts were correct based on the validated deposit slip and cash receipt summary.	JG	2/18/XY	R-412 R-441
c. Determine if the cash collection amounts were posted to the correct customer's accounts receivable master file.	JG	2/18/XY	R-412 R-441
8. Reconcile cash receipts recorded in the cash receipts journal to cash and accounts receivable recorded in the general ledger for the month of March.	JG	2/18/XY	R-421
9. Scan the monthly cash receipts journal for large, unusual, or related party transactions and perform follow-up procedures for each one identified.	JG	2/18/XY	R-431
10. Select a sample of 30 cash summaries prepared throughout the year and perform the following:	JG	2/16/XY	R-313
a. Obtain the related validated deposit slip and determine if cash collection was properly accounted for in the cash receipts journal.	JG	2/19/XY	R-413 R-441
11. Scan the general journal for the write-off of specific customer accounts and examine credit memo and other supporting documents for customer write-offs greater than $1,000.	JG	2/19/XY	R-432
12. Obtain a lead schedule for revenue cycle accounts and perform the following:	JG	2/16/XY	R-200
a. Agree the prior year balances to prior year audit schedules.	JG	2/16/XY	R-200
b. Agree current year balances to the general ledger.	JG	2/16/XY	R-200

The Winery at Chateau Americana
Revenue Cycle Audit Program

For the Year Ended December 31, 20XX

Reference: *R-103*
Prepared by: *JG*
Date: *2/20/XY*
Reviewed by: _____

Audit Procedures	Initial	Date	A/S Ref.
13. Obtain an aged trial balance printout of year-end customer accounts receivable balances and perform the following:	*JG*	*1/02/XY*	*N/A*
a. Foot the year-end aged trial balance and agree amount to the general ledger and lead schedule.	*JG*	*2/16/XY*	*R-200*
b. Scan the year-end aged trial balance for unusual, related party or credit balances and perform follow-up procedures for each one identified.	*JG*	*2/19/XY*	*R-511*
c. Test the aging of the aged accounts receivable trial balance by examining supporting sales documents for five customers.	*JG*	*2/20/XY*	*R-500*
d. Inquire of the office manager concerning large old outstanding receivable balances.	*JG*	*2/20/XY*	*R-501*
e. Obtain the last 5 bill of ladings issued before year-end and determine if they were properly included in the year-end customer ledgers and aged trial balance printout.	*JG*	*2/20/XY*	*R-502*
f. Obtain the first 5 bill of ladings issued after year-end and determine if they were properly excluded from the year-end customer ledgers and aged trial balance printout.	*JG*	*2/20/XY*	*R-502*
14. Select a sample of the 20 largest customer balances from the aged trial balance and perform the following:	*JG*	*1/02/XY*	*R-314*
a. Confirm the balances directly with the customers using positive confirmations.			*R-520*
b. Examine documentation supporting subsequent cash collections for positive confirmations not returned.		*N/A*	*R-520*
15. Perform the following analytical procedures:			
a. Compare accounts receivable turnover to prior year results.	*JG*	*2/20/XY*	*R-510*
b. Compare the percent aging of accounts receivable to prior year results.	*JG*	*2/20/XY*	*R-510*
b. Compare the allowance for bad debts as a percent of accounts receivable to prior year results.	*JG*	*2/20/XY*	*R-510*

The Winery at Chateau Americana
Revenue Cycle Audit Program

Reference:	R-104
Prepared by:	JG
Date:	3/05/XY
Reviewed by:	

For the Year Ended December 31, 20XX

Audit Procedures	Initial	Date	A/S Ref.
16. Review board of directors' meeting minutes for indication of the factoring or pledging of accounts receivable.	JG	3/05/XY	R-503
17. Inquire of management concerning the:			
a) Factoring or pledging of receivables.	JG	3/05/XY	R-503
b) Existence of related party and/or noncurrent receivables.	JG	3/05/XY	R-503
18. Conclude as to the fair presentation of revenue cycle accounts in all material respects.			R-200

The Winery at Chateau Americana
Revenue Cycle - Sales Flowchart

For the Year Ended December 31, 20XX

Reference:	*R-110*
Prepared by:	*JG*
Date:	*11/14/XX*
Reviewed by:	

Sales Department

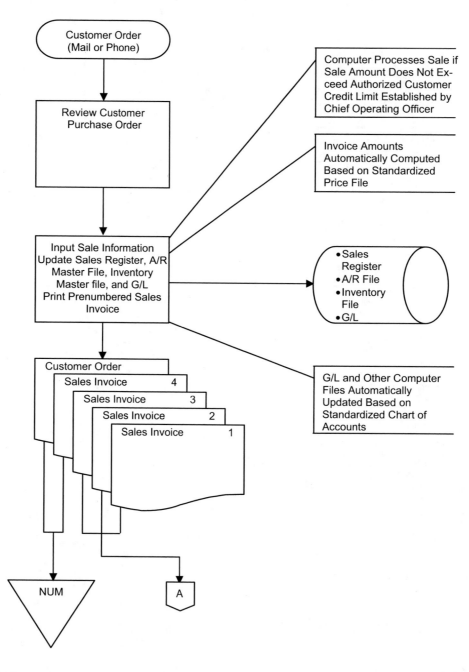

Customer Order (Mail or Phone)

Review Customer Purchase Order

Computer Processes Sale if Sale Amount Does Not Exceed Authorized Customer Credit Limit Established by Chief Operating Officer

Invoice Amounts Automatically Computed Based on Standardized Price File

Input Sale Information Update Sales Register, A/R Master File, Inventory Master file, and G/L Print Prenumbered Sales Invoice

- Sales Register
- A/R File
- Inventory File
- G/L

G/L and Other Computer Files Automatically Updated Based on Standardized Chart of Accounts

Customer Order
Sales Invoice 4
Sales Invoice 3
Sales Invoice 2
Sales Invoice 1

NUM

A

Legend:
NUM - filed numerically by Sales Invoice number
A - off-page connector

Assurance - 63

Ingraham / Jenkins

The Winery at Chateau Americana
Revenue Cycle - Sales Flowchart

For the Year Ended December 31, 20XX

Reference: _R-111_
Prepared by: _JG_
Date: _11/14/XX_
Reviewed by: _____

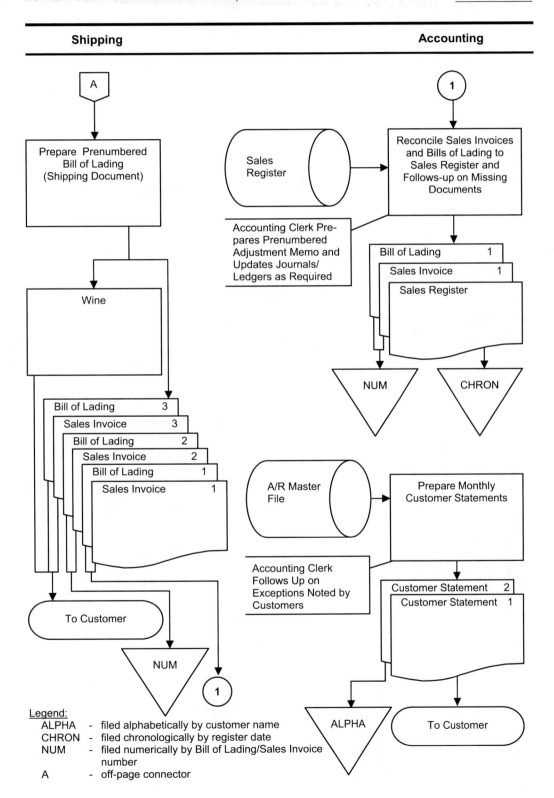

Shipping	Accounting

Legend:
ALPHA - filed alphabetically by customer name
CHRON - filed chronologically by register date
NUM - filed numerically by Bill of Lading/Sales Invoice number
A - off-page connector

Assurance - 64

The Winery at Chateau Americana
Revenue Cycle - Cash Receipts Flowchart

For the Year Ended December 31, 20XX

Reference:	*R-112*
Prepared by:	*JG*
Date:	*11/14/XX*
Reviewed by:	

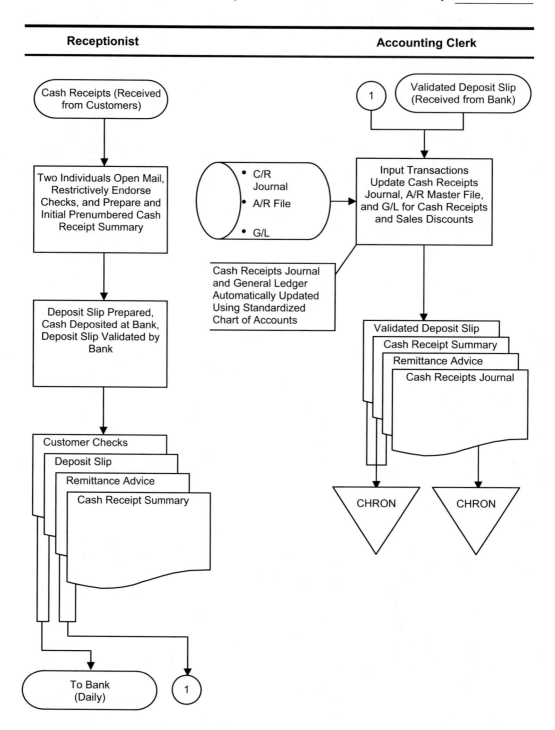

Legend:
  CHRON - filed chronologically by summary/journal date.

Ingraham / Jenkins

The Winery at Chateau Americana
Revenue Cycle - Cash Receipts Flowchart

Reference: _R-113_
Prepared by: _JG_
Date: _11/14/XX_
Reviewed by: _____

For the Year Ended December 31, 20XX

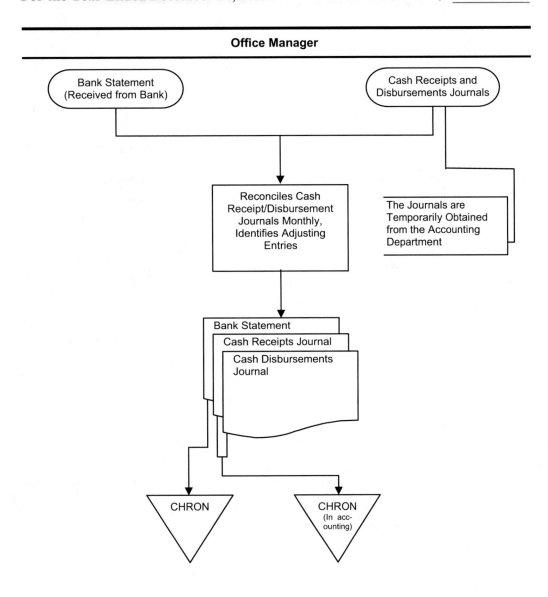

Office Manager

Bank Statement (Received from Bank)

Cash Receipts and Disbursements Journals

Reconciles Cash Receipt/Disbursement Journals Monthly, Identifies Adjusting Entries

The Journals are Temporarily Obtained from the Accounting Department

Bank Statement

Cash Receipts Journal

Cash Disbursements Journal

CHRON

CHRON (In accounting)

Legend:
CHRON - filed chronologically by statement/journal date.

Assurance - 66

The Winery at Chateau Americana
Revenue Cycle - Planned Audit Risk Matrix

Reference: _R-180_
Prepared by: _JG_
Date: _11/14/XX_

Year Ended December 31, 20XX

Reviewed by: _____

Tolerable Misstatement: $40,000, G6	Reference	Existence*	Rights /Obligations	Valuation	Presentation/Disclosure	Completeness**
Acceptable Audit Risk	G5	L	L	L	L	L
Initial Inherent Risk – Sales		M		M	L	H
Initial Inherent Risk – Cash Collections		H		H	L	H
Initial Inherent Risk – Accounts Receivables		M	L	M	L	L
Planned Control Risk – Sales		M		M	H	M
Planned Control Risk – Cash Collections		M		M	H	M
Planned Detection Risk – Sales		M		M	M	M
Planned Detection Risk – Cash Collections		M		M	M	M
Planned Detection Risk – Accounts Receivable		M	M	M	M	M

Planned Inherent Risk should be assessed as:
  High (H) unless the combination of inherent risk factors present justify a lower assessment.
  Medium (M) if the combination of inherent risk factors present justify this assessment.
  Low (L) if the combination of inherent risk factors present justify this assessment.
Factors justifying a lower inherent risk assessment are:
  High management integrity, Low motivation to materially misstate for external parties,
  Repeat engagement, No material prior year misstatements, No related party transactions,
  Routine transactions, Limited judgement required to correctly record transactions, Low
  susceptibility to defalcation, Stable business environment.

Planned Control Risk should be assessed as:
  Low (L) if control activity(ies) reduces the likelihood of a material misstatement to a
    negligible level and persuasive tests of controls are planned.
  Medium (M) if control activity(ies) reduces the likelihood of a material misstatement to a
    negligible level and moderately persuasive tests of controls are planned or control
    activity(ies) reduces the likelihood of a material misstatement to a moderate level and
    persuasive tests of controls are planned.
  High (H) if control activity(ies) does not reduce the likelihood of a material misstatement to
    a reasonable level or no tests of controls are planned.

Planned Detection Risk should be assessed as:
  Low (L) if persuasive substantive tests are planned.
  Medium (M) if moderately persuasive substantive tests are planned.
  High (H) if minimal substantive tests are planned.

Note: * completeness for cash collections, ** existence for cash collections

	Audited Balance 12/31/XW	**Unaudited Balance 12/31/XX**			**Adjusted Balance 12/31/XX**

The Winery at Chateau Americana
Revenue Cycle - Lead Schedule

Reference: *R-200*
Prepared by: *JG*
Date: *2/16/XY*

For the Year Ended December 31, 20XX

Reviewed by: _____

Account	Audited Balance 12/31/XW	Unaudited Balance 12/31/XX	Adjustments Debit	Credit	Adjusted Balance 12/31/XX
Accounts Receivable	$ 4,913,697 √	$ 5,347,094 *f, GL*			
Allowance for Bad Debts	$97,460 √	$106,375 *GL*			
Net Sales	$ 20,189,194 √	$ 21,945,422 *GL*			
Bad Debt Expense	$9,957 √	$10,974 *GL*			

Conclusion: _____

Tickmark Legend

√ - *Agreed to prior year audit schedules without exception (audit step 12a).*

GL - *Agreed to 12/31/20XX general ledger without exception (audit step 12b).*

f - *Agreed to the footed balance of the 12/31/20XX accounts receivable customer ledgers and 12/31/20XX aged accounts receivable trial balance without exception (audit step 13a).*

The Winery at Chateau Americana
Revenue Cycle - Proposed Adjusting Entry Schedule

For the Year Ended December 31, 20XX

Reference: _R-210_
Prepared by: _JG_
Date: _2/20/XY_
Reviewed by: _____

Account	Debit	Credit
dr. Bad debt expense	$13,488	
cr. Accounts receivable		$13,488
Explanation: To eliminate the uncollectible receivable balance of $13,488 from accounts receivable while still maintaining an allowance for bad debts balance of 2% of A/R (see R-501).		
Explanation:		
Explanation:		
Explanation:		

The Winery at Chateau Americana
Tests of Transactions Sample Plan -
Revenue Cycle Sales Transactions
For the Year Ended December 31, 20XX

Reference: *R-310*
Prepared by: *JG*
Date: *2/16/XY*
Reviewed by: _____

Sampling Frame	Beg. Doc. # or Page #	End. Doc. # or Page #	Sample Size
Lines recorded in the sales register during the year	*Page 1 (Line 1)*	*Page 166 (Line 1,992)*	*30*

Sample Selection Method:

The sample was selected by using the "=randbetween(1,1992)" Microsoft Excel spreadsheet function. Line numbers drawn twice were discarded and a new line number was selected using the Excel "randbetween" function.

Sample: *Line number starting with line 1 on page 1 to line 1,992 on page 166*

Sample Item	Sample Ref.	Sample Item	Sample Ref.	Sample Item	Sample Ref.	Sample Item	Sample Ref.
1	*4*	*16*	*904*				
2	*43*	*17*	*908*				
3	*111*	*18*	*945*				
4	*148*	*19*	*960*				
5	*154*	*20*	*1077*				
6	*276*	*21*	*1241*				
7	*311*	*22*	*1284*				
8	*348*	*23*	*1381*				
9	*435*	*24*	*1561*				
10	*444*	*25*	*1633*				
11	*459*	*26*	*1756*				
12	*560*	*27*	*1757*				
13	*657*	*28*	*1821*				
14	*716*	*29*	*1906*				
15	*767*	*30*	*1985*				

The Winery at Chateau Americana
Tests of Transactions Sample Plan –
Revenue Cycle Sales Transactions
For the Year Ended December 31, 20XX

Reference:	*R-311*
Prepared by:	*JG*
Date:	*2/16/XY*
Reviewed by:	

Sampling Frame	Beg. Doc. # or Page #	End. Doc. # or Page #	Sample Size
Bill of ladings (shipping documents) issued during the year	*134617*	*136608*	*30*

Sample selection method:

The sample items were selected by using the "=randbetween (134617,136608)" Microsoft Excel spreadsheet function. Bill of ladings drawn twice were discarded and a new random number was selected using the Excel "randbetween" function.

Sample: *Bill of Lading Number*

Sample Item	Sample Ref.	Sample Item	Sample Ref.	Sample Item	Sample Ref.	Sample Item	Sample Ref.
1	*134628*	*16*	*135449*				
2	*134657*	*17*	*135467*				
3	*134687*	*18*	*135675*				
4	*134711*	*19*	*135785*				
5	*134776*	*20*	*135980*				
6	*134846*	*21*	*136245*				
7	*134942*	*22*	*136260*				
8	*134949*	*23*	*136266*				
9	*134950*	*24*	*136356*				
10	*135111*	*25*	*136378*				
11	*135114*	*26*	*136421*				
12	*135251*	*27*	*136425*				
13	*135329*	*28*	*136528*				
14	*135358*	*29*	*136637*				
15	*135382*	*30*	*136728*				

The Winery at Chateau Americana
Tests of Transactions Sample Plan –
Revenue Cycle Cash Receipts
For the Year Ended December 31, 20XX

Reference: _R-312_
Prepared by: _JG_
Date: _2/16/XY_
Reviewed by: _____

Sampling Frame	Beg. Doc. # or Page #	End. Doc. # or Page #	Sample Size
Lines recorded in the cash receipt journal during the year	*Page 1 (Line 1)*	*Page 178 (Line 2,133)*	*30*

Sample Selection Method:

The sample was selected by using the "=randbetween(1,2133)" Microsoft Excel spreadsheet function. Line numbers drawn twice were discarded and a new line number was selected using the Excel "randbetween" function.

Sample: *Line number starting with line 1 on page 1 to line 2,133 on page 178*

Sample Item	Sample Ref.	Sample Item	Sample Ref.	Sample Item	Sample Ref.	Sample Item	Sample Ref.
1	69	16	1152				
2	86	17	1157				
3	98	18	1226				
4	364	19	1351				
5	387	20	1387				
6	526	21	1424				
7	563	22	1435				
8	622	23	1458				
9	827	24	1466				
10	831	25	1545				
11	859	26	1679				
12	900	27	1755				
13	985	28	1758				
14	1000	29	1920				
15	1048	30	2091				

The Winery at Chateau Americana
Nonstatistical Tests of Transactions Sample Plan –
    Revenue Cycle Cash Receipt Transactions
For the Year Ended December 31, 20XX

Reference:	R-313
Prepared by:	JG
Date:	2/16/XY
Reviewed by:	

Sampling Frame	Beg. Doc. # or Page #	End. Doc. # or Page #	Sample Size
Cash receipt summaries prepared during the year	*5468*	*5719*	*30*

Sample selection method:

The sample items were selected by using the "=randbetween(5468,6179)" Microsoft Excel spreadsheet function. Cash summary sheets drawn twice were discarded and a new random number was selected using the Excel "randbetween" function.

Sample: *Cash Receipt Summary Sheet Number*

Sample Item	Sample Ref.	Sample Item	Sample Ref.	Sample Item	Sample Ref.	Sample Item	Sample Ref.
1	5473	16	5593				
2	5483	17	5616				
3	5484	18	5618				
4	5487	19	5619				
5	5494	20	5624				
6	5515	21	5646				
7	5519	22	5653				
8	5520	23	5663				
9	5525	24	5666				
10	5534	25	5671				
11	5535	26	5675				
12	5538	27	5692				
13	5552	28	5695				
14	5558	29	5712				
15	5569	30	5714				

The Winery at Chateau Americana
Nonstatistical Tests of Transactions Sample Plan –
Revenue Cycle Sales Transactions
For the Year Ended December 31, 20XX

Reference: _R-314_
Prepared by: _JG_
Date: _1/02/XY_
Reviewed by: _____

Sampling Frame	Beg. Doc. # or Page #	End. Doc. # or Page #	Sample Size
Lines recorded on the aged accounts receivable trial balance	_Page 1 (Line 1)_	_Page 2 (Line 81)_	_20_

Sample Selection Method:

The sample was selected by taking the 20 customers with the largest outstanding balances at year-end.

Sample: Customer _line number starting with line 1 on page 1 to line 81 on page 2_

Sample Item	Sample Ref.	Sample Item	Sample Ref.	Sample Item	Sample Ref.	Sample Item	Sample Ref.
_1_	_0501_	_16_	_3502_				
_2_	_0502_	_17_	_3801_				
_3_	_0504_	_18_	_3803_				
_4_	_0701_	_19_	_4301_				
_5_	_0901_	_20_	_4601_				
_6_	_0902_						
_7_	_1001_						
_8_	_1301_						
_9_	_2001_						
_10_	_2101_						
_11_	_2201_						
_12_	_3001_						
_13_	_3201_						
_14_	_3302_						
_15_	_3501_						

The Winery at Chateau Americana
Tests of Transactions -
    Revenue Cycle Cash Receipt Transactions
For the Year Ended December 31, 20XX

Reference:	*R-400*
Prepared by:	*JG*
Date:	*2/18/XY*
Reviewed by:	

Procedure:

Observations and inquires were made of the office receptionist regarding the handling of cash receipt mail and preparation of cash summary sheets. Consistent with established company policy, cash receipt envelopes are always opened by the office receptionist in the presence of one other company employee and the cash receipt is immediately recorded on a cash summary sheet.

Exceptions/Misstatements Identified:

No exceptions or misstatements were noted as a result of performing audit

procedures 5 and 6.

Follow-up procedures performed:

No follow-up procedures are necessary.

Ingraham / Jenkins

The Winery at Chateau Americana
Nonstatistical Tests of Controls Evaluation –
Revenue Cycle Sales Transactions
For the Year Ended December 31, 20XX

Reference: _R-410_
Prepared by: _JG_
Date: _2/17/XY_
Reviewed by: _____

Sampling Frame: *Lines recorded in the sales register during the year*

Attribute	RCL	Sample Size	SDR	TDR	ASR
Purchase order, shipping document, and sales invoice look authentic and reasonable.	M	30		5%	
Sales register amount is correct based on sales invoice and shipping document.	M	30		5%	
Sales invoice is posted to correct customer's accounts receivable master file.	M	30	0%	5%	5%

Conclusion:

Legend:
ASR - Allowance for Sampling Risk (TDR-SDR)
RCL - Risk of Assessing Control Risk Too Low (L – Low or M – Moderate)
SDR - Sample Deviation Rate
TDR - Tolerable Deviation Rate

The Winery at Chateau Americana
Nonstatistical Tests of Controls Evaluation –
**   Revenue Cycle Sales Transactions**
For the Year Ended December 31, 20XX

Reference: _R-411_
Prepared by: _JG_
Date: _2/17/XY_
Reviewed by: _____

Sampling Frame: *Bill of ladings (shipping documents) issued during the year*

Attribute	RCL	Sample Size	SDR	TDR	ASR
Bill of lading is properly accounted for in sales register.	*M*	*30*	*0%*	*5%*	*5%*

Conclusion:

The results of audit procedure 4a support a reduced control risk assessment for the completeness and valuation of sales as no deviations from company policy were noted. Therefore, no changes to the planned audit program are required.

Legend:
ASR - Allowance for Sampling Risk (TDR-SDR)
RCL - Risk of Assessing Control Risk Too Low (L – Low or M – Moderate)
SDR - Sample Deviation Rate
TDR - Tolerable Deviation Rate

The Winery at Chateau Americana
Nonstatistical Tests of Controls Evaluation –
Revenue Cycle Cash Receipts
For the Year Ended December 31, 20XX

Reference: _R-412_
Prepared by: _JG_
Date: _2/18/XY_
Reviewed by: _____

Sampling Frame: *Lines recorded in the cash receipt journal during the year*

Attribute	RCL	Sample Size	SDR	TDR	ASR
Validated bank deposit slip and cash summary sheet look authentic and reasonable.	*M*	*30*	*0%*	*5%*	*5%*
Cash receipt journal amount is correct based on deposit slip and cash summary sheet.	*M*	*30*	*0%*	*5%*	*5%*
Cash collection amount is posted to correct customers accounts receivable master file.	*M*	*30*	*0%*	*5%*	*5%*

Conclusion:

The results of audit procedures 7a, b, and c support a reduced control risk assessment for the existence and valuation of cash receipts as no deviations from company policy were noted. Therefore, no changes to the planned audit program are required.

Legend:
ASR - Allowance for Sampling Risk (TDR-SDR)
RCL - Risk of Assessing Control Risk Too Low (L – Low or M – Moderate)
SDR - Sample Deviation Rate
TDR - Tolerable Deviation Rate

The Winery at Chateau Americana
Nonstatistical Tests of Controls Evaluation –
Revenue Cycle Cash Receipts
For the Year Ended December 31, 20XX

Reference: _R-413_
Prepared by: _JG_
Date: _2/19/XY_
Reviewed by: _____

Sampling Frame: Cash summary sheets prepared _during the year_

Attribute	RCL	Sample Size	SDR	TDR	ASR
Cash summary sheet is properly accounted for in cash receipt journal.	M	30	0%	5%	5%

Follow-up procedures performed:

The results of audit procedure 10a support a reduced control risk assessment for the completeness and valuation of cash receipts as no deviations from company policy were noted. Therefore, no changes to the planned audit program are required.

Legend:
ASR - Allowance for Sampling Risk (TDR-SDR)
RCL - Risk of Assessing Control Risk Too Low (L – Low or M – Moderate)
SDR - Sample Deviation Rate
TDR - Tolerable Deviation Rate

The Winery at Chateau Americana
Tests of Transactions –
    Revenue Cycle Sales Transactions
For the Year Ended December 31, 20XX

Reference:	*R-420*
Prepared by:	*JG*
Date:	*2/17/XY*
Reviewed by:	

Procedure:
Sales recorded in the sales register were reconciled to sales and accounts receivable recorded in the general ledger for the month of November.

Exceptions/Misstatements Identified:
No exceptions or misstatements were noted as a result of performing audit
procedure 2.

Follow-up procedures performed:
No follow-up procedures are necessary.

The Winery at Chateau Americana	Reference:	*R-421*
Tests of Transactions –	Prepared by:	*JG*
Revenue Cycle Cash Receipt Transactions	Date:	*2/18/XY*
For the Year Ended December 31, 20XX	Reviewed by:	

Procedure:

Cash receipts recorded in the cash receipts journal were reconciled to cash and accounts receivable recorded in the general ledger for the month of March.

Exceptions/Misstatements Identified:

No exceptions or misstatements were noted as a result of performing audit procedure 8.

Follow-up procedures performed:

No follow-up procedures are necessary.

The Winery at Chateau Americana
Unusual Transactions - Revenue Cycle
   Sales Register
For the Year Ended December 31, 20XX

Reference: _R-430_
Prepared by: _JG_
Date: _2/17/XY_
Reviewed by: _____

Date	Account Description or Customer of Unusual Transactions Identified	Ref.	Account IDs	Amount
	No unusual transactions identified.			

Follow-up procedures performed:

No follow-up procedures are necessary.

The Winery at Chateau Americana
Unusual Transactions - Revenue Cycle
Cash Receipts Journal
For the Year Ended December 31, 20XX

Reference: *R-431*
Prepared by: *JG*
Date: *2/18/XY*
Reviewed by: _____

Date	Account Description or Payer of Unusual Transactions Identified	Ref.	Account IDs	Amount
	No unusual transactions identified.			

Conclusion/Follow-up procedures performed:

No follow-up procedures are necessary.

The Winery at Chateau Americana
Unusual Transactions - Revenue Cycle
   General Journal - Customer Write-offs
For the Year Ended December 31, 20XX

Reference: _R-432_
Prepared by: _JG_
Date: _2/19/XY_
Reviewed by: _____

Date	Account Description or Customer of Unusual Transactions Identified	Ref.	Account IDs	Amount
	No unusual transactions identified.			

Follow-up procedures performed:

No follow-up procedures are necessary.

The Winery at Chateau Americana
Nonstatistical Substantive Tests Evaluation –
Revenue Cycle Sales Transactions
For the Year Ended December 31, 20XX

Reference: _R-440_
Prepared by: _____
Date: _____
Reviewed by: _____

Misstatements:	Recorded Amount	Audited Amount	Misstatement Amount
Total sample misstatement			
Projected misstatement:			
Total sample misstatement			
Dollar value of sample		÷	_$727,107_
Percentage sample dollar misstatement		=	
Dollar value of population per register		×	_$21,945,490_
Projected population dollar misstatement		=	
Allowance for sampling risk			
Tolerable misstatement			_$40,000_
Projected population dollar misstatement		–	
Recorded adjustments		+	
Allowance for sampling risk		=	
Conclusions:			

The Winery at Chateau Americana
Nonstatistical Substantive Tests Evaluation –
Revenue Cycle Cash Receipts Transactions
For the Year Ended December 31, 20XX

Reference:	*R-441*	
Prepared by:	*JG*	
Date:	*2/19/XY*	
Reviewed by:		

Misstatements:	Recorded Amount	Audited Amount	Misstatement Amount
No missatements were identified as a result of performing audit procedures 7a-c and 10.			
Total sample misstatement			*$0*
Projected misstatement:			
Total sample misstatement			*$0*
Dollar value of sample		÷	*$ 662,470*
Percentage sample dollar misstatement		=	*$0*
Dollar value of population per journal		×	*$25,233,126*
Projected population dollar misstatement		=	*$0*
Allowance for sampling risk			
Tolerable misstatement			*$40,000*
Projected population dollar misstatement		–	*$0*
Recorded adjustments		+	*$0*
Allowance for sampling risk		=	*$40,000*

Conclusions:

The results of audit procedures 7a-c and 10 support the completeness, existence, valution, and presentation and disclosure of cash receipts in all material respects. Therefore, no changes to the planned audit program are required.

The Winery at Chateau Americana
Tests of Balances – Revenue Cycle
   Accounts Receivable
For the Year Ended December 31, 20XX

Reference:	*R-500*
Prepared by:	*JG*
Date:	*2/20/XY*
Reviewed by:	

Procedure:

The proper aging of the aged accounts receivable trial balance was verified by examining the supporting sales invoices for the following five customers: Blue Ridge Beverage Company, Johnson Brothers Company, Premier Wine and Spirits, Southern Wine and Spirits, Young's Market Company.

Exceptions/Misstatements Identified:

No exceptions or misstatements were noted as a result of performing audit procedure 13c.

Follow-up procedures performed:

No follow-up procedures are necessary.

The Winery at Chateau Americana
Inquires – Revenue Cycle
    Accounts Receivable
For the Year Ended December 31, 20XX

Reference: *R-501*
Prepared by: *JG*
Date: *2/20/XY*
Reviewed by: _____

Inquires of:	*Office Manager*
Question:	**Response:**
The collectibility of the Fine Wine and Spirits, Inc. receivable balance of $13,488 was discussed with the office manager as it was over a year old.	*Per the office manager, CA has stopped selling to Fine Wine and Spirits because of the lack of payment and has referred the balance to a collection agency. The office manager does not believe the company will collect on this balance.*
The collectibility of the Desert Beverage Company receivable balance of $6,221 was discussed with the office manager as it was almost a year old.	*Per the office manager, CA had negotiated at year-end a payment plan of $1,037 over the next six months starting in January. A review of the January and February 20XY cash receipts reveals that two payments totaling $2,074 were received From Desert Beverage Co. This balance appears collectible.*

Follow-up procedures performed:

No other receivable balances listed on the aged trial balance were identified as unusually large and old. Therefore, no change to the planned audit program is necessary. Based on the discussions with the office manager and analytic procedures performed related to the collection of receivables (see R-510). The following adjusting entry is proposed (see R-210):

    dr. Bad debt expense $13,488
      cr. Accounts receivable $13,488

This entry will eliminate the uncollectible receivable balance of $13,488 from accounts receivable account while still maintaining an allowance for bad debts balance at 2% of accounts receivable.

The Winery at Chateau Americana
Tests of Balances – Revenue Cycle
    Accounts Receivable
For the Year Ended December 31, 20XX

Reference: _R-502_
Prepared by: _JG_
Date: _2/20/XY_
Reviewed by: _____

Procedure:

The last bill of lading issued before December 31, 20XX was 136608. The sales invoices and purchase orders supporting the last five bill of ladings issued before year-end and first five bill of ladings issued after year-end were examined and traced to proper inclusion/exclusion in/from the December 31, 20XX accounts receivable customer ledgers.

Exceptions/Misstatements Identified:

No exceptions or misstatements were noted as a result of performing audit

procedures 13e and f.

Follow-up procedures performed:

No follow-up procedures are necessary.

The Winery at Chateau Americana
Tests of Balances – Revenue Cycle
    Accounts Receivable
For the Year Ended December 31, 20XX

Reference:	*R-503*
Prepared by:	*JG*
Date:	*3/1/XY*
Reviewed by:	

Procedure:

The board of directors' meeting minutes issued from 1/1/20XX through 3/1/20XY were reviewed for indication of the factoring or pledging of accounts receivable. Additionally, inquiries were made of the chief financial officer concerning the factoring or pledging of receivables and/or the existence of related party/noncurrent receivables.

Exceptions/Misstatements Identified:

No exceptions or misstatements were noted as a result of performing audit

procedures 16, 17a, and 17b.

Follow-up procedures performed:

No follow-up procedures are necessary.

The Winery at Chateau Americana
Ratio Analysis - Revenue Cycle

For the Year Ended December 31, 20XX

Reference:	R-510
Prepared by:	JG
Date:	2/20/XY
Reviewed by:	

Ratio Description	20XX Ratio Amount	20XW Ratio Amount	Conclusion/Follow-up Procedures Performed
Accounts Receivable Turnover	4.36	4.74	Per the office manager the turnover and aging of receivables has worsened slightly as the company started offering more favorable credit terms to select customers to encourage higher sales volume. The office manager believes that the allowance for bad debts of $200,000 is sufficient to cover any uncollectible balances.

Percent of Receivables:
    0 to 60 days old
    61 to 120 days old
    121 to 180 days old
    greater than 181 days old
	42.6%
	34.9%
	15.9%
	6.6%
		46.8%
		34.2%
		14.3%
		4.7%	

Allowance for Bad Debts as Percent of Accounts Receivable	2.0%	2.0%	Based on the review of the A/R aged trial balance (see R-501), past history, and current economic conditions the allowance percent of 2% of A/R is reasonable.

Ingraham / Jenkins

The Winery at Chateau Americana
Unusual Transactions - Revenue Cycle Printout of
Aged Accounts Receivable Trial Balance
For the Year Ended December 31, 20XX

Reference: _R-511_
Prepared by: _JG_
Date: _2/19/XY_
Reviewed by: _____

Date	Account Description or Customer of Unusual Transactions Identified	Ref.	Account IDs	Amount
	No unusual transactions identified.			

Follow-up procedures performed:

No follow-up procedures are necessary.

The Winery at Chateau Americana
Nonstatistical Tests of Balance Evaluation –
Revenue Cycle Accounts Receivable
For the Year Ended December 31, 20XX

Reference: *R-520*
Prepared by: _____
Date: _____
Reviewed by: _____

Misstatements:	Recorded Amount	Audited Amount	Misstatement Amount
Total Sample Misstatement			

Projected Misstatement:		
Total Sample Misstatement		
Dollar Value of Sample	÷	$1,785,704
Percentage Sample Dollar Misstatement	=	
Dollar Value of Population per G/L	×	$5,240,719
Projected Dollar Misstatement for Accounts Receivable	=	

Allowance for Sampling Risk		
Tolerable Misstatement		$40,000
Projected Dollar Misstatement for Accounts Receivable	−	
Recorded Adjustments	+	
Allowance for Sampling Risk	=	

Conclusions:

The Winery at Chateau Americana			
Chart of Accounts			
Account Description	**Account Number**	**Account Description**	**Account Number**
General Checking Account	111000	Sales	410000
Payroll Checking Account	112000	Sales Discounts	420000
Money Market Account	113000	Sales Returns and Allowances	430000
Savings Account	114000	Gains/Loss Marketable Securities	452000
Petty Cash	119000	Dividend Income	491000
Accounts Receivable	121000	Interest Income	492000
Allowance for Bad Debts	129000	Cost of Goods Sold	510000
Inventory- Production	141000	Wages and Salary Expense	601000
Inventory - Finished Goods	145000	Sales Commission Expense	601500
Prepaid Expenses	150000	FICA Tax Expense	602100
Land and Buildings	160000	Medicare Tax Expense	602200
Equipment	170000	FUTA Tax Expense	602300
Accumulated Depreciation	180000	SUTA Tax Expense	602400
Investments	191000	Utilities Expense	611000
Accounts Payable	210000	Irrigation & Waste Disposal	
Federal Income Tax Withheld	222100	Expense	611300
FICA Withheld	222200	Landscaping Expense	612000
Medicare Withheld	222300	Advertising Expense	621000
FICA Payable - Employer	223100	Marketing Expense	623000
Medicare Payable - Employer	223200	Festivals & Competitions Expense	624000
Unemployment Taxes Payable	223300	Telephone Expense	631000
Federal Income Taxes Payable	235000	Internet & Computer Expense	632000
Property Taxes Payable	236000	Postage Expense	633000
Mortgages Payable	240000	Legal & Accounting Fees	641000
Notes Payables	261000	Office Supplies Expense	651000
Common Stock	310000	Data Processing Expense	660000
Paid in Capital Excess Par -		Depreciation Expense	670000
Common	311000	Travel and Entertainment Expense	680000
Dividends - Common	312000	Other Insurance Expense	691000
Retained Earnings	390000	Medical Insurance Expense	692000
		Workmen's Compensation	
		Insurance	693000
		Other Employee Benefit Expense	699000
		Dues and Subscription Expense	700000
		Federal Income Tax Expense	711000
		Property Tax Expense	712000
		Repairs and Maintenance Expense	721000
		Automobile Expense	731000
		Lease Expense	740000
		Bad Dept Expense	791000
		Miscellaneous Expense	792000
		Interest Expense	793000

Note: Pages 95 to 106 contain documentation required to complete two of the open audit procedures shown on the audit program on pages 59 to 62. Document for Audit Procedure 1 is available on pages 95 to 100 and documentation for Audit Procedure 14 is available on pages 101 to 106.

	The Winery at Chateau Americana Sales Register for Audit Procedure 1* For the Period From January 1, 20XX to December 31, 20XX				
Date	**G.L. Account ID - Account Description**	**Customer No.**	**Invoice No.**	**Debit Amount**	**Credit Amount**
01/10/XX (43)	121000 - Accounts Receivable 410000 - Sales	0501	13713	16,186.80	16,186.80
03/19/XX (348)	121000 - Accounts Receivable 410000 - Sales	3301	14081	8,373.60	8,373.60
06/12/XX (716)	121000 - Accounts Receivable 410000 - Sales	0901	14386	11,566.80	11,566.80
11/20/XX (1633)	121000 - Accounts Receivable 410000 - Sales	1301	15303	11,444.40	11,444.40
12/11/XX (1821)	121000 - Accounts Receivable 410000 - Sales	3802	15491	10,220.40	10,220.40

*Abstracted from the Sales Register using exact format of the actual Sales Register. Note that the number in parenthesis under the transaction date is not normally included in the Sales Register. This number is provided as it represents the line number of the transaction in the Sales Register.

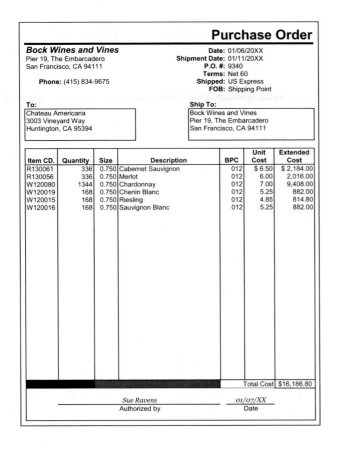

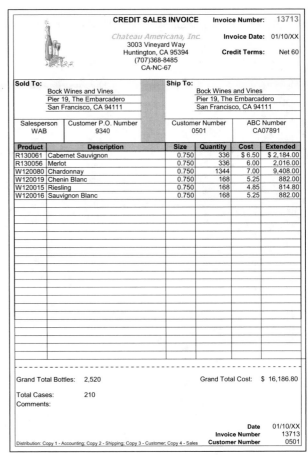

Purchase Order

Bock Wines and Vines
Pier 19, The Embarcadero
San Francisco, CA 94111

Phone: (415) 834-9675

Date: 01/06/20XX
Shipment Date: 01/11/20XX
P.O. #: 9340
Terms: Net 60
Shipped: US Express
FOB: Shipping Point

To:
Chateau Americana
3003 Vineyard Way
Huntington, CA 95394

Ship To:
Bock Wines and Vines
Pier 19, The Embarcadero
San Francisco, CA 94111

Item CD.	Quantity	Size	Description	BPC	Unit Cost	Extended Cost
R130061	336	0.750	Cabernet Sauvignon	012	$ 6.50	$ 2,184.00
R130056	336	0.750	Merlot	012	6.00	2,016.00
W120080	1344	0.750	Chardonnay	012	7.00	9,408.00
W120019	168	0.750	Chenin Blanc	012	5.25	882.00
W120015	168	0.750	Riesling	012	4.85	814.80
W120016	168	0.750	Sauvignon Blanc	012	5.25	882.00

Total Cost $16,186.80

Sue Ravens — Authorized by
01/07/XX — Date

CREDIT SALES INVOICE

Invoice Number: 13713

Chateau Americana, Inc.
3003 Vineyard Way
Huntington, CA 95394
(707)368-8485
CA-NC-67

Invoice Date: 01/10/XX
Credit Terms: Net 60

Sold To:
Bock Wines and Vines
Pier 19, The Embarcadero
San Francisco, CA 94111

Ship To:
Bock Wines and Vines
Pier 19, The Embarcadero
San Francisco, CA 94111

Salesperson	Customer P.O. Number	Customer Number	ABC Number
WAB	9340	0501	CA07891

Product	Description	Size	Quantity	Cost	Extended
R130061	Cabernet Sauvignon	0.750	336	$ 6.50	$ 2,184.00
R130056	Merlot	0.750	336	6.00	2,016.00
W120080	Chardonnay	0.750	1344	7.00	9,408.00
W120019	Chenin Blanc	0.750	168	5.25	882.00
W120015	Riesling	0.750	168	4.85	814.80
W120016	Sauvignon Blanc	0.750	168	5.25	882.00

Grand Total Bottles: 2,520

Grand Total Cost: $ 16,186.80

Total Cases: 210

Comments:

Date 01/10/XX
Invoice Number 13713
Customer Number 0501

Distribution: Copy 1 - Accounting; Copy 2 - Shipping; Copy 3 - Customer; Copy 4 - Sales

---

Date 01/10/XX	Uniform Bill of Lading	

Ship From

Name: Chateau Americana, Inc.
Address: 3003 Vineyard Way
City/State/Zip: Huntington, CA 95394
SID No.: 122448

Bill of Lading Number: 134659

Carrier Name: US Express
Trailer Number: KLDF 897
Serial Number: 000123123

Ship To

Name: Bock Wines and Vines
Address: Pier 19, The Embarcadero
City/State/Zip: San Francisco, CA 94111
CID No.: 244888

Special Instructions:

Freight Charge Terms: (Freight charges are prepaid unless marked otherwise)
Prepaid: ☐ Collect: ☑ 3rd Party: ☐
☐ (check box): Master bill of lading with attached underlying bills of lading.

Customer Order Information

Description of Items	Quantity	Weight	Pallet/Slip (circle one)	Additional Shipper Information
Wine	210	7,140	(Y) N	
			Y N	
			Y N	
			Y N	
Grand Total	210	7,140		

Where the rate is dependent on value, shippers are required to state specifically in writing the agreed or declared value of the property is specifically stated by the shipper to be not exceeding _____ per _____.

COD Amount: $ _____ N/A
Free Terms:
☐ Collect
☐ Prepaid
☐ Customer check acceptable

Note: Liability limitation for loss or damage in this shipment may be applicable. See 49 USC §14706 (c) (1) (A) & (B)

Received, subject to individually determined rates or contracts that have been agreed upon in writing between the carrier and shipper, if applicable, otherwise to the rates, classifications and rules that have been established by the carrier and are available to the shipper, on request, and to all applicable state and federal regulations.

The carrier shall not make delivery of this shipment without payment of and all other lawful charges.

Shipper Signature *Jerry Richards*

Shipper Signature/Date

This is to certify that the above named materials are properly classified, packaged, marked and labeled, and are in proper condition for transportation according to the applicable regulations of the DOT.

Jerry Richards 01/10/XX

Trailer Loaded:
☐ By shipper
☑ By Driver

Carrier Signature/Pickup Date

Carrier acknowledges receipt of packages and required placards. Carrier certifies emergency response information was made available and/or carrier has the DOT emergency response guidebook or equivalent documentation in the vehicle. **Property described above is received in good order, except as noted.**

Frank Loren 01/10/XX

Distribution: Copy 1 - Accounting; Copy 2 - Shipping; Copy 3- Customer

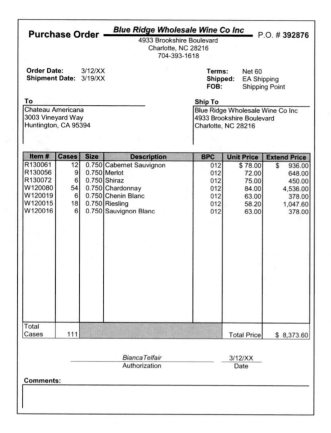

Purchase Order — **Blue Ridge Wholesale Wine Co Inc**

4933 Brookshire Boulevard
Charlotte, NC 28216
704-393-1618

P.O. # **392876**

Order Date: 3/12/XX	Terms: Net 60
Shipment Date: 3/19/XX	Shipped: EA Shipping
	FOB: Shipping Point

To
Chateau Americana
3003 Vineyard Way
Huntington, CA 95394

Ship To
Blue Ridge Wholesale Wine Co Inc
4933 Brookshire Boulevard
Charlotte, NC 28216

Item #	Cases	Size	Description	BPC	Unit Price	Extend Price
R130061	12	0.750	Cabernet Sauvignon	012	$ 78.00	$ 936.00
R130056	9	0.750	Merlot	012	72.00	648.00
R130072	6	0.750	Shiraz	012	75.00	450.00
W120080	54	0.750	Chardonnay	012	84.00	4,536.00
W120019	6	0.750	Chenin Blanc	012	63.00	378.00
W120015	18	0.750	Riesling	012	58.20	1,047.60
W120016	6	0.750	Sauvignon Blanc	012	63.00	378.00
Total Cases	111				Total Price	$ 8,373.60

Bianca Telfair   3/12/XX
Authorization   Date

Comments:

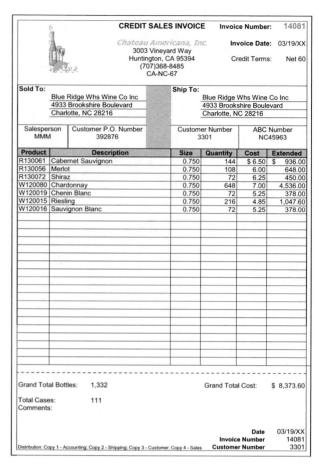

CREDIT SALES INVOICE

Invoice Number: 14081

Chateau Americana, Inc.
3003 Vineyard Way
Huntington, CA 95394
(707)368-8485
CA-NC-67

Invoice Date: 03/19/XX

Credit Terms: Net 60

Sold To:
Blue Ridge Whs Wine Co Inc
4933 Brookshire Boulevard
Charlotte, NC 28216

Ship To:
Blue Ridge Whs Wine Co Inc
4933 Brookshire Boulevard
Charlotte, NC 28216

Salesperson	Customer P.O. Number	Customer Number	ABC Number
MMM	392876	3301	NC45963

Product	Description	Size	Quantity	Cost	Extended
R130061	Cabernet Sauvignon	0.750	144	$ 6.50	$ 936.00
R130056	Merlot	0.750	108	6.00	648.00
R130072	Shiraz	0.750	72	6.25	450.00
W120080	Chardonnay	0.750	648	7.00	4,536.00
W120019	Chenin Blanc	0.750	72	5.25	378.00
W120015	Riesling	0.750	216	4.85	1,047.60
W120016	Sauvignon Blanc	0.750	72	5.25	378.00

Grand Total Bottles: 1,332

Grand Total Cost: $ 8,373.60

Total Cases: 111
Comments:

Date	03/19/XX
Invoice Number	14081
Customer Number	3301

Distribution: Copy 1 - Accounting; Copy 2 - Shipping; Copy 3 - Customer; Copy 4 - Sales

---

Date 03/19/XX	Uniform Bill of Lading

Ship From
Name: Chateau Americana, Inc.
Address: 3003 Vineyard Way
City/State/Zip: Huntington, CA 95394
SID No.: 122448

Bill of Lading Number: 134964

Carrier Name: EA Shipping

Trailer Number: 7777 SOU

Serial Number: 022323444

Ship To
Name: Blue Ridge Whs Wine Co Inc
Address: 4933 Brookshire Boulevard
City/State/Zip: Charlotte, NC 28216
CID No.: 883229

Special Instructions:

Freight Charge Terms: (Freight charges are prepaid unless marked otherwise)
Prepaid: ☐   Collect: ☒   3rd Party: ☐
☐ (check box): Master bill of lading with attached underlying bills of lading.

Customer Order Information

Description of Items	Quantity	Weight	Pallet/Slip (circle one)	Additional Shipper Information
Wine	111	3,774	Ⓨ N	
			Y N	
			Y N	
			Y N	
Grand Total	111	3,774		

Where the rate is dependent on value, shippers are required to state specifically in writing the agreed or declared value of the property as follows: "The agreed or declared value of the property is specifically stated by the shipper to be not exceeding _____ per _____.

COD Amount: $ _____ N/A
Free Terms:
☐ Collect
☐ Prepaid
☐ Customer check acceptable

Note: Liability limitation for loss or damage in this shipment may be applicable. See 49 USC §14706(c)(1)(A)&(B)

Received, subject to individually determined rates or contracts that have been agreed upon in writing between the carrier and shipper, if applicable, otherwise to the rates, classifications and rules that have been established by the carrier and are available to the shipper, on request, and to all applicable state and federal regulations.

The carrier shall not make delivery of this shipment without payment of and all other lawful charges.

Shipper Signature   _Jerry Richards_

Shipper Signature/Date	Trailer Loaded:	Carrier Signature/Pickup Date
This is to certify that the above named materials are properly classified, packaged, marked and labeled, and are in proper condition for transportation according to the applicable regulations of the DOT.	☐ By shipper ☒ By Driver	Carrier acknowledges receipt of packages and required placards. Carrier certifies emergency response information was made available and/or carrier has the DOT emergency response guidebook or equivalent documentation in the vehicle. Property described above is received in good order, except as noted.
Jerry Richards 03/19/XX		_Basi Abbas_ 03/19/XX

Distribution: Copy 1 - Accounting; Copy 2 - Shipping; Copy 3- Customer

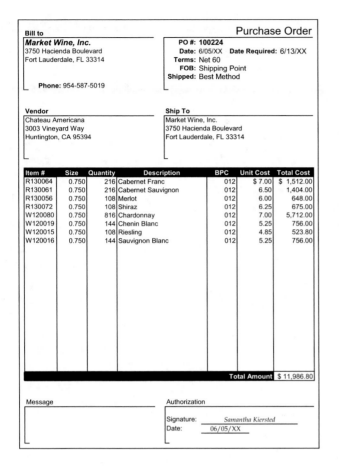

Purchase Order

Bill to
Market Wine, Inc.
3750 Hacienda Boulevard
Fort Lauderdale, FL 33314

Phone: 954-587-5019

PO #: 100224
Date: 6/05/XX   **Date Required:** 6/13/XX
Terms: Net 60
FOB: Shipping Point
Shipped: Best Method

Vendor
Chateau Americana
3003 Vineyard Way
Huntington, CA 95394

Ship To
Market Wine, Inc.
3750 Hacienda Boulevard
Fort Lauderdale, FL 33314

Item #	Size	Quantity	Description	BPC	Unit Cost	Total Cost
R130064	0.750	216	Cabernet Franc	012	$ 7.00	$ 1,512.00
R130061	0.750	216	Cabernet Sauvignon	012	6.50	1,404.00
R130056	0.750	108	Merlot	012	6.00	648.00
R130072	0.750	108	Shiraz	012	6.25	675.00
W120080	0.750	816	Chardonnay	012	7.00	5,712.00
W120019	0.750	144	Chenin Blanc	012	5.25	756.00
W120015	0.750	108	Riesling	012	4.85	523.80
W120016	0.750	144	Sauvignon Blanc	012	5.25	756.00

Total Amount $ 11,986.80

Message

Authorization
Signature: *Samantha Kiersted*
Date: 06/05/XX

CREDIT SALES INVOICE   Invoice Number: **14386**

Chateau Americana, Inc.
3003 Vineyard Way
Huntington, CA 95394
(707)368-8485
CA-NC-67

Invoice Date: 6/12/XX
Credit Terms: Net 60

Sold To:
Market Wine, Inc.
3750 Hacienda Boulevard
Fort Lauderdale, FL 33314

Ship To:
Market Wine, Inc.
3750 Hacienda Boulevard
Fort Lauderdale, FL 33314

Salesperson	Customer P.O. Number	Customer Number	ABC Number
MMM	100224	0901	FLS11132

Product	Description	Size	Quantity	Cost	Extended
R130064	Cabernet Franc	0.750	216	$ 7.00	$ 1,512.00
R130061	Cabernet Sauvignon	0.750	216	6.50	1,404.00
R130056	Merlot	0.750	108	6.00	648.00
R130072	Shiraz	0.750	108	6.25	675.00
W120080	Chardonnay	0.750	816	7.00	5,712.00
W120019	Chenin Blanc	0.750	144	5.25	756.00
W120015	Riesling	0.750	108	4.85	523.80
W120016	Sauvignon Blanc	0.750	144	5.25	756.00

Grand Total Bottles: 1,860   Grand Total Cost: $ 11,986.80

Total Cases: 155
Comments:

Date: 6/12/XX
Invoice Number: 14386
Customer Number: 0901

Distribution: Copy 1 - Accounting; Copy 2 - Shipping; Copy 3 - Customer; Copy 4 - Sales

---

Date 06/12/XX	Uniform Bill of Lading

Ship From

Name: *Chateau Americana, Inc.*
Address: *3003 Vineyard Way*
City/State/Zip: *Huntington, CA 95394*
SID No.: *122448*

Bill of Lading Number: 135332

Carrier Name: *Crossway Deliveries*

Ship To
Name: *Market Wine, Inc.*
Address: *3750 Hacienda Boulevard*
City/State/Zip: *Fort Lauderdale, FL 33314*
CID No.: *456987*

Trailer Number: *ABC 3210*

Serial Number: *000456789*

Special Instructions:

Freight Charge Terms: (Freight charges are prepaid unless marked otherwise)
Prepaid: ☐   Collect: ☒   3rd Party: ☐
(check box): Master bill of lading with attached underlying bills of lading.

Customer Order Information

Description of Items	Quantity	Weight	Pallet/Slip (circle one)		Additional Shipper Information
Wine	155	5,270	Ⓨ	N	
			Y	N	
			Y	N	
			Y	N	
Grand Total	155	5,270			

COD Amount: $ N/A
Free Terms:
☐ Collect
☐ Prepaid
☐ Customer check acceptable

Note: Liability limitation for loss or damage in this shipment may be applicable. See 49 USC §14706© (1) (A) & (B)

Received, subject to individually determined rates or contracts that have been agreed upon in writing between the carrier and shipper, if applicable, otherwise to the rates, classifications and rules that have been established by the carrier and are available to the shipper, on request, and to all applicable state and federal regulations.

The carrier shall not make delivery of this shipment without payment of and all other lawful charges.

Shipper Signature: *Jerry Richards*

Shipper Signature/Date

This is to certify that the above named materials are properly classified, packaged, marked and labeled, and are in proper condition for transportation according to the applicable regulations of the DOT.

Jerry Richards   06/12/XX

Trailer Loaded:
☐ By shipper
☒ By Driver

Carrier Signature/Pickup Date

Carrier acknowledges receipt of packages and required placards. Carrier certifies emergency response information was made available and/or carrier has the DOT emergency response guidebook or equivalent documentation in the vehicle. Property described above is received in good order, except as noted.

Santos Padilla   6/12/XX

Distribution: Copy 1 - Accounting; Copy 2 - Shipping; Copy 3- Customer

Purchase Order

Pacific Wine & Spirits Co
2701 South Western Avenue
Chicago, IL 60608
Phone: 773-247-8000

To:
Chateau Americana
3003 Vineyard Way
Huntington, CA 95394

Ship To:
Pacific Wine & Spirits Co
2701 South Western Avenue
Chicago, IL 60608

Date	P.O. No.	Terms	F.O.B. Point	Ship Via
11/14/XX	455698	Net 60	Shipping Point	Best Method

Item #	Cases	Size	Description	BPC	Unit Cost	Total Cost
R130064	24	0.750	Cabernet Franc	012	$ 84.00	$ 2,016.00
R130061	24	0.750	Cabernet Sauvignon	012	78.00	1,872.00
R130056	12	0.750	Merlot	012	72.00	864.00
R130072	6	0.750	Shiraz	012	75.00	450.00
W120080	48	0.750	Chardonnay	012	84.00	4,032.00
W120019	12	0.750	Chenin Blanc	012	63.00	756.00
W120015	12	0.750	Riesling	012	58.20	698.40
W120016	12	0.750	Sauvignon Blanc	012	63.00	756.00

| Total | 150 | | | | Total | $ 11,444.40 |

Cresent Belcher   11/14/XX
Authorized by   Date

Comments:

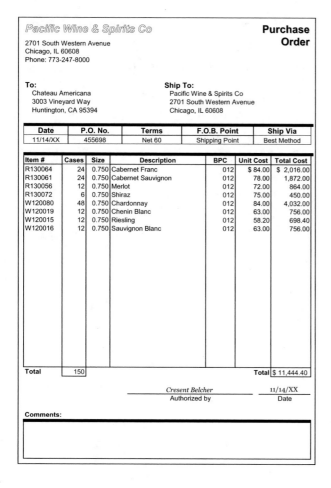

CREDIT SALES INVOICE

Invoice Number: 15303

Chateau Americana, Inc.
3003 Vineyard Way
Huntington, CA 95394
(707)368-8485
CA-NC-67

Invoice Date: 11/20/XX

Credit Terms: Net 60

Sold To:
Pacific Wine & Spirits Co
2701 South Western Avenue
Chicago, IL 60608

Ship To:
Pacific Wine & Spirits Co
2701 South Western Avenue
Chicago, IL 60608

Salesperson	Customer P.O. Number	Customer Number	ABC Number
CEZ	455698	1301	IS48489

Product	Description	Size	Quantity	Cost	Extended
R130064	Cabernet Franc	0.750	288	$ 7.00	$ 2,016.00
R130061	Cabernet Sauvignon	0.750	288	6.50	1,872.00
R130056	Merlot	0.750	144	6.00	864.00
R130072	Shiraz	0.750	72	6.25	450.00
W120080	Chardonnay	0.750	576	7.00	4,032.00
W120019	Chenin Blanc	0.750	144	5.25	756.00
W120015	Riesling	0.750	144	4.85	698.40
W120016	Sauvignon Blanc	0.750	144	5.25	756.00

Grand Total Bottles: 1,800

Grand Total Cost: $ 11,444.40

Total Cases: 150

Comments:

Date 11/20/XX
Invoice Number 15303
Customer Number 1301

Distribution: Copy 1 - Accounting; Copy 2 - Shipping; Copy 3 - Customer; Copy 4 - Sales

---

Date 11/20/XX   **Uniform Bill of Lading**

Ship From

Name: Chateau Americana, Inc.
Address: 3003 Vineyard Way
City/State/Zip: Huntington, CA 95394
SID No.: 122448

Bill of Lading Number: 136249

Carrier Name: Crossway Deliveries

Ship To
Name: Pacific Wine & Spirits Co
Address: 2701 South Western Avenue
City/State/Zip: Chicago, IL 60608
CID No.: 617493

Trailer Number: DDR 7192

Serial Number: 000123123

Special Instructions:

Freight Charge Terms: (Freight charges are prepaid unless marked otherwise)
Prepaid: ☐   Collect: ☒   3rd Party: ☐
(check box): Master bill of lading with attached underlying bills of lading.

Customer Order Information

Description of Items	Quantity	Weight	Pallet/Slip (circle one)	Additional Shipper Information
Wine	150	5,100	Ⓨ N	
			Y N	
			Y N	
			Y N	
Grand Total	150	5,100		

COD Amount: $ N/A
Free Terms:
☐ Collect
☐ Prepaid
☐ Customer check acceptable

Where the rate is dependent on value, shippers are required to state specifically in writing the agreed or declared value of the property as follows: "The agreed or declared value of the property is specifically stated by the shipper to be not exceeding _____ per _____.

Note: Liability limitation for loss or damage in this shipment may be applicable. See 49 USC §14706 (c) (1) (A) & (B)

Received, subject to individually determined rates or contracts that have been agreed upon in writing between the carrier and shipper, if applicable, otherwise to the rates, classifications and rules that have been established by the carrier and are available to the shipper, on request, and to all applicable state and federal regulations.

The carrier shall not make delivery of this shipment without payment of and all other lawful charges.

Shipper Signature   *Jerry Richards*

Shipper Signature/Date

This is to certify that the above named materials are properly classified, packaged, marked and labeled, and are in proper condition for transportation according to the applicable regulations of the DOT.

Jerry Richards   11/20/XX

Trailer Loaded:
☐ By shipper
☒ By Driver

Carrier Signature/Pickup Date

Carrier acknowledges receipt of packages and required placards. Carrier certifies emergency response information was made available and/or carrier has the DOT emergency response guidebook or equivalent documentation in the vehicle. Property described above is received in good order, except as noted.

Rich Venditti   11/20/XX

Distribution: Copy 1 - Accounting; Copy 2 - Shipping; Copy 3- Customer

Purchase Order

P.O. No.: **198885**
Date: 12/03/XX

To:
Chateau Americana
3003 Vineyard Way
Huntington, CA 95394

Ship To:
Phila Wine Company
940 South 9th Street
Philadelphia, PA 19147
Phone: 215-733-0655

Ship Via	F.O.B. Point	Terms
Best Method	Shipping Point	Net 60

Item #	Quantity	Size	Description	BPC	Unit Cost	Total Cost
R130064	168	0.750	Cabernet Franc		7.00	1,176.00
R130061	252	0.750	Cabernet Sauvignon		6.50	1,638.00
R130056	72	0.750	Merlot		6.00	432.00
W120080	732	0.750	Chardonnay		7.00	5,124.00
W120015	144	0.750	Riesling		4.85	698.40
W120016	144	0.750	Sauvignon Blanc		5.25	756.00
S140000	36	0.750	Sparkling Brut		11.00	396.00

| Total | 1548 | | | | Total | $ 10,220.40 |

Georgia Morock   12/03/XX
Authorized by   Date

Comments:

CREDIT SALES INVOICE   Invoice Number: 15491

Chateau Americana, Inc.
3003 Vineyard Way
Huntington, CA 95394
(707)368-8485
CA-NC-67

Invoice Date: 12/11/XX

Credit Terms: Net 60

Sold To:
Phila Wine Company
940 South 9th Street
Philadelphia, PA 19147

Ship To:
Phila Wine Company
940 South 9th Street
Philadelphia, PA 19147

Salesperson	Customer P.O. Number	Customer Number	ABC Number
FEW	198885	3802	PA009821

Product	Description	Size	Quantity	Cost	Extended
R130064	Cabernet Franc	0.750	168	$ 7.00	$ 1,176.00
R130061	Cabernet Sauvignon	0.750	252	6.50	1,638.00
R130056	Merlot	0.750	72	6.00	432.00
W120080	Chardonnay	0.750	732	7.00	5,124.00
W120015	Riesling	0.750	144	4.85	698.40
W120016	Sauvignon Blanc	0.750	144	5.25	756.00
S140000	Sparkling Brut	0.750	36	11.00	396.00

Grand Total Bottles: 1,548   Grand Total Cost: $ 10,220.40

Total Cases: 129
Comments:

Date 12/11/XX
Invoice Number 15491
Customer Number 3802

Distribution: Copy 1 - Accounting; Copy 2 - Shipping; Copy 3 - Customer; Copy 4 - Sales

---

Date 12/11/XX	Uniform Bill of Lading

Ship From

Name: Chateau Americana, Inc.
Address: 3003 Vineyard Way
City/State/Zip: Huntington, CA 95394
SID No.: 122448

Bill of Lading Number: 136437

Carrier Name: *Crossway Deliveries*

Trailer Number: CEF 5824

Ship To
Name: Phila Wine Company
Address: 940 South 9th Street
City/State/Zip: Philadelphia, PA 19147
CID No.: 463728

Serial Number: 000360087

Special Instructions:

Freight Charge Terms: (Freight charges are prepaid unless marked otherwise)
Prepaid: ☐   Collect: ☒   3rd Party: ☐
(check box): Master bill of lading with attached underlying bills of lading.

Customer Order Information

Description of Items	Quantity	Weight	Pallet/Slip (circle one)	Additional Shipper Information
Wine	129	4,386	(Y) N	
			Y N	
			Y N	
			Y N	
Grand Total	129	4,386		

COD Amount: $ _____ N/A
Free Terms:
☐ Collect
☐ Prepaid
☐ Customer check acceptable

Where the rate is dependent on value, shippers are required to state specifically in writing the agreed or declared value of the property as follows: "The agreed or declared value of the property is specifically stated by the shipper to be not exceeding _____ per _____.

Note: Liability limitation for loss or damage in this shipment may be applicable. See 49 USC §14706(c)(1)(A)&(B)

Received, subject to individually determined rates or contracts that have been agreed upon in writing between the carrier and shipper, if applicable, otherwise to the rates, classifications and rules that have been established by the carrier and are available to the shipper, on request, and to all applicable state and federal regulations.

The carrier shall not make delivery of this shipment without payment of all other lawful charges.

Shipper Signature   *Jerry Richards*

Shipper Signature/Date	Trailer Loaded:	Carrier Signature/Pickup Date

This is to certify that the above named materials are properly classified, packaged, marked and labeled, and are in proper condition for transportation according to the applicable regulations of the DOT.

☐ By shipper
☒ By Driver

Carrier acknowledges receipt of packages and required placards. Carrier certifies emergency response information was made available and/or carrier has the DOT emergency response guidebook or equivalent documentation in the vehicle. Property described above is received in good order, except as noted.

Jerry Richards   12/11/XX   *Tom Greer*   12/11/XX

Distribution: Copy 1 - Accounting; Copy 2 - Shipping; Copy 3- Customer

The Winery at Chateau Americana
Accounts Receivable Aged Trial Balance for Audit Procedure 14*
As of December 31, 20XX

Customer	Customer ID	Total Balance	Days Old			
			0 - 60	61 - 120	121 - 180	Over 180
Atlanta Wholesale Wine	1001	$151,696.20	$151,696.20			
Bock Wines and Vines	0501	$210,198.20	$171,946.40	$38,251.80		
Bolliger, Inc.	0701	$163,570.80	$163,570.80			
Pinnacle Wine Company	3201	$184,610.40	$135,978.00	$48,632.40		
Vintage Wine Company	0502	$255,169.80	$207,893.40	$47,276.40		

*Abstracted from the Accounts Receivable Aged Trial Balance using exact format of the actual Accounts Receivable Aged Trial Balance.

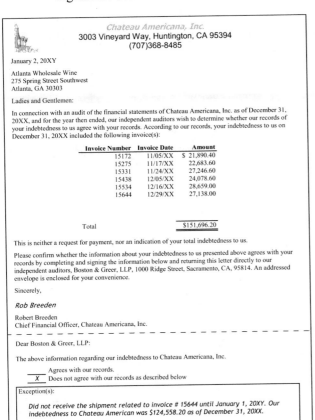

Chateau Americana, Inc.
3003 Vineyard Way, Huntington, CA 95394
(707)368-8485

January 2, 20XY

Atlanta Wholesale Wine
275 Spring Street Southwest
Atlanta, GA 30303

Ladies and Gentlemen:

In connection with an audit of the financial statements of Chateau Americana, Inc. as of December 31, 20XX, and for the year then ended, our independent auditors wish to determine whether our records of your indebtedness to us agree with your records. According to our records, your indebtedness to us on December 31, 20XX included the following invoice(s):

Invoice Number	Invoice Date	Amount
15172	11/05/XX	$ 21,890.40
15275	11/17/XX	22,683.60
15331	11/24/XX	27,246.60
15438	12/05/XX	24,078.60
15534	12/16/XX	28,659.00
15644	12/29/XX	27,138.00
	Total	$151,696.20

This is neither a request for payment, nor an indication of your total indebtedness to us.

Please confirm whether the information about your indebtedness to us presented above agrees with your records by completing and signing the information below and returning this letter directly to our independent auditors, Boston & Greer, LLP, 1000 Ridge Street, Sacramento, CA, 95814. An addressed envelope is enclosed for your convenience.

Sincerely,

Rob Breeden

Robert Breeden
Chief Financial Officer, Chateau Americana, Inc.

- -

Dear Boston & Greer, LLP:

The above information regarding our indebtedness to Chateau Americana, Inc.

_____ Agrees with our records.

__X__ Does not agree with our records as described below

Exception(s):

Did not receive the shipment related to invoice # 15644 until January 1, 20XY. Our indebtedness to Chateau American was $124,558.20 as of December 31, 20XX.

Name and Title (please print): ___Blake Conroe, Accounts Payable Clerk___

Signature: *Blake Conroe*   Date: _1/7/XY_

CREDIT SALES INVOICE   Invoice Number: **15644**

Chateau Americana, Inc.   Invoice Date: 12/29/XX
3003 Vineyard Way
Huntington, CA 95394   Credit Terms: Net 60
(707)368-8485
CA-NC-67

Sold To: **Ship To:**

Atlanta Wholesale Wine   Atlanta Wholesale Wine
275 Spring Street Southwest   275 Spring Street Southwest
Atlanta, GA 30303   Atlanta, GA 30303

Salesperson MMM	Customer P.O. Number 11332	Customer Number 1001	ABC Number GA3141

Product	Description	Size	Quantity	Cost	Extended
R130064	Cabernet Franc		204	$7.00	$ 1,428.00
R130061	Cabernet Sauvignon		204	6.50	1,326.00
R130056	Merlot		144	6.00	864.00
R130072	Shiraz		144	6.25	900.00
W120080	Chardonnay		1824	7.00	12,768.00
W120019	Chenin Blanc		396	5.25	2,079.00
W120015	Riesling		300	4.85	1,455.00
W120016	Sauvignon Blanc		600	5.25	3,150.00
S140000	Sparkling Brut		288	11.00	3,168.00

Grand Total Bottles: 4,104   Grand Total Cost: $ 27,138.00

Total Cases: 342

Comments:
   Rush delivery

	Date	12/29/XX
	Invoice Number	15644
	Customer Number	1001

Distribution: Copy 1 - Accounting; Copy 2 - Shipping; Copy 3 - Customer; Copy 4 - Sales

---

Purchase Order   *Atlanta Wholesale Wine*   P.O. No.: **11332**
275 Spring Street Southwest
Atlanta, GA 30303
404-522-3358

To: **Ship To:**

Chateau Americana   Atlanta Wholesale Wine
3003 Vineyard Way   275 Spring Street Southwest
Huntington, CA 95394   Atlanta, GA 30303

Date	Terms	F.O.B. Point	Ship Via
12/24/XX	Net 60	Shipping Point	Best Method

Item #	Cases	Size	Description	Unit Cost	Total Cost
R130064	17	750ML	Cabernet Franc	$ 84.00	$ 1,428.00
R130061	17	750ML	Cabernet Sauvignon	78.00	1,326.00
R130056	12	750ML	Merlot	72.00	864.00
R130072	12	750ML	Shiraz	75.00	900.00
W120080	152	750ML	Chardonnay	84.00	12,768.00
W120019	33	750ML	Chenin Blanc	63.00	2,079.00
W120015	25	750ML	Riesling	58.20	1,455.00
W120016	50	750ML	Sauvignon Blanc	63.00	3,150.00
S140000	24	750ML	Sparkling Brut	132.00	3,168.00
				Total	$ 27,138.00

Jean Kalicki   12/24/XX
Authorized by   Date

Comments:

Date 12/29/XX	Uniform Bill of Lading	

Ship From

Name: *Chateau Americana, Inc.*
Address: *3003 Vineyard Way*
City/State/Zip: *Huntington, CA 95394*
SID No.: *122448*

Bill of Lading Number: **136590**

Ship To

Name: Atlanta Wholesale Wine
Address: 275 Spring Street Southwest
City/State/Zip: Atlanta, GA 30303
CID No.: 002996

Carrier Name: *EA Shipping*

Trailer Number: 4578 CAL

Serial Number: 000111789

Special Instructions:

Freight Charge Terms: (Freight charges are prepaid unless marked otherwise)
Prepaid: ☐   Collect: ☒   3rd Party: ☐
☐ (check box): Master bill of lading with attached underlying bills of lading.

Customer Order Information

Description of Items	Quantity	Weight	Pallet/Slip (circle one)	Additional Shipper Information
Wine	342	11,628	(Y) N	
			Y N	
			Y N	
			Y N	
Grand Total	342	11,628		

Where the rate is dependent on value, shippers are required to state specifically in writing the agreed or declared value of the property as follows: "The agreed or declared value of the property is specifically stated by the shipper to be not exceeding _____ per _____.

COD Amount: $ N/A

Free Terms:
☐ Collect
☐ Prepaid
☐ Customer check acceptable

Note: Liability limitation for loss or damage in this shipment may be applicable. See 49 USC $14706 (c) (1) (A) & (B)

Received, subject to individually determined rates or contracts that have been agreed upon in writing between the carrier and shipper, if applicable, otherwise to the rates, classifications and rules that have been established by the carrier and are available to the shipper, on request, and to all applicable state and federal regulations.

The carrier shall not make delivery of this shipment without payment of and all other lawful charges.

Shipper Signature   *Jerry Richards*

Shipper Signature/Date	Trailer Loaded:	Carrier Signature/Pickup Date

This is to certify that the above named materials are properly classified, packaged, marked and labeled, and are in proper condition for transportation according to the applicable regulations of the DOT.

☐ By shipper
☒ By Driver

Carrier acknowledges receipt of packages and required placards. Carrier certifies emergency response information was made available and/or carrier has the DOT emergency response guidebook or equivalent documentation in the vehicle. Property described above is received in good order, except as noted.

Jerry Richards   12/29/XX   *Sam Souza*   12/29/XX

Distribution: Copy 1 - Accounting; Copy 2 - Shipping; Copy 3- Customer

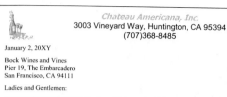

Chateau Americana, Inc.
3003 Vineyard Way, Huntington, CA 95394
(707)368-8485

January 2, 20XY

Bock Wines and Vines
Pier 19, The Embarcadero
San Francisco, CA 94111

Ladies and Gentlemen:

In connection with an audit of the financial statements of Chateau Americana, Inc. as of December 31, 20XX, and for the year then ended, our independent auditors wish to determine whether our records of your indebtedness to us agree with your records. According to our records, your indebtedness to us on December 31, 20XX included the following invoice(s):

Invoice Number	Invoice Date	Amount
14944	10/09/XX	$ 18,501.00
15072	10/24/XX	19,750.80
15158	11/03/XX	19,337.60
15252	11/14/XX	20,206.80
15335	11/24/XX	23,826.00
15406	12/01/XX	22,042.80
15465	12/08/XX	24,682.80
15551	12/18/XX	30,303.60
15619	12/26/XX	31,546.80
Total		$210,198.20

This is neither a request for payment, nor an indication of your total indebtedness to us.

Please confirm whether the information about your indebtedness to us presented above agrees with your records by completing and signing the information below and returning this letter directly to our independent auditors, Boston & Greer, LLP, 1000 Ridge Street, Sacramento, CA, 95814. An addressed envelope is enclosed for your convenience.

Sincerely,

Rob Breeden

Robert Breeden
Chief Financial Officer, Chateau Americana, Inc.

- -

Dear Boston & Greer, LLP:

The above information regarding our indebtedness to Chateau Americana, Inc.

_____ Agrees with our records.

___X___ Does not agree with our records as described below

Exception(s):

Mailed check on 12/30/20XX for $18,501.00 (check number 25386), our outstanding balance was $191,697.20 on 12/31/20XX.

Name and Title (please print):   Diana Meiburg, Controller

Signature: *Diana Meiburg*   Date: *1/9/20XY*

Grand Total Bottles:	2,640	Grand Total Cost:	$ 18,501.00
Total Cases:	220		
Comments: Rush delivery			
		Date	10/09/XX
		Invoice Number	14944
		Customer Number	0501

Distribution: Copy 1 - Accounting; Copy 2 - Shipping; Copy 3 - Customer

---

Bank of Huntington   Customer Receipt

All items credited subject to verification, collection, and conditions of the Rules and Regulations of this Bank and as otherwise provided by law. Payments are accepted when credit is applied to outstanding balances and not upon issuance of this receipt. Transactions received after the Bank's posted cut-off time or Saturday, Sunday, and Bank Holidays, are dated and considered received as of the next business day.

Please retain this receipt until you receive your account statement.

00406 018 057167 01-03-XY 16:52 DEP BUS
640665135 000000000739601109 $131,677.20

86-15-2007C 06-2001

Cash Receipt Summary   # 5719

Chateau Americana
3003 Vineyard Way
Huntington, CA 95394

Date : *1/2/XY*
Preparer 1 Initial: *MSB*
Preparer 2 Initial: *GLH*

Customer/Description	Ref./Customer #	Invoice #	Amount
Bock Wines and Vines	0501	14944	$ 18,501.00
Glazer's Distributors of Ohio	3502	15163	12,365.40
Louis Carufel Wine Co	0503	15154	16,255.20
Bacchus Wine Wholesale Distribution	0902	15175	13,203.60
Prestige Wine Cellars	4301	15192	10,996.20
American Vineyards	3501	15129	12,533.40
Veritas Distributors Inc	2201	15189	14,125.80
Fine Wine Selection Company	0301	15170	11,164.20
Mountain Wine Distributing Company	0601	15121	13,581.60
World Vintage Imports Inc	2101	15153	8,950.80
Total			$ 131,677.20

Chateau Americana, Inc.
3003 Vineyard Way, Huntington, CA 95394
(707)368-8485

January 2, 20XY

Bolliger, Inc.
88 Viaduct Road
Stamford, CT 06907

Ladies and Gentlemen:

In connection with an audit of the financial statements of Chateau Americana, Inc. as of December 31, 20XX, and for the year then ended, our independent auditors wish to determine whether our records of your indebtedness to us agree with your records. According to our records, your indebtedness to us on December 31, 20XX included the following invoice(s):

Invoice Number	Invoice Date	Amount
15156	11/03/XX	$ 23,532.00
15233	11/12/XX	25,116.00
15308	11/21/XX	29,407.20
15431	12/04/XX	23,710.80
15542	12/17/XX	30,110.40
15618	12/26/XX	31,694.40
Total		$163,570.80

This is neither a request for payment, nor an indication of your total indebtedness to us.

Please confirm whether the information about your indebtedness to us presented above agrees with your records by completing and signing the information below and returning this letter directly to our independent auditors, Boston & Greer, LLP, 1000 Ridge Street, Sacramento, CA, 95814. An addressed envelope is enclosed for your convenience.

Sincerely,

Rob Breeden

Robert Breeden
Chief Financial Officer, Chateau Americana, Inc.

- -

Dear Boston & Greer, LLP:

The above information regarding our indebtedness to Chateau Americana, Inc.

   _X_   Agrees with our records.
         Does not agree with our records as described below

Exception(s):

N/A

Name and Title (please print):   Arnoldo Tucci, Accounts Payable Manager

Signature: *Arnoldo Tucci*   Date: _1/13/XY_

Chateau Americana, Inc.
3003 Vineyard Way, Huntington, CA 95394
(707)368-8485

January 2, 20XY

Pinnacle Wine Company
345 Underhill Blvd.
Syosset, New York 11791

Ladies and Gentlemen:

In connection with an audit of the financial statements of Chateau Americana, Inc. as of December 31, 20XX, and for the year then ended, our independent auditors wish to determine whether our records of your indebtedness to us agree with your records. According to our records, your indebtedness to us on December 31, 20X included the following invoice(s):

Invoice Number	Invoice Date	Amount
15047	10/21/XX	$ 24,129.60
15132	10/31/XX	24,502.80
15235	11/12/XX	26,086.80
15312	11/21/XX	29,254.80
15403	12/01/XX	23,710.80
15525	12/15/XX	26,086.80
15612	12/26/XX	30,838.80

Total $184,610.40

This is neither a request for payment, nor an indication of your total indebtedness to us.

Please confirm whether the information about your indebtedness to us presented above agrees with your records by completing and signing the information below and returning this letter directly to our independent auditors, Boston & Greer, LLP, 1000 Ridge Street, Sacramento, CA, 95814. An addressed envelope is enclosed for your convenience.

Sincerely,

Rob Breeden

Robert Breeden
Chief Financial Officer, Chateau Americana, Inc.

- -

Dear Boston & Greer, LLP:

The above information regarding our indebtedness to Chateau Americana, Inc.

   _X_ Agrees with our records.

   _____ Does not agree with our records as described below

Exception(s):

Name and Title (please print):   Maurice Vasser, Assistant Controller

Signature: *Maurice Vasser*   Date: _1/14/20XY_

Chateau Americana, Inc.
3003 Vineyard Way, Huntington, CA 95394
(707)368-8485

January 2, 20XY

Vintage Wine Company
2650 Commerce Way
Los Angeles, Ca 90040

Ladies and Gentlemen:

In connection with an audit of the financial statements of Chateau Americana, Inc. as of December 31, 20XX, and for the year then ended, our independent auditors wish to determine whether our records of your indebtedness to us agree with your records. According to our records, your indebtedness to us on December 31, 20XX included the following invoice(s):

Invoice Number	Invoice Date	Amount
15038	10/20/XX	$ 22,206.00
15123	10/30/XX	25,070.40
15217	11/10/XX	26,769.60
15299	11/19/XX	27,058.80
15337	11/24/XX	29,340.00
15440	12/05/XX	27,598.80
15488	12/11/XX	28,096.80
15550	12/18/XX	30,463.20
15611	12/26/XX	38,566.20
Total		$255,169.80

This is neither a request for payment, nor an indication of your total indebtedness to us.

Please confirm whether the information about your indebtedness to us presented above agrees with your records by completing and signing the information below and returning this letter directly to our independent auditors, Boston & Greer, LLP, 1000 Ridge Street, Sacramento, CA, 95814. An addressed envelope is enclosed for your convenience.

Sincerely,

Rob Breeden

Robert Breeden
Chief Financial Officer, Chateau Americana, Inc.

— —

Dear Boston & Greer, LLP:

The above information regarding our indebtedness to Chateau Americana, Inc.

_____ Agrees with our records.

___X___ Does not agree with our records as described below

Exception(s):
Invoice # 15611 included an over shipment of 70 cases of Chardonnay (Product # W120080) at $84 a case. The 70 cases were shipped back to Chateau Americana on 12/29/XX. Our records indicated that our indebtedness to Chateau American was $249,289.80 on December 31, 20XX.

Name and Title (please print):   Rachel Parks, Controller

Signature: *Rachel Parks*   Date: _1/15/XY_

Credit Memo

Chateau Americana, Inc.
3003 Vineyard Way
Huntington, CA 95394

Phone: (707)368-8485

Credit Memo: **2896**	
Date: 1/5/XY	Sales Person: WAB
Customer Number: 0502	Customer PO No: 287654
Amount Net: $5,880.00	

Credit To: Vintage Wine Company

Comments:

Over-shipped customer 70 cases of Chardonnay

		Price	
Item # / Description	Quantity	Unit Price	Amount
W120080 / Chardonnay	840	$7.00	$5,880.00

Customer Name: Vintage Wine Company		Credit Amount: $5,880.00

Chateau Americana
3003 Vineyard Way
Huntington, CA 95394
Phone: (707)368-8485

Credit Date: 1/5/XY

Credit Memo #: **2896**

Customer Number: 0502

Distribution: Copy 1 - Accounting; Copy 2 - Customer

Receiving Report

Date Received: 12/31/XX
Receiving Report #: **17263**

Received From	Purchase Order #
Vintage Wine Company	Credit Sales Invoice # 15611
Freight Carrier	**Received by**
West Cost Shipping	BH

Quantity	Item #	Size	Description
840	W120080	0.750	70 Cases of Chardonnay

Condition:

Excellent

Distribution: Copy 1 - Accounting; Copy 2 - Purchasing; Copy 3 - Receiving

COMPLETING THE AUDIT:
The Winery At Chateau Americana

LEARNING OBJECTIVES

After completing and discussing this case, you should be able to:

- Understand and identify audit procedures to detect contingent liabilities and commitments
- Understand and identify audit procedures to detect subsequent events
- Understand and evaluate information relevant to the assessment of the going concern assumption
- Evaluate and recognize potential limitations of responses to letters of inquiry sent to legal counsel
- Identify information that must be included in a management representation letter
- Understand and evaluate a summary of unadjusted differences schedule
- Prepare an audit report that is appropriate in light of client circumstances
- Understand the required communications with those charged with governance

INTRODUCTION

Your firm's first audit of Chateau Americana is drawing to a close and your partner, Claire Helton, has just informed you that the next couple of days will be devoted to wrapping up the engagement. She plans to present the firm's audit report to the winery's chief financial officer next week; however, there are a number of audit procedures that remain open on this year's audit program and must be completed prior to next week's meeting.

Several client interviews were conducted by Elise Simpson, another senior auditor assigned to the engagement. You will find transcripts of these interviews and the accompanying documents useful in completing the open items.

INTERVIEW TRANSCRIPTS

Elise: Good morning Edward. I have several questions to ask you to help with completing our audit. Are you aware of any contingent liabilities that should be disclosed in the financial statements?

Edward: You've already received the letter from our attorney regarding the lawsuit filed by a former employee. We hope to resolve the suit in the very near future. I'm not aware of any other lawsuits or contingencies.

Elise: Have there been similar suits filed against your company in the past?

Edward: No, this is the first employee-initiated suit of this type. We've made every attempt to maintain excellent working conditions and relationships with our employees.

Elise: Does the company have any sales or purchase contracts?

Edward: We don't have any sales contracts, but we do have several purchase contracts that we use to secure our supply of grapes. We've maintained purchase agreements with the same growers for the past 12 years and we've never been disappointed by either the quality of their product or the contract terms. Under the terms of these agreements we are required to purchase a predetermined amount of grapes at prices based on existing market conditions, although some contracts establish minimum purchase prices.

Elise: I suppose such contracts can be beneficial or detrimental.

Edward: That's precisely why we're so methodical in establishing sales projections that we use to calculate our inventory requirements.

Elise: Does the company have any other commitments, such as equipment or building leases?

Edward: I personally own some of the production equipment that I lease to the company. I believe Rob provided a copy of the lease agreement to someone on the audit team. There are no other leases or commitments of any type.

Elise: My last question relates to subsequent events. Are you aware of any event that has occurred since the balance sheet date that requires either adjustment to or disclosure in the financial statements? For example, have there been any changes in the company's capital stock or long-term debt, or any unusual adjustments since the end of the year?

Edward: Rob and I met with representatives from the financial institutions that we have loans with several weeks ago to discuss the possibility of restructuring our long term debt. Given the recent downward trends in interest rates, we decided to attempt to secure a lower rate and shorter repayment terms for our debt. Although we're still negotiating, we expect to reach an agreement within the next week or two.

Otherwise, there have been no changes to our debt or capital structure and there have definitely been no unusual adjustments to our financial statements.

After meeting with Edward, Elise met with Rob Breeden, CA's chief financial officer.

Elise: Hi Rob. Thanks for meeting with me this morning. I need to talk with you about several issues so that we can finalize our audit in time for your and Claire's meeting next week. First, are you aware of any contingent liabilities that should be disclosed in the financial statements?

Rob: No, our only current litigation relates to a lawsuit filed by a former employee. We're working very hard through our attorney to resolve the suit.

Elise: Are you likely to offer a settlement to the individual?

Rob: I can't say with any certainty what we'll do. Our attorney is still in the process of researching the case and formulating a position for us. We've never had a suit such as this brought against our company, so we're in new territory. I can tell you that Edward feels very strongly about resolving the case as quickly as possible and keeping it out of the press.

Elise: Could you tell me a little about the case?

Rob: William Simmons worked for the winery for six years prior to the accident. He was a dependable and competent employee according to his supervisor. As I understand it, William was injured while he was repairing one of our large storage tanks. The insurance report states that he fell when his safety harness broke. He sustained several broken ribs, a broken arm and a broken leg. He contends that the company was negligent in maintaining the equipment. We're not convinced that he was using it properly.

Elise: Do you have any idea of what the maximum settlement could be?

Rob: The suit seeks damages of $500,000, or almost 20 times the former employee's prior year's earnings.

Elise: Turning to a different subject now. Tell me about any sales or purchase contracts.

Rob: We don't enter into sales contracts. However, because we rely on outside growers for almost 75% of our grapes, we do contract with growers to ensure a flow of grapes. We've had agreements with a number of the same growers for many years. Based on my experience, the contract terms are relatively favorable. The greatest benefit to us is that we're assured a flow of inventory.

Elise: Do the agreements set minimum prices?

Rob: We obviously use these contracts to ensure a continuous source of grapes. While most of the contracts call for prices to be based on market conditions, several establish minimum purchase prices. However, we've been able to negotiate prices that we believe still provide a great deal of protection for us.

Elise: Edward mentioned that you are very careful in forecasting your grape needs. Who is responsible for the forecasting process?

Rob: I oversee the process. Our calculations are based on sales projections developed by our sales manager, Susan Platt. She has more years of experience in the wine industry than most of us and has always done a very competent job for us. After Susan finishes her calculations she and I meet with Taylor, the company's vice president of marketing, to go over the numbers.

Elise: Does the company have any commitments?

Rob: We lease certain production equipment from Edward. I think I may have mentioned that to you when were discussing related party transactions. Our total monthly lease payments are approximately $9,000. We have no other leases or commitments.

Elise: Have there been any subsequent events since the end of the year? Also, have there been changes in the company's capital stock or long-term debt, or any unusual adjustments since the end of the year?

Rob: You may be interested to know that Edward and I have had several meetings with our creditors in recent weeks to negotiate changes in our loan terms. I have been talking to Edward about our need to take advantage of the recent interest rates drops. Edward finally has agreed to pursue a shorter payback period in hopes of extinguishing our debt earlier than originally planned.

Elise: Have you reached an agreement with the financial institutions?

Rob: Nothing definite at this point. We're in the process of working out the details. I'm hopeful that we'll agree on new terms within the next several weeks.

◆◆

The following documents are relevant to the completion of your firm's audit of Chateau Americana's financial statements and may be found on the following pages:

1. Draft of the current year's financial statements
2. Summary of Unadjusted Differences (prepared by the audit team)
3. Attorney's Response to Audit Inquiry Letter
4. Minutes from the company's Board of Directors meetings

The Winery at Chateau Americana, Inc.
Balance Sheets as of December 31, 20XX – 20XV
(In Thousands)

Draft - for Internal Use Only

ASSETS

	20XX	20XW	20XV
CURRENT ASSETS			
Cash	$ 3,005	$ 2,992	$ 3,281
Accounts receivable (net of allowance)	5,241	4,816	3,703
Investments	3,095	2,081	2,294
Production inventories	11,578	10,407	9,107
Finished goods inventories	4,015	3,902	3,567
Prepaid expenses	142	85	69
Total Current Assets	27,076	$ 24,283	$ 22,021
PROPERTY, PLANT & EQUIPMENT	30,230	28,135	27,612
Less accumulated depreciation	15,277	14,096	13,185
Net Property, Plant & Equipment	14,953	14,039	14,427
TOTAL ASSETS	$ 42,029	$ 38,322	$ 36,448

LIABILITIES AND SHAREHOLDERS' EQUITY

	20XX	20XW	20XV
CURRENT LIABILITIES			
Accounts payable	$ 4,988	$ 3,683	$ 2,221
Accrued expenses	599	569	640
Notes payable	813	654	891
Current portion of long term debt	410	525	464
Payroll taxes withheld and payable	100	95	96
Federal income tax payable	172	157	134
Total Current Liabilities	7,082	5,683	4,446
LONG TERM DEBT	7,229	6,918	7,983
TOTAL LIABILITIES	14,311	12,601	12,429
SHAREHOLDERS' EQUITY			
Common stock (No par value, 5,000,000 shares authorized, 45,000 shares issued)	90	90	90
Additional paid-in capital	3,567	3,567	3,567
Retained earnings	24,061	22,064	20,362
Total Shareholders' Equity	27,718	25,721	24,019
TOTAL LIABILITIES AND SHAREHOLDERS' EQUITY	$ 42,029	$ 38,322	$ 36,448

Draft - for Internal Use Only

The Winery at Chateau Americana, Inc.
Statements of Income for Years Ended December 31, 20XX – 20XV
(In Thousands)

Draft - for Internal Use Only

	20XX	20XW	20XV
Sales	$ 21,945	$ 20,189	$ 18,170
Cost of goods sold	11,543	10,525	9,777
Gross profit	10,402	9,664	8,393
Selling, general and administrative expenses	7,017	6,824	6,218
Operating income	3,386	2,840	2,175
Interest expense	360	211	257
Provision for income taxes	1,028	927	483
Net income	$ 1,997	$ 1,702	$ 1,435

Draft - for Internal Use Only

Summary of Unadjusted Differences

Client: The Winery at Chateau Americana, Inc.
Year ended: December 31, 20XX

Reference: CA-4
Prepared by: WJ, 3-2-XY
Approved:

				Possible Misstatements Overstatements / (Understatements)			
Audit Schedule Reference	Description of Misstatement	Type of Misstatement	Total Amount	Current Assets	Noncurrent Assets	Current Liabilities	Income Before Taxes
R-210	Write-off of customer account receivable	P	($13,488)	($13,488)			
E-210	Unrecorded accounts payable	P	61,917	(31,200)	($20,717)	($61,917)	10,000
I-210	Unrecorded capital acquisitions	A	48,610	48,610	(48,610)		
I-210	Misstatement in depreciation expense	A	13,368		13,368		13,368
				$	$	$	$

	Possible Overstatement (Understatement)	Materiality
Total Assets	$	$1,050,725
Income Before Taxes	$	$99,850

Conclusion:

McKenna, Harmon, & Jacobs
First Union Square Place
1450 California Avenue
Napa, CA 41008

March 12, 20XY

Boston & Greer, LLP
1000 Ridge Street
Sacramento, CA, 95814

Re: The Winery at Chateau Americana, Inc.

Dear Sirs:

By letter dated, March 1, 20XY, Mr. Rob Breeden, Chief Financial Officer of The Winery at Chateau Americana, Inc., (the "Company") has requested us to furnish you with certain information in connection with your examination of the accounts of the Company as of December 31, 20XX.

While this firm represents the Company on a regular basis, our engagement has been limited to specific matters as to which we were consulted by the Company.

Subject to the foregoing and to the last paragraph of this letter, we advise you that since January 1, 20XX we have not been engaged to give substantive attention to, or represent the Company in connection with, material loss contingencies coming within the scope of clause (a) of Paragraph 5 of the Statement of Policy referred to in the last paragraph of this letter, except as follows:

On November 21, 20XX, a suit was filed against The Winery at Chateau Americana, Inc. by a former employee who is seeking damages for injuries sustained while employed by the Company. The suit alleges that William Simmons (the "Employee") was injured as a result of the Company's negligent maintenance of workplace safety equipment as required by the Occupational Safety & Health Administration. In addition, the suit claims that Simmons was not instructed in the proper use of the safety equipment as required by applicable federal and state laws. According to the suit, Simmons was performing routine maintenance on one of the Company's wine storage tanks when a safety harness he was wearing failed. The fall resulted in a loss of work time, hospitalization, and significant physical therapy.

In preparation of providing this letter to you, we have reviewed the merits of the claim against the Company. After careful consideration, we are unable to express an opinion as to the merits of the litigation at this time. The Company believes there is absolutely no merit to the litigation.

The information set forth herein is as of March 12, 20XY, the date on which we commenced our internal review procedures for purposes of preparing this response, except as otherwise noted, and we disclaim any undertaking to advise you of changes which thereafter may be brought to our attention.

This response is limited by, and in general accordance with, the ABA Statement of Policy Regarding Lawyers' Responses to Auditors' Requests for Information (December 1975); without limiting the generality of the foregoing, the limitations set forth in such Statement on the scope and use of this response (Paragraphs 2 and 7) are specifically incorporated herein by reference, and any description herein of any "loss contingencies" is qualified in its entirety by Paragraph 5 of the Statement and the accompany Commentary (which is an integral part of the Statement). Consistent with the last sentence of Paragraph 6 of the ABA Statement of Policy and pursuant to the Company's request, this will confirm as correct the Company's understanding as set forth in its audit inquiry letter to us that whenever, in the course of performing legal services for the Company with respect to a matter recognized to involve an unasserted possible claim or assessment that may call for financial statement disclosure, we have formed a professional conclusion that the Company must disclose or consider disclosure concerning such possible claim or assessment, we, as a matter of professional responsibility to the Company, will so advise the Company and will consult with the Company concerning the question of such disclosure and the applicable requirements of Statement of Financial Accounting Standards No. 5.

Very truly yours,

McKenna, Harmon, & Jacobs

Napa, CA

The Winery at Chateau Americana, Inc.

CA-203
PBC/AG
3/05/XY

Board of Directors Meeting
Minutes – March 3, 20XY

The quarterly meeting of the Board of Directors of The Winery at Chateau Americana, Inc. was held at the Company's offices on Wednesday, March 3, 20XY. Mr. Edward Summerfield, Chairman of the Board, called the meeting to order at 9:30 a.m. Eastern Standard Time.

Present at the meeting:

Mr. Edward Summerfield, Chairman of the Board
Ms. Taylor Summerfield, Vice President of Marketing and Member of the Board
Mrs. Charlotte Summerfield, Member of the Board
Mr. Rob Breeden, Chief Financial Officer and Member of the Board
Mr. Bill Jameson, Member of the Board
Ms. Susan Martinez, Member of the Board
Mr. Terrence Dillard, Member of the Board
Mr. Harry West, Outside Legal Counsel (Present only for discussion of pending litigation)

Action Items

1. **Approval of the Minutes**. On a motion duly made and seconded, the Board approved the minutes as distributed of the meeting of Wednesday, December 3, 20XX.

2. **Creation of Committees**. As Chairman of the Board, Mr. Summerfield recommended that the Board establish an Audit Committee. Mr. Summerfield stated that the Company's audit firm had suggested that establishing such a committee would be beneficial to the Company in improving its corporate governance structure.

   On a motion duly made and seconded, the Board adopted the following resolution:

   Resolved, That the Board accepts the Chairman's recommendation to establish an Audit Committee effective as soon as such a committee can be formed.

3. **Nomination and Election of Committee Members**. Mr. Terrence Dillard nominated Ms. Susan Martinez to be the Chair of the Audit Committee and nominated Mr. Bill Jameson and Mrs. Charlotte Summerfield to be members of the Committee.

   On a motion duly made and seconded, the Board adopted the following resolutions:

Resolved, That the Board elects Ms. Susan Martinez as Chair of the Audit Committee and Mr. Bill Jameson and Mrs. Charlotte Summerfield as members of the Committee for a term of one year that shall begin immediately and that shall conclude at the close of the March 20XZ quarterly Board meeting; and

Resolved Further, That the Board directs Ms. Martinez to adopt such practices as may be appropriate to assist the Committee in fulfilling its corporate governance responsibilities. The Committee shall meet no less than two times per year immediately preceding regularly scheduled quarterly Board meetings. Such requirement shall not be construed as limiting the Committee's prerogative to meet more frequently. Further, the Board understands the Committee will meet privately with the Company's auditor to discuss any matters it deems appropriate.

4. **Report on Pending Litigation – Confidential and Proprietary** – Executive Session. A confidential and proprietary supplemental issue paper was distributed at the meeting. Mr. Harry West, partner at McKenna, Harmon, & Jacobs, provided an update regarding the status of the lawsuit filed by William Simmons against the Company. Mr. West recommended that the matter be discussed in Executive Session because this item is about pending litigation matters that are subject to attorney-client privilege.

On a motion duly made and seconded, the Board adopted the following resolution:

Resolved, That the Board determines that discussion of an update on pending litigation to which the Company is a party shall be conducted in Executive Session.

Information Items

1. **Restructuring of Long-term Debt**. Mr. Rob Breeden reported that he and Mr. Summerfield have had several meetings with representatives of financial institutions from whom the Company has borrowed funds to discuss renegotiating the current terms of the Company's debt. Although no agreement has been reached, Mr. Breeden stated that he believes the Company will be able to successfully renegotiate debt terms with all related financial institutions.

2. **Update on New Accounting Firm**. Mr. Rob Breeden informed the Board that the Company has been very pleased with the service provided by the recently appointed firm of Boston & Greer, LLP. Mr. Breeden stated that he anticipates receiving the firm's audit report on the Company's financial statements in the coming week. Mr. Jameson inquired whether the firm had identified any significant accounting matters during the course of the audit. Mr. Breeden stated that no significant matters had been identified.

There being no further business, Mr. Summerfield adjourned the meeting at 11:25 a.m. Eastern Standard Time.

REQUIREMENTS

Completing an audit is a challenging process that requires auditors to make a number of critically important decisions. The following questions relate to some of these issues. You should answer these questions prior to completing the "open" audit procedures on the audit program.

1. ASC Topic 450 - *Contingences*, (formerly SFAS No. 5 - *Accounting for Contingencies*) prescribes how companies must treat contingent liabilities in various circumstances. The likelihood that a contingency will arise in any given situation may be considered as probable, reasonably possible, or remote. If an auditor believes that an attorney's response is ambiguous as to the possible outcome of pending litigation, how may an auditor obtain evidence to assess the need for a possible accrual of a loss contingency or disclosure of the matter in the notes to the financial statements? You may wish to refer to SAS No. 12, *Inquiry of a Client's Lawyer Concerning Litigation, Claims, and Assessments*, for help in answering this question.

2. Describe three to five audit procedures that auditors commonly perform to search for contingencies.

3. SAS No. 59, *The Auditor's Consideration of an Entity's Ability to Continue as a Going Concern*, requires auditors to perform an evaluation of an entity's ability to continue as a going concern as part of each audit. Describe several audit procedures that may be used in the auditor's evaluation of going concern. What audit documentation is required if an auditor concludes there is substantial doubt about an entity's ability to continue as a going concern?

4. Generally accepted auditing standards require auditors to obtain written representations from management as part of each audit. To what extent should an auditor rely solely on a client's written representations? At what point in the audit should a representation letter be obtained and as of what date should the client make the representations? What are the implications of management's refusal to provide requested representations?

5. Claire Helton, the engagement partner has been very impressed with your work on Chateau Americana. As a consequence, she has asked you to identify the appropriate audit report for the company. Assuming that each of the following situations is independent from the others, determine the type of audit report which is most appropriate.

    a. Assume that subsequent to year-end, but before issuance of the audit report that one of Chateau Americana's customers filed bankruptcy. The customer's year-end account receivable was $50,750, an immaterial amount. Chateau Americana's CFO indicates that he neither wants to write-off the customer's account, nor record a specific reserve.

    b. Assume the litigation discussed in the case is settled subsequent to year-end for $200,000. The financial statements for the year ended 12/31/20XX did not include a loss accrual. The company does not want to include disclosure regarding the settlement in the financial statements.

CAST: Completing the Audit

    c. The company renegotiates certain terms associated with its long term debt subsequent to year-end. The new terms are more favorable than the previous terms, but the principal amount of the outstanding debt did not change as a consequence of the renegotiation. No disclosure is being provided in the financial statements.

    d. A flood destroys one-third of the company's vineyard shortly after year-end. The company is currently attempting to secure access to more grapes from the open market. While the company had some insurance on its vineyards, it appears likely that the company will not be indemnified for the full market value of its loss. The value of the lost inventory is material to the financial statements. Management does not intend to include a footnote in the financial statements.

6. Subsequent to year-end, Chateau Americana's board of directors passed a resolution to establish an audit committee. Does this action require any response by your audit team? Describe matters that your firm may discuss with such a committee in future years. Is your audit team required to have such discussions with Chateau Americana's audit committee?

The Winery at Chateau Americana
Partial Audit Program for Completing the Audit

For the Year Ended December 31, 20XX

Reference:	CA-100
Prepared by:	AG
Date:	3/15/XY
Reviewed by:	

	Audit Procedures	Initial	Date	A/S Ref.
1.	Request the client to send letters of inquiry to attorneys from whom the client has obtained legal services from during the year.	AG	3/15/XY	CA-201
2.	Review the response received from the client's attorney for information related to contingencies. Document issues related to ongoing or pending litigation.			CA-202
3.	Obtain a copy of the minutes of all meetings of the board of directors subsequent to year end.	AG	3/05/XY	CA-203
4.	Review the minutes of the board of directors meeting for subsequent events affecting the current year financial statements. Note items for follow-up during next year's audit.			CA-204
5.	Complete the Summary of Unadjusted Differences. Conclude whether the financial statements are fairly stated in all material respects.			CA-4
6.	Prepare a memo to summarize your assessment of the validity of the going concern assumption for Chateau Americana.			CA-205
7.	Document matters to be included in the current year's management representation letter.			CA-206

The Winery at Chateau Americana
Review of Attorneys Letters
For the Year Ended December 31, 20XX

Reference: _CA-202_
Prepared by: _____
Date: _____
Reviewed by: _____

Matters related to ongoing litigation:

Matters related to pending litigation:

The Winery at Chateau Americana
Review of Minutes of the Board of Directors Meetings
For the Year Ended December 31, 20XX

Reference: _CA-204_
Prepared by: _____
Date: _____
Reviewed by: _____

Notes regarding subsequent events affecting the current year financial statements:

Planning notes regarding next year's audit:

The Winery at Chateau Americana
Assessment of Going Concern Assumption
For the Year Ended December 31, 20XX

Reference: _CA-205_
Prepared by: _____
Date: _____
Reviewed by: _____

Comments:

The Winery at Chateau Americana
Matters for Management Representation Letter
For the Year Ended December 31, 20XX

Reference: _CA-206_
Prepared by: _____
Date: _____
Reviewed by: _____

Matters to be included in the current year management represent letter: